an uncertain beginning

MISTER BOFFO

by Joe Martin

GROWING UP BLUE-COLLAR:

an uncertain beginning

Ross Alan Bachelder

Growing Up Blue-Collar: An Uncertain Beginning

Copyright © 2025 by Ross Alan Bachelder

Printed in the United States of America

Published By
The Publishing Pad
www.thepublishingpad.com

Paperback ISBN: 978-1-963732-19-1
Hardback ISBN: 978-1-963732-22-1

This book was produced in coordination with
Artful Endeavors New England (AENE), Berwick, Maine.

PRAISE FOR *GROWING UP BLUE-COLLAR: AN UNCERTAIN BEGINNING*

"In Growing Up Blue-Collar: An Uncertain Beginning, we learn from author, artist, and musician Ross Alan Bachelder what it was like for him to grow up in a Midwestern blue-collar family, and how being labeled "blue-collar" has continued to affect him—not always favorably—for eight tumultuous, up-and-down decades. Now living in Maine, he's penned 27 thematically connected essays, some darkly humorous, others emotionally unsettling, for this book. Whether your collar happens to be sky blue, cloud white, or, like that of the author himself, a fascinating blend of the two, *Growing Up Blue-Collar*—his fourth book—is a finely crafted, intellectually stimulating read."

—*Writer, Winslow Farm founder, and environmental activist*
Sarah Porter Boudreau, Falmouth, Maine

"Polymath Ross Alan Bachelder has always been on an insatiable quest for usable knowledge and new experiences, and in *Growing Up Blue-Collar,* his drive to learn shines through with blinding, invigorating light. His writing is imaginative and willy-nilly, with twists and turns across an experiential terrain in which he explores and puts into motion some of his sharpest, most playfully irreverent observations. And yet best of all, his heart always manages to be in the right place."

—*Artist, teacher, art conservator, and lover of the outdoors/islands*
Tom Glover, Dover, New Hampshire

"Arts multiple Ross Alan Bachelder is at it again! *Growing Up Blue-Collar: An Uncertain Beginning*—his fourth book—is bursting with the kind of dark humor, gut-wrenching self-revelations, and profound insights that only the product of a struggling blue-collar family could hope to summon up from so deep within himself. *Growing Up Blue-Collar* may be built around a series of essays, but rest assured: it's anything but academically stuffy. No ivory-tower pretentiousness, no aggravating machismo here—just a no-holds-barred intellectual salad, spiced with colorful anecdotes and, in countless places, lessons to be learned about the human condition."

—Encaustic artist, jewelry maker, and born nurturer
Anne Strout, Falmouth, Maine

DEDICATION

To my blue-collar intellectual friend Mike Plumer:
fifty rewarding years of trying our damnedest to learn
what this thing called life really means.

TABLE OF CONTENTS

PREFACE

The book you're about to read—*Growing Up Blue-Collar: An Uncertain Beginning*—may seem at first glance to be no more than a highly formulaic, painfully predictable memoir, yet another long-winded life story to add to the ever-expanding list of books in that particular genre. Where there are humans, there will be memoirs; it's pretty much inevitable.

But this is really *much, much more* than a memoir. Sure, it's replete with memorable incidents that can only have happened to this one man on the remote, farm-country perimeter of the Rust Belt city he grew up in. It's *also* a colorful, multifaceted, straight-from-the-heart look at the blue-collar/white-collar divide.

Part I looks at the origin, meaning, and influence of the term *blue-collar*, then presents a roundup of some influential champions of the rights of blue-collar workers.

Part II will take you through my one-room-school days in rural southern Michigan; my high school years both treacherous and triumphant; my battles with family, identity, and college life; my graduate work at Eastern Michigan University in Ypsilanti; and, finally, in 1974, my move to Maine.

Part III is an exploration of the building blocks of one man's personality and outlook on the world—in this case, a man born into not white-collar privilege but blue-collar uncertainty.

The story of my early life strikes me as a classic example of the kind of roller-coaster blue-collar melodrama that many thousands of people around the country—people a whole lot like me, and maybe you, too—have struggled through while searching for an acceptable place within the blue-collar, white-collar hierarchy.

As this book should make perfectly clear, I wasn't born rich and have no desire to *be* rich. I'm happy to report that you won't find even one little ounce of either Elon or The Donald in *this* man's psyche. And I'm even more proud to say that when it comes to the kind of wealth that really matters—a wealth of insights, empathies, cultural experiences, and intellectual passions—I, a man now in my early eighties and still actively growing, am rich beyond measure.

ACKNOWLEDGMENTS

Special thanks to cartoonist **Joe Martin** for allowing me to include the brilliant *Mister Boffo* comic strip that is the frontispiece for this book.

The day I saw that strip in my newspaper (it must have been 11/13/1999), I instantly fell in love with it, clipped it out, and pinned it to a wall of my writing room, where it has been enshrined for more than twenty-five years now. Not only is the strip beautifully drawn, it's also wise, insightful, and quietly hilarious. It's a spot-on encapsulation of my very own blue-collar/white-collar history, and I knew from the moment I first conceived of this book that I wanted that strip to be at the very top of it. And so, to my everlasting good fortune, it is.

INTRODUCTION

What would it be like to have had your future guaranteed the moment you left the Sweet Inner Sanctum of your mother's womb? What if your path to maturity had been paved with emeralds and written in stone? Immune to poverty, even before conception?

What if, like the most unimaginably affluent luminaries in Zurich or Abu Dhabi, Oslo or Copenhagen, you'd been simply born rich? *Privileged! Powerful! Financially buff*—with absolutely no need to aspire to anything because you already knew your future? You'd have been pampered, socially advantaged at every turn, and guaranteed success in a profession, whether you had proven aptitude and genuine interest in it or not.

So be it. After all, you didn't choose to be born a child of privilege, did you! And I—unquestionably a man from what most people could reasonably call humble beginnings—didn't choose *my* lot in life, either. So I guess I really have no good reason to envy you for your good fortune, do I.

Or maybe I do!

That's because, for those of us *not* born to privilege, the answer to the urgent question of who we actually are is more elusive than a butter-rubbed eel. Despite decades of living, I for one have failed to come even close to answering that question. And yet it's always worth trying, isn't it? So let's give it a shot:

That Blue-Collar Feeling Defined: Nine Critical Points

To be blue-collar is to drive by houses larger, more artfully designed, and more attractively situated than yours and wonder, "Will I ever be able live like that?"

To be blue-collar is to choose the cheapest possible options, whether you're shopping for a home, a car, a shirt, or something as simple as a restaurant side dish.

To be blue-collar is to watch with envy as the more affluent people in your community travel to distant lands, frequently and without any apparent financial worry.

To be blue-collar is to assume that to travel to any destination beyond the local ones you've already been to is an unjustifiable waste of money.

To be blue-collar is to view highly successful people as "privileged" and "spoiled" and, because of it, most likely undeserving of their success.

To be blue-collar is to assume that any higher educational facility other than a state university or a community college is for the moneyed class and therefore unavailable to you.

To be blue-collar is to assume that because you aren't living the high life, there's either something fundamentally wrong with you or you're simply not smart enough and skilled enough to have achieved such lofty goals.

To be blue-collar is to feel that if you were only more physically attractive, you'd be more successful.

To be blue-collar is to feel that you'll never be able to escape fully from your less privileged, less-than-glamorous lifestyle.

I'll be revisiting those Nine Critical Points later in this book, but for now, perhaps I should simply say *no mas*, acknowledge that I really am blue-collar through and through, and stop fretting about it.

Fine, I suppose. But then what?

Growing Up Blue-Collar, the book you're about to read. *That's* what.

The overarching subject of this book, then, will be the long-ago shotgun wedding of the words *blue* and *collar* and their continuing effect on my lifestyle, thought processes, sense of self, and creative endeavors of every kind.

It will also be my valiant attempt to provide answers to the *Who am I* question—not just for *you* the reader, and not just for *me* the writer, but for the two of us together, in tandem. I'd like to think that by pouring out to you the contents of my heart and my way of thinking—by examining in great detail the circumstances, people, and events that led to the blue-collar part of me—I'll have contributed in some meaningful way to a greater understanding of the dramatic day-to-day differences between the blue-collar and white-collar mentalities.

At this point you may wonder why I've chosen to call the twenty-seven commentaries in my book "essays" instead of the standard book-industry label, "chapters."

To begin with, I simply like the word *essay*. Always have and always will! To me it's a remarkably pleasant-sounding word. But more importantly, it automatically confers a certain status on its users.

Essay. I mean, just listen to yourself as you say it! Is it not an elegant, emphatically sibilant word, decidedly European in flavor? And does it not announce to the rest of the world—perhaps especially here in America, which has always been more than a little jealous of Europe's long, rich history in the arts—that with such a word in one's vocabulary, one must surely be well educated and well positioned within the social hierarchy? The answer cannot be anything but *yes*.

And of course the word *essay* is anything but the kind of blue-collar word we as a culture expect "working-class" people to use in everyday conversation. That word has been corralled and then expropriated by who else but the academics, a large and influential group of people who, by and large, take excessive pride in employing a more exotic, more nuanced, more arcane vocabulary than the rest of us poor souls who live outside the Halls of Academe. We're talking words like *confluence, extemporaneously,* and *desultory,* but of course the list isn't just endless, it's downright intimidating. And yet, while they would like very much to think so, the word *essay* is not and never will be the exclusive property of the Intelligentsia. Sorry, folks—like every other word, in any language you can name, that word belongs to *all* of us!

So you see, by intentionally pitting the word *essay* against the phrase *blue-collar,* I'm attempting to make what I consider to be a critically important point: that "working-class" people should never shy away from the use of 24-karat words like *essay* out of some irrational, deeply ingrained fear that the word will somehow come across as pretentious—as belonging not to themselves but to some other, more sophisticated and more privileged segment of the population.

As my younger years unfolded, I never, ever thought of myself as "blue-collar." Indeed, I'd never heard or seen the phrase. And when I finally did, I had no idea what it meant. My guess is that I scratched my head and thought, *What? A blue collar on a white shirt? That's ridiculous!*

I decided more than a year ago that I wanted to delve deeply into the blue-collar experience as I've lived it for more than eighty years now. I knew that I didn't want my book to be just one more long-winded, heavily footnoted treatise on "The History and Social Ramifications of the Blue-Collar Phenomenon." *Leave that to the scholars*, I said to myself. *It's their own hyper-academic playground—their fun-filled intellectual sandbox—and they're welcome to it.*

Incidentally, it isn't my intent here to dis the academics. Indeed, at one time, while a graduate teaching fellow in the English department at Eastern Michigan University, I wanted nothing more than to *be* one of them. I was a devoted reader of the *Chronicle of Higher Education* and had been accepted into doctoral programs at three Midwestern universities: Wayne State University, the University of Toledo, and the University of Michigan. But my yearning to embark on a cross-country adventure (more about that later) proved stronger than my wish to become an academic, so off I went to New England and what quickly turned out to be a very different life as a maverick, aesthetically driven freelancer—an authentic, true-blue, round-the-clock *arts multiple.*

Scholars like **Steven Naifeh** and **Gregory White Smith**, authors of *Van Gogh: The Life*; **Heather Clark**, author of *Red Comet: The Short Life and Blazing Art of Sylvia Plath*; and **David Nasaw**, author of *The Last Million: Europe's Displaced Persons from World War to Cold War* deserve thunderous applause for their scholarly achievements. But I finally realized that the more sedentary, tradition-bound lifestyle of the typical academic would never have been a good fit for me—a footloose, independent-minded, intellectually restless soul if there ever was one.

Had I become an academic, I might still have written a book about the blue-collar experience, but it would undoubtedly have been very different from the book you're reading now. Why? Because it would have been a matter of *publish or perish*. For me to have had any hope of actually getting published, I'd have had to write only in the "appropriate," academically high-toned literary style. And for a born rebel like me, that would have been a recipe for abject failure.

Fortunately, for me *and* you, that never happened. And the good news, as I see it, is that the book I've actually written is in every respect temperamentally *me* and therefore fully authentic. I realize that some might see it as too casual a style for my purposes—a little too colloquial and "loosey-goosey" to be taken seriously as an attempt to explain the nexus and nuances of the blue-collar/white-collar divide. But I need to remind all the well-meaning guardians of propriety—and there are masses of them around every corner—that there really is room for a more conversational style when delving deeply into important societal issues.

We're almost ready to go now, but first, a brief, highly condensed overview of the obsessions that led to *Growing Up Blue-Collar.*

To have been born into a family that had no clear sense of itself—a group of ill-focused kin armed only with a fragile, loosely tied grab bag of uncertainties—has been not unlike crossing the Atlantic without a sail or walking the entire perimeter of planet Earth on a ribbon of shifting, oozing quicksand.

Who on Earth am I? I continue to ask myself, decades after my arrival. *And what is likely to be my future?* Like countless others in human history, I've been struggling all my life to know *where* and indeed *whether* I actually fit, reasonably well, into the world of ideas, ambition, and accomplishment.

Que sera, sera, they say. *Whatever will be, will be.* And yet, as much as I may yearn for a more solid footing, the future really isn't mine to see. *Que sera, sera,* indeed!

But enough of this insecurity. I'm really not a fatalist! And besides, it's time for us to get down to business. The color blue is calling, and I'm ever so glad to know I'll have you along for the ride!

PART I

What Does *Blue-Collar* Mean?

ESSAY 1

BLUE and COLLAR:
Two Words in Search of a Mate

"The market for poetry is believed to be those with a college education, and that's whom the publisher targets. The blue-collar crowd is not supposed to read Horace, nor is the farmer in his overalls Montale or Andrew Marvell [. . .]. This is dumb as well as dangerous."[1]
—Joseph Brodsky

Blue and *collar*: two words, each centuries old, each with its own rich linguistic history, its own unique charm, its own utilitarian, written and spoken value.

Anyone can see that those two words, when employed separately, really have nothing in common other than perhaps the simple fact that . . . well, they're both *words*.

But when those words—or perhaps any other two unrelated words, for example, *pro* and *life, white* and *nationalist, neck* and *tie*—are brought together and, with the help of one simple, unbiased hyphen, suddenly coupled like two train cars, they can immediately take on an entirely different and elaborately interwoven

---

1. Joseph Brodsky, "Poet Laureate/Consultant in Poetry Joseph Brodsky delivering a lecture to open the 1991–1992 literary season" [audio], Library of Congress Archive of Recorded Poetry and Literature, 1991, https://www.loc.gov/item/92758604/.

Links to sources in the footnotes can be found at:
www.artsaplenty.me/gubc-sources

meaning. And within the everyday world of common usage, they quickly become well-nigh inseparable.

One could begin the story of the shotgun marriage of *blue* and *collar* in the tiny, relatively nondescript town of Alden, Iowa.

Alden, a little patch of Midwest serenity whose population has never cracked a thousand, was founded in 1855 by Massachusetts native Henry Alden. Though it was small, for decades it attracted shoppers, traders, and visitors from miles around, in part because of its nationally known, culturally vibrant lyceum. Even today, Alden is understandably proud, not just of its lyceum and its library—the smallest Carnegie Foundation library in America— but of what must surely be its most illustrious onetime resident, character actor **Gordon Wynnivo Jones**.

Jones wasn't just some bit-part player. He worked frequently with John Wayne, Lou Costello, and other world-famous entertainers, and he is remembered fondly for playing the Green Hornet in the first of two movie serials based on their predecessor, the radio program of the same name.

But how, you might be asking, can a tiny, out-of-the-way town in north central Iowa possibly have anything to do with a discussion about the coupling of two seemingly disparate words?

There really is a reason, and a good one. For it turns out that the first known use of *blue-collar* to describe labor-intensive jobs was in the *Alden News* in 1924.

Etymologist Barry Popik tells us that the term *blue-collar* was likely a reference to the darker, more rugged fabrics laborers wore, in contrast to the typical office worker's white shirt. Coveralls, in particular, were often blue, and the blue work shirt became emblematic of labor and trades.[2]

It's also worth noting that denim, more than any other fabric, is known for being resistant to stains and grime. And who else but

---

2. Popik, Barry, "Blue Collar," The Big Apple, January 24, 2010, https://barrypopik. com/blog/blue_collar.

the working class are the people most frequently forced to do battle with a relentless tide of stains, grime, and other unwelcome substances? Certainly not the dollar-swamped high rollers in Monaco, or those do-nothing hoity-toities down in West Palm Beach—people who see dirt and grime only in Western films, dish-soap promos, and their own ostensibly pure and squeaky-clean imaginations.

So it seems fitting that the concept of a "blue-collar" workforce—an enormously influential, life-changing way of looking at the labor hierarchy in early-twentieth-century America—came about not just in the minds of college-educated economists but as a direct consequence of the clothes on the aching backs of working-class men and women.

THE COLOR BLUE
IN HISTORY, SCIENCE, LITERATURE, AND THE ARTS

"The colour blue means you have left
the drabness of day-to-day reality to be
transported into—not a world of fantasy,
it's not a world of fantasy—but a world of
freedom where you can say what you like and
what you don't like. This has been expressed
forever by the colour blue, which is
really sky blue."
—Louise Bourgeois[3]

Blue. Nice color! Nice word, too—even if linguists do trace it back to a 6,500-year-old root which they represent, rather unappealingly, as *bʰleh₁-.

One has to admit that just pronouncing the word *blue* is a linguistically sensuous, quasi-erotic pleasure. Words like *cabbage* or *cauliflower* just don't seem to have the same titillating punch when pronounced.

So how do we produce the sound of the word *blue*? Well, we all kinda know, intuitively, how it's done, don't we? To begin with, the lips pair off and then protrude—you know, as they do when we pucker up and prepare to plant a kiss on the moist, plump lips

3. Louise Bourgeois with L. Rinder, *Louise Bourgeois: Drawings and Observations*, Little, Brown & Co., 1995.

of some irresistible creature—your Significant Other, or perhaps a dog, a cat, or your Aunt Persephone's pet aardvark. Then they—the lips, I mean—quietly come together and, with the help of one modest puff of air followed immediately by one mildly percussive slap of the tongue against the roof of your mouth, produce the sound "bloo." And *presto*—you've just hatched another bilabial fricative, which in this case happens to be the word for the color blue!

So universally prevalent is the color blue that, like peanut butter and jelly or sheets and pillows, we take it—and every other imaginable color—pretty much for granted. But artists *don't*, and neither do fashion designers, color theorists, social scientists, and marketers of everything from lipstick to leotards—people necessarily obsessed with the relationship between color and temperament, pigments and personality.

YouGov, a marketing research firm headquartered in London, once conducted a worldwide survey whose results led to the conclusion that blue is "the most popular color in 10 countries across four continents—including China."[4]

Cool, huh? Also, a remarkably wide array of books, both fiction and nonfiction, have been devoted either entirely or partially to the analysis of the color blue—its chemical properties; its ubiquitous presence in popular culture; and its connection to politics, religion, and the global economy.

In his book *On Being Blue: A Philosophical Enquiry*, novelist and essayist **William H. Gass** does his best, with a steady outpouring of humor, insight, and brutal honesty, to catalog every usage of the color blue everywhere around us. Blue book, blue moon, blue Monday, blue laws, blue balls, blueberries. Does the color blue ever take a vacation? Not really!

In his book *Blue: The History of a Color*, historian **Michel Pastoureau** points out that the color blue, if it existed at all in

---

4. William Jordan, "Why is blue the world's favorite color?", YouGov US, May 12, 2015, https://today.yougov.com/international/articles/12335-why-blue-worlds-favorite-color.

Western culture other than in the natural elements, was not destined to become the world's most beloved color until long after the Upper Paleolithic age—when, some 44,000 years ago, the oldest known art was produced on cave walls in South Sulawesi, Indonesia. The dominant colors in nearly all those paintings were red and black. It wasn't until humans finally learned how to extract blue pigments from natural sources that the color blue began to play a critical role in their social, religious, and creative lives.

Theoretical physicist **Stephen Hawking** knew that blue is "one of the three colors that quarks have" in the theory of quantum chromodynamics. "One cannot have a single quark on its own," wrote Hawking, "because it would have a color (red, green, or blue). Instead, a red quark has to be joined to a green and a blue quark by a 'string' of gluons (red + green + blue = white). Such a triplet constitutes a proton or a neutron."[5]

Well, of *course*, Stephen! We knew this all along.

Bravo to scholars, scientists, and the Eternally Curious! What would we do without at least some of them? But the truth is that most of us have never needed to turn to scholarship to find examples of the color blue in our lives. Like dogs and cats, fast food and foolish behavior, it's all around us. I needed only a minute or two to compile my own list of examples, and I've no doubt it would be just as easy for you. So here we go!

- **Thomas Gainsborough**'s painting *The Blue Boy*, originally titled *A Portrait of a Young Gentleman*, was unveiled at London's Royal Academy of Arts in 1770. The brilliant blue suit immediately caused a stir, given the period's preference for warm, red tones in the style of Florentine artists.
- The song "When the Blue Moon Turns to Gold Again," featuring Wiley Walker and Gene Sullivan, was first published

---

5. Stephen Hawking, *A Brief History of Time*, Bantam Books, 1998, chapter 5.

in 1941. It was then recorded by **Elvis Presley** in 1957, **Hank Snow** in 1962, and **Merle Haggard** in 1977.

- A dish called *cordon bleu* (or *schnitzel cordon bleu)*, thought to have originated in Brig, Switzerland in the early 1940s, is a dish of meat wrapped around cheese (or with cheese filling), then breaded and pan-fried or deep-fried.
- The song "My Blue Heaven" charted for twenty-six weeks in 1927, stayed at number one for thirteen weeks, and sold over five million copies worldwide.
- *Sacrebleu* is a very old-fashioned French curse, which—in the same way that a genuine Scot would rather be dead than be seen wearing a tam—is rarely used by the French these days. An English equivalent would be "My goodness!" or "Golly gosh!" The word was once considered very offensive, but these days, saying *sacrebleu* in public—at least here in monolingual America—might, at worst, cause people within hearing distance to whisper, "Oh, those French—they're so pretentious!"
- **Wassily Kandinsky**, a pioneering abstractionist with a formidable, science-based knowledge of both music and color, used the color blue to great effect in a landscape entitled *Der Blaue Reiter* (The Blue Rider).
- **Louise Bourgeois**, a proudly unconventional sculptor, painter, and printmaker, had an intensely emotional affection for the color blue and employed it in many of her artworks, including *Blue Is the Color of Your Eyes* and *VIII Blue Dress*, both drypoint prints.
- **Yves Klein**, a media darling who was famous for his artworks in several media including sculpture, was equally passionate about the color blue but insisted on using only his signature, patented pigment—International Klein Blue—in many of his artworks. For him, the color blue had deep spiritual and religious meaning. Klein even ventured into performance art, staging events in which nude women,

covered head to toe in lush blue paint and transformed into "living brushes," would use their moving bodies to create large murals. Their appearance in the documentary film *Mondo Cane* helped make Klein an international force in the visual arts.

- The film *Der Blaue Engel* (The Blue Angel), a cinematic musical comedy-drama starring **Marlene Dietrich**, was released in 1930.

In a far more personal vein, I have to assume that, like all other young males destined since the dawn of time to find themselves in the midst of arousal, Klein must have known a whole lot about "blue balls"—the very essence and pinnacle of testicular pain and sexual frustration. Me, too; been there, suffered that. And so, I imagine, have the vast majority of my *readers* of the male persuasion—though most of them would rather not talk about it, not with their doctor and especially not with their very first, *let's-get-acquainted* date. 'T ain't no fun! But fear not; I'll return now to the topic of blue in art and culture.

Altogether, according to Goodreads.com, more than nine hundred books with the word *blue* in the title have been published, including **Elizabeth Kada**'s *A Patch of* Blue, **John Guare**'s *The House of Blue Leaves*, **Walter Mosley**'s *Devil in a Blue Dress*, **Toni Morrison**'s *The Bluest Eye*, and **Theodor Seuss Geisel**'s *One Fish, Two Fish, Red Fish, Blue Fish*. One can't help wondering if any other color has come even *close* to appearing in the title of a book so often.

In film, blue has come to symbolize a wide range of emotions including coldness, isolation, melancholy, passivity, calm, faith, spirituality, loyalty, tranquility, unity, and trust.

Leni Riefenstahl was a gifted actor and dancer turned photographer who produced critically acclaimed films during the Germany's troublesome Wehrmacht Era. In 1932, she directed a black-and-white film of fairy tale sensibilities called *The Blue Light* (*Das blaue Licht* in German).

In the film, set in the magical mountaintop village of Santa Maria, Riefenstahl plays the lead role of Junta—a witch conceived by Riefenstahl and her collaborators as a "sympathetic character." In effect, she was what today we would proudly call a "good witch."

In Santa Maria, the light of the full moon shines through a crack in an Alpine peak and illuminates a crystal grotto, creating a blue glow that lures young men to their deaths. Because the film so effectively celebrated the beauty of Germany's legendary Alpine region, it was featured in the prestigious Vienna Film Festival and found favor in London, Paris, New York City, and other major population centers mesmerized by the region's breathtaking scale and—dare I say it?—Purple Mountain Majesty.

But even *that* wasn't enough. *The Blue Light* eventually caught the attention of an admiring Adolf Hitler. He was so impressed with Riefenstahl's work that he eventually commissioned her to make propaganda films for him.

What happened to Riefenstahl and her soaring reputation after the fall of the Third Reich is a fascinating story that's been told innumerable times in countless fora around the world. So there's really no need to relive it here.

And yet it's abundantly clear that, in spite of being cloaked in the dark and sinister shadows of the Third Reich, the color blue was celebrated and revered. Such was—and continues to be—the staggering, invincible power of that universally beloved color in every corner, good and bad, of the known universe.

ALL ABOUT THE COLLAR:

The Good, the Bad, and the Diabolical

"White collar conservative flashin' down the street, pointing that plastic finger at me, they're hopin' soon my kind will drop and die, but I'm gonna wave my freak flag high."[6]
—Jimi Hendrix

Collar. I'll admit that it sounds disappointingly prosaic, but *come on now!* One could surely do worse than to fall in love with a word like *collar.* So don't be discouraged; the word has a surprisingly rich history, perhaps especially after the 1920s, when it was finally coupled, in popular culture, with the word *blue.*

The English word *collar* dates back to the Middle Ages, so one would be wise to get over the idea that it's always had the word *blue* attached to it. Because it *hasn't.*

So, let's hear some of what Wiktionary has to say about this harmless little six-letter word.

Collar (noun): "Clothes that encircle the neck," such as "a decorative band or other fabric around the neckline"; or, "a part of harness designed to distribute the load around the shoulders of a

---

6. Jimi Hendrix, "The Jimi Hendrix Experience—If 6 Was 9 (Official Audio)", JimiHendrixVEVO, June 14, 2024, https://www.youtube.com/watch?v=pt0AqikB98A/.

draft animal." Collar (verb): "To grab or seize by the collar or neck"; or, "To place a collar on, to fit with one."[7]

Sounds innocent enough.

I mean, other than our friends the sadomasochists' well-documented penchant for deriving erotic pleasure from inflicting pain—remember *Fifty Shades of Grey*?—it's hard for me to imagine even one little hint of romance or eroticism in the word *collar*. Not from the way it feels and sounds when pronounced, not thanks to its wide-ranging utilitarian uses within the material world, and not for any good reason I can think of.

How dreary, compared to the luxury of nuance available in the word *blue*, is the word *collar*! Or *is* it?

The answer is *not really*. The truth is that one can find a rich array of synonyms for the word *collar*—synonyms that remove it from the realm of the prosaic to the glamor, glory, and gut-wrenching truth of history.

Some, not surprisingly, land on the positive side of possibilities.

Take, for instance, the word *rabato*, meaning a "stiff collar, wired or starched, worn in the 16th and 17th centuries; sometimes used as a support for the ruff."[8] Who wouldn't want to be seen in one of those?

Or *gorget:* "A crescent-shaped ornamental metal plate suspended around the neck from the crescent's points by a length of chain or ribbon, used to indicate rank or authority [. . .] worn as part of a dress military uniform by officers."[9]

And of course one wouldn't want to fail to pay homage to **Ruth Bader Ginsburg**'s remarkably diverse collection of jabots!

Jabot? Good God—I've just learned a new word! And here's how Wiktionary defines it: "A cascading or ornamental frill down the

---

7. Various contributors, "Collar," Wiktionary, https://en.wiktionary.org/wiki/collar.

8. Various contributors, "Rabato," Wiktionary, https://en.wiktionary.org/wiki/rabato.

9. Various contributors, "Gorget," Wiktionary, https://en.wiktionary.org/wiki/gorget.

front of a blouse, shirt, etc."[10] Think George Washington! In Gilbert Stuart's iconic portrait of him, he's wearing, a snow-white wig and a jabot more than worthy of our nation's first president.

Anyway, Justice Ginsburg—who must still be rolling over in her grave, 24/7, as she posthumously watches the integrity of SCOTUS melt away like cheap butter in a red-hot frying pan— and her esteemed colleague **Sandra Day O'Connor** decided one day that their judicial robes, designed originally for only male accoutrements in the neck region, needed to learn to accommodate something decidedly *female* now that the Fairer Sex had found a place at the Big Table.

And so, during her tenure as an associate justice, Ginsburg began commissioning what finally became a unique collection of more than twenty jabots (or *collars*, to use the vernacular), each to be worn on special occasions and designed to represent her official opinion, whether concurring or dissenting, on various social issues brought before the Supreme Court. Today, the Jewish Museum in New York City has **Elinor Carucci**'s impressive still-life photographs of the collars in its permanent collection.

Well fine, then. We've now established that there are a great many wholesome—some would even say *noble*—reasons for the existence of a collar. All right already! But when it comes to its *negative* possibilities, history offers up a veritable free-falling cornucopia of examples.

Take, for instance, the *necktie*—an item most people consider a harmless and either discreetly or noisily playful fashion accessory.

I know, I know. The necktie isn't really a collar! But let's face it: a necktie is so intimately related to and dependent upon a shirt collar that it may as well *be* a shirt collar. It's for that reason I think it only fair to include it on my list of collars with less than entirely admirable intentions.

---

10. Various contributors, "Jabot," Wiktionary, https://en.wiktionary.org/wiki/jabot.

Many people consider the necktie an absolutely foolproof barometer of occupational status and aesthetic good taste. It's meant to function as a style statement, and it often does so with remarkable skill and authority. Ask any man who's worn one: there's nothing quite like showing up at work one morning wearing a tie you spent a great deal of your precious time and money choosing, then being greeted with a tidal wave of smiley-faced water-cooler kudos.

And yet in some ways, a tie can be a decidedly negative force in the life of the man who's *forced* by his superiors to wear one as a condition of employment. It's then that the necktie can quickly become more a liability than an asset.

Why a liability? Because, like the collar itself, a necktie inhibits the natural function of the human neck, which is both the essential bridge between our heads and torsos and the gateway through which all food, water, O_2 and CO_2 must pass in order to reach their all-important destinations.

And it's not just physical discomfort that can turn an innocent necktie into the very symbol of physical restriction, status labeling, and mind control.

Many years ago, recently arrived in southern Maine and working as a freelance writer, I wrote a column for the now-defunct *Somersworth–Berwick Free Press* entitled "Neck Tyranny." In the column I described the necktie as less a style statement than a nefarious, culturally ingrained tool employed to control, clamp down, and inhibit the actions of the poor souls—usually men, of course—who, as the self-appointed "breadwinners" of their families, were forced to wear it and the collar needed to accommodate it.

In the hands of a workplace superior, a well-designed necktie can easily become little more than a velvet Vise-Grip. Dress codes that require neckties have been able to induce an intractable kind of large-group conformity—the kind of unspoken workplace regimentation that serves the needs of superiors while conveniently neglecting the needs of their underlings.

One sure way to see rigid, collar-based conformity in action is to review images from the past half-dozen federal election cycles showing presidential candidates lined up on the debate stage for yet another photo-op. Politically speaking, any candidate who dared to show up on debate night wearing jeans and a tank top instead of a suit and tie would be sentencing himself to death by occupational guillotine. (Women candidates have their own version of the suit, blessedly free of the necktie; instead, they must suffer in heels.) The same thing would happen if a candidate wore all the right clothing but forgot to pin the required flag pin to her lapel—in the eyes of many, an even *worse* political sin.

To even unintentionally abuse a perfectly good collar or necktie, simply by failing to maintain it properly, can lead a man into trouble. Remember when, back in 1959, the song "Lipstick on Your Collar" reached number three on the UK charts? Unless that lipstick can be proven to have come from one's very own Significant Other, it has no place on the collar of a respectable, socially responsible, maritally faithful male. Nor, of course, is it a good idea to dribble food or beverage down onto one's tie, especially if one happens to be in the midst of a job interview.

In the Necktie as Status Indicator department, have you ever noticed that men on trial are almost always dressed to meet a certain standard, regardless of how they attire themselves outside of court? The accused may wear threadbare jeans and grubby tees year-round, but nonetheless he glides into the courtroom decked out in a sport coat, dress slacks, and—surprise, surprise!—a carefully selected, class-conscious *necktie*. And he's always wearing a look of manufactured contrition on his face—another strategy compliments of the defense.

At moments like these, it's hard not to want to ask, for the thousandth time, *will men ever really learn*? What reputable collar wants to be seen with a spaghetti-stained cravat or a beer-soaked tie?

Such is the power, in a social Darwinist climate, of one little flimsy, ostensibly stylish strip of cloth to slap a hard-to-shake label on the wearer.

But enough about the necktie as enabler! It's time now to move on to a handful of far more negative examples of collars employed for all the wrong reasons.

We all know that the most deplorable uses—or shall we say *abuses*—of the very *idea* of a collar can be traced back to the prisons and dungeons of medieval history—those and a great many subsequent historical eras including, sadly, our very own Civil War.

Now, I should think that in the interest of painful truth and scholarly inclusiveness, we really need to take a mercifully brief tour of some of the more horrific examples. So please, if your stomach can take it, won't you come with me?

Let us begin our tour with the *spike collar*. For some, I imagine, this will prove to have been a fortuitous choice. After all, its execrable purposes—and perhaps especially its unique methodology—must have made it the envy of hardcore torture enthusiasts everywhere.

This clever, low-tech instrument—proudly employed in the twelfth and thirteenth centuries at the Castle of the Counts in Belgium and, centuries later, in the American Civil War—was placed around a prisoner's neck while he was standing in the center of a room. The collar was then fastened with ropes to the four walls, and if the prisoner moved so much as an inch in either direction, the spikes—an equal opportunity purveyor of punishment—would impale him—or of course *her*—through the throat.

I'm pretty sure you'll agree that, like the spike collar, the *pillory* also had a certain sick-minded charm about it. This device consisted of hinged wooden boards forming holes through which the head and/or various limbs were inserted. The boards were then locked together to secure the captive.

Pillories were set up to display people in marketplaces, crossroads, and other public areas. Victims of this punishment were forced to bend forward and stick their head and hands out in front of them—an especially uncomfortable predicament for anyone subjected to it. But of course the main purpose of the pillory was to publicly humiliate the victim.

Sometimes, demeaning strategies like that simply weren't enough. So to make the offender's experience as unpleasant as possible, the crowd would often pelt them with rotten food, mud, offal, dead animals, and even animal excrement. It's hard for us today, living as we do in what we like to consider a more sophisticated time, to imagine what could be a more offal (sic) experience than this.

I feel duty-bound to mention just *one* more device—the *slave collar*—sent long ago, along with its twisted inventor, down the Road to Eternal Damnation.

According to the Henry Ford Museum in Dearborn, Michigan—which has at least one slave collar on display in its vast collection of Americana—"the wealth and power of Southern plantation owners depended upon a large labor force of enslaved people."[11] No surprise there, huh?

Anyway, slaves with a reputation for running away—how dare they!—might have had to wear a slave collar, a cast-iron device remarkably like the collar we routinely put on Man's Best Friend but with a series of long, upturning hooks protruding from it like an excess of horizontal TV aerials.

Why, you ask? This instrument of discouragement was pretty straightforward. When the slave collar was drafted into service, either as punishment (for *what*—being caught learning to read? Stealing a moldy slice of leftover bread for your hungry toddler?) or to prevent the wearer from running away, its design was pretty much guaranteed to cause severe injury to the wearer. If the hooks were suddenly caught on a bush or tree limb—a guaranteed

---

11. Henry Ford Museum, "Slave Collar, circa 1860," The Henry Ford, retrieved June 10, 2025, https://www.thehenryford.org/collections-and-research/digital-collections/artifact/344612/.

outcome for someone in a hurry for some urgent, life-or-death reason—they'd cause a violent jerking to the individual's head and neck, and presto! Mission accomplished! Lots more pain, intimidation, entrapment, and humiliation, and no more running away.

How appallingly cruel human beings can be as they employ their inventiveness in the service of control, dehumanization, and destruction, all in the name of dominance!

Funny how that pesky little word, *collar*, keeps showing up in unexpected places, wearing many different costumes according to either its needs or its wishes. Like the word *blue*, the word *collar* has weathered many cultural storms, bringing lightness, darkness, or perhaps just a welcome whiff of humor in its wake.

In the '60s, in her book *The Female Eunuch*, radical feminist **Germaine Greer** shed unique light on the idea of a collar with her assertion that "no woman wants to find out that she has a twat like a horse-collar."[12]

So you see, the word *collar*, no less than the word *blue*, has had a long and colorful history. And it's painfully obvious that not all of the collars were the *good* kind of collars.

And it was when those two words—*blue* and *collar*—were first married, more than a century ago, that Western culture would never again be quite the same.

---

12. Germaine Greer, *The Female Eunuch*, McGraw-Hill, 1971, 30.

BLUE-COLLAR LUMINARIES:

The Cream of the Crop

"I have been forty years a slave and
forty years free and would be here forty years
more to have equal rights for all."[13]
—Sojourner Truth

There've been a great many well-known and lesser-known (but no less important) blue-collar advocates over the years—journalists, historians, academics, union organizers, social activists, and creatives of nearly every aesthetic discipline. Not surprisingly, a select few of them have earned places of honor in the colorful, often violent history of the American workforce.

It's more than likely that at least some of the following luminaries never thought of themselves as blue-collar advocates (in part because the term didn't appear in public dialogue until that fateful moment in 1924 when it landed in the *Alden News*). And yet, as I see it, their determination to improve the rights, conditions, and opportunities of poor, working-class people everywhere more than qualifies them to be described as legitimate contributors to the blue-collar ethos.

---

13. Henry Martyn Parkhurst, *Proceedings of the First Anniversary of the American Equal Rights Association: Held at the Church of the Puritans, New York, May 9 and 10, 1867*, Robert J. Johnston, Printer, 1867, 20.

I'll begin with a man named **Oscar Micheaux**. Born in Metropolis, Illinois, he was one of thirteen children. His father, Calvin Micheaux, was born into slavery and was finally freed as a result of Abraham Lincoln's Emancipation Proclamation.

Oscar Micheaux moved in 1901 to Chicago, where he wrote and published several novels dealing with issues of fundamental importance to Blacks. He sold his books door to door to readers who included many sympathetic White laborers. Micheaux's second novel, *The Homesteader*, was adapted into a film that launched his career as a filmmaker, making him the first known African-American filmmaker and director.

Eventually, thanks to Lincoln's Homestead Act, Micheaux became a property owner in South Dakota. He was the only African-American homesteader for miles around, but his success there finally earned him the grudging respect and admiration of his neighbors.

In his thirty-year career, Micheaux made more than forty films, two of which have been deemed "culturally, historically, and aesthetically significant" by the National Film Registry. His films, in which Black actors were cast in roles as successful professionals in various occupations, helped Micheaux become a major player in the movement to combat racism and racial inequality. And if the issues he dealt with weren't blue-collar in nature, I don't know what issues could legitimately claim to be.

Eric Hoffer, born in the Bronx, New York, had no formal education. At the age of seven, he lost the better part of his eyesight, and yet he'd already learned to read both English and German fluently. Nearly blind until his sight inexplicably returned at the age of fifteen, he ended up falling in love with books. "I was seized with an enormous hunger for the printed word," said Hoffer.[14]

---

14. The Eric Hoffer Project, "Eric Hoffer Biography," retrieved June 6, 2025 from http://www.hofferproject.org/HPhoffer.html.

When in 1920 his father died, Hoffer was suddenly forced to fend for himself. He found work in California work camps and gold mines, educating himself in his spare time with the help of library cards from a dozen different small-town libraries. During the Great Depression he continued to read and write, and beginning in 1943, while still in California, he worked three days a week as a longshoreman.

Altogether, Hoffer authored ten books, but it was his first book—*The True Believer*, published in 1951 while he was still working as a longshoreman in San Francisco—that brought him national fame as a highly motivated, self-educated writer, respected philosopher, and passionate advocate for the rights of working-class people. In 1983, during the presidency of Ronald Reagan, Hoffer was awarded the Presidential Medal of Freedom. Noted commentator Eric Sevareid once described him as "the most important working-class writer in America."[15]

Studs Terkel, the Pulitzer Prize–winning author and oral historian, is famous for having chronicled the lives of Americans from the Great Depression into the early twenty-first century. He may have been born in New York City, but he will forever be associated with the city of Chicago, where he lived beginning at age nine while his parents ran a rooming house called the Wells-Grand Hotel. It was at the Wells-Grand that he interacted with a wide array of working-class people who became the subject of his early oral history documents.

Terkel eventually studied at the University of Chicago Law School, but after failing his first bar examination, he decided he didn't really want to be a lawyer. Instead, he joined the Works Progress Administration's Federal Writers' Project, where he wore a great many hats including radio actor, news commentator, sportscaster, and disc jockey. Without really having to try, Terkel became the living prototype of the successful blue-collar laborer—a

15. Ibid.

man who, in spite of having few credentials, managed to turn his winning personality, sharply-honed oratorial skills, and love for average humanity into a stellar career as a communicator. By doing things *his* way, he became an irresistible example of the virtues of hard work, ingenuity, and left-leaning, people-centered idealism.

And we mustn't fail to pay homage to **Gene Kelly**, legendary actor, self-described blue-collar dancer, and choreographer.

Born in 1912 into a blue-collar family in Pittsburgh, Pennsylvania, Eugene Curran Kelly showed athletic prowess at an early age. In the beginning he hated dancing, partly because he'd been forced to take dance lessons and partly because other children teased him about engaging in what people at the time considered an inherently "feminine" form of expression. So, for a while, he quit.

But in his sixteenth year he returned to dancing, got serious about it as an artform, and found ways to make money with his precocious skills as a dancer. He eventually built a stellar career as a masculinity-flavored, close-to-the-ground dancer and choreographer. It was well known in the entertainment industry that Kelly rebelled against female-trained male dancers who, as he saw it, were too light on their feet—too unnaturally "girlish" in their approach to dancing. His style of male dance was noticeably more physical, more heavily athletic in the male sense of the word. Kelly himself said: "I wanted to dance for the Common Man."[16]

No airy, sugar-coated stage movements for *this* guy! By consciously differentiating his dancing style from that of top-hatted High Society dancers like Fred Astaire, Kelly guaranteed himself a unique place in dance history with unforgettable performances in critically praised films like *Anchors Aweigh, An American in Paris, Singin' in the Rain,* and a host of other films too numerous to be mentioned here.

---

16. Jack Tewksbury, "Oral History: Gene Kelly, Dancing for the Common Man," Hollywood Foreign Press Association and Golden Globes, LLC, April 3, 2019, https://goldenglobes.com/articles/oral-history-gene-kelly-dancing-for-the-common-man/.

Pete Seeger was far more than a beloved singer of American folk music; he was also a civil rights activist, an environmentalist, and a thoroughly committed advocate for the rights of disadvantaged men, women, and children. His music served the poor, the oppressed, and the exploited, and because of it he has become a legendary figure not just in North America but around the world.

During the McCarthy era, Seeger was blacklisted, along with the other members of the folk group The Weavers, for his decidedly leftist political views. In the early '60s he re-emerged as a public figure, singing protest music in support of international disarmament, civil rights, workers' rights, and environmental causes.

Seeger wrote a great many memorable songs, including "Where Have All the Flowers Gone?", "If I Had a Hammer," "Kisses Sweeter Than Wine," and "Turn! Turn! Turn!" He also played a major role in popularizing the spiritual "We Shall Overcome."

Ray Bradbury, the prolific and celebrated author of *Fahrenheit 451*, *Dandelion Wine*, *The Martian Chronicles*, and a host of other best-selling books, was as self-made—as blue-in-the-collar—as anyone could possibly be. And like author and philosopher Eric Hoffer, Bradbury had America's public libraries to thank for what he became.

When he was nineteen, his family couldn't afford to send him to college, so he went to the library. "Three days a week I read every possible book," he recalled. "At the age of 27 I [completed] almost the entire library instead of university. So I got my education in a library and for free. When a person wants something, they will find a way to achieve it."[17]

Pete Hamill, cartoonist, essayist, editor, novelist, globe-hopping journalist, and the author of *A Drinking Life: A Memoir*, struggled mightily to put his tough-guy, blue-collar Brooklyn roots behind him and find a place in the white-collar world. Always scrappy

---

17. AVA News Service, "Mendocino County Today: Friday, Sept. 15, 2023 [link: Library Education]", *Anderson Valley Advertiser*, https://theava.com/archives/227986#39.

and temperamental like his father—and, like so many men in the Depression era, convinced that drinking was what *real* men did—he became a proud and very public drunk. When he finally realized that alcohol was about to put an end to his hopes of lasting fame and notoriety, he turned himself around and rebuilt his reputation as a gifted and universally beloved journalist—becoming the pride of New York City and the epitome of its spirit.

Michael Moore, firebrand social critic and the creator of *Roger & Me, Bowling for Columbine, Fahrenheit 9/11,* and a host of other over-the-top box office hits, has more than earned his place on my list of blue-collar luminaries. The man has enough awards in his curriculum vitae to pave I-95 from the outskirts of Miami to the Canadian border and back again. But, like many people who've achieved so much, he has also been the target of intense, openly harsh criticism.

While Moore is beloved by political progressives around the world for his high-octane left-wing political activism and his devotion to issues affecting the blue-collar community, he has also been accused (unfairly, I think) of hypocrisy. Some of his more vocal critics have excoriated him for having become a temperamentally difficult wheeler and dealer "posing" as a onetime Flint, Michigan, pro-union working stiff.

Such critics are fond of pointing out that Moore has never punched a time clock, is worth more than fifty million dollars at last count, and owns nine homes, including a Manhattan condo the size of three spacious, top-dollar New York City apartments. The price of success? Perhaps. But there will always be people who find intense pleasure in trying their best to remove the successful from their perceived thrones of superiority.

Michael Moore, who as of this writing is seventy-one years old, appears to have done it all. So what, we might ask, if anything is left for him to do? One possibility is retirement. But for a man with Moore's astronomical drive and breathtaking list of accomplishments, retirement is more than likely out of the question. We need just to sit back, wait patiently, and see what he'll be pulling out of his hat the *next* time around.

My, oh my. All that talent, energy, and idealism! By addressing the most urgent social issues of the day, people like Micheaux, Hoffer, Terkel, Kelly, Seeger, Hamill, and Moore (pun not intended, but so very appropriate!) made the world a far better place than it would have been without their input.

But of course it isn't just men who have made such important contributions to the betterment of blue-collar humankind. To suggest otherwise would be both patently untrue and shamefully irresponsible.

Here, then, is a highly selective shortlist of *women* who've made lasting contributions to the quality of life of working-class people everywhere.

Abolitionist and civil rights advocate **Sojourner Truth** was born into slavery but eventually freed by the Emancipation Proclamation. She spent most of her life working as a teacher and investigative reporter, documenting lynchings and racial violence in the US during the late 1800s and early 1900s.

In 1851, at the Ohio Woman's Rights Convention in Akron, Truth delivered a stirring extemporaneous address which eventually became known as "the Ain't I a Woman speech."[18]

Truth eventually travelled internationally to expose the rampant, endemic racism occurring in her own country. She continued to fight on behalf of women and African-Americans until her death. Among her many accomplishments, she is gratefully remembered for helping to recruit Black troops for the Union Army.

How proud she would have been to learn that in 2009, a bust of her was unveiled in the visitor center at the United States Capitol

---

18. The most accurate version of Sojourner Truth's famous speech is not the dialect-laden one concocted by Frances Gage in 1863, but rather the nearly contemporaneous account published by Marius Robinson in the *Anti-Slavery Bugle* in 1851. See Leslie Podell, "Compare the Two Speeches," The Sojourner Truth Project, https://www.thesojournertruthproject.com/compare-the-speeches/.

Building, making her the first African-American woman to have a statue there.

Ida Tarbell, a writer, investigative journalist, biographer, and lecturer, was one of the leading reformers of the Progressive Era, which bridged the late nineteenth and early twentieth centuries. She was also one of the earliest proponents of investigative journalism. As America's first great woman journalist, she set a stellar example for other women seeking careers in what had always been the male-dominated field of journalism.

In *The History of the Standard Oil Company*, her most important book, Tarbell revealed the illegal ways in which John D. Rockefeller had come to monopolize the early oil industry. Yet she was objective enough and fair enough to praise him for his many accomplishments.

Among Tarbell's most important contributions to the profession of journalism were her meticulous research, her across-the-board fairness, and her all-embracing intellectual integrity.

Journalist and social activist **Ida B. Wells-Barnett** battled sexism, racism, and violence. Through her many years of careful research and inspired writing, she shed light on the conditions of African-Americans throughout the South.

Born into slavery during the Civil War, Wells-Barnett was blessed with politically active parents who valued education. Both her mother and her father were struck down by yellow fever when Ida was only sixteen, yet their impact on their daughter was cemented.

In 1892, after one of her friends was lynched, Wells-Barnett began focusing her energies on the problem of White mob violence. Her pamphlet entitled *Southern Horrors: Lynch Law in All Its Phases*—a full-throated, truly eloquent exposé—so enraged her White detractors that they burned her printing press and drove her from Memphis to Chicago, where she continued to report on discrimination and violence against African-Americans wherever and whenever it was happening.

Over the next few years, Wells-Barnett traveled internationally, speaking on the subject of lynching and openly confronting White suffragists who had failed to speak out against it. Because of her stance, she was often ridiculed and ostracized by women's suffrage organizations in the United States.

Southern California feminist, lesbian activist, and blue-collar trades advocate **Pat Williams** went to college for social work but found job opportunities lacking. Instead of pursuing a master's, she decided to go in a blue-collar direction. In 1979, she entered the Operating Engineer apprenticeship program in Los Angeles—one of the first women to do so.

But she didn't stop there. A hard-driving, remarkably determined champion of workplace equality, she eventually earned the respect of legions of men who actively—and often derisively—doubted her ability to work in blue-collar trades. But she hung tough, refused to be intimidated, then went on to become a district representative and vice president of Operating Engineers Local 501.

Altogether, Williams spent thirty-two years as a building and maintenance engineer in Los Angeles. Even after retirement, while an appointee to the City of Los Angeles Commission on the Status of Women, she continued to work tirelessly to improve employment opportunities and working conditions for women.

Williams' accomplishments, against formidable odds, were really quite stunning. Women like her have continued, in ways small and large, to make significant contributions to the betterment of the blue-collar workforce in matters of safety, on-the-job quality of life, and fair wages. Their names may have faded from history, but their accomplishments cannot be denied and will not easily be forgotten.

PART II

A Blue-Collar Childhood

GROWING UP RURAL:

My Blue-Collar, Southern Michigan Roots

"People in small towns, much more than in cities, share a destiny."[19]
—Richard Russo

I was born and raised in southern Michigan—the lowest portion of the Lower Peninsula—by post–World War II parents who, like most people, had hopes and dreams more modest than lofty, but no less noble for that.

For all intents and purposes, I was a blank slate—not just when I came roaring down my mother's birth canal and into the Outer World, and not just while I was still wriggling in the cradle, but on through my early childhood and well into my adolescent years. Like countless other children born in the Eisenhower era, I appeared to have no personal vision to call my own, no truly active imagination, no burning desire, no great sense of future. My only obligation as a child was to fit in with everyone around me; obey authority; be content with my life as it was; never, ever sass my parents; and—most importantly—stay the hell out of trouble.

---

19. Bruce Weber, "Richard Russo, Happily at Home in Winesburg East," *The New York Times*, July 2, 2004, https://www.nytimes.com/2004/07/02/books/richard-russo-happily-at-home-in-winesburg-east.html.

But in 1949, just as Harry Truman was settling into his new job as president of the United States—sorry, Mr. Dewey; guess it just wasn't your time, huh!—my parents and their two children (me and an older brother) abruptly pulled up anchor, left the heavily industrial city of Jackson, Michigan (population 51,000 at that time), and moved straight up Route 127, thirteen miles north. I finally learned, a few years later, that they'd made the Big Move for only one clear-cut reason: to get as far away as possible from a network of relatives they'd grown sick and tired of visiting because, like so many other people, they'd begun to feel pressured into doing so whether they felt like it or not.

Now, instead of living in the bustling, quasi-sophisticated city of Jackson—known as the birthplace of the Jaxon steam car, the Coney Island hot dog, and *(uh-oh)* the Republican Party—we were hanging our hats out in the country. Our new home was only twenty minutes from Jackson State Prison (at the time the largest walled prison in the world, with six thousand inmates) and a ten-minute bike ride from the ultra-conservative, decidedly inelegant, redder-than-red village of Rives Junction.

White-collar is the last phrase anyone then would have used to describe Rives Junction, known by the locals as "Rives." *Folksy*, yes. *White-collar*? Not a chance!

That our new home happened to be that close to such a notorious prison was no small matter. We eventually learned that on occasion, its parolees had a nasty habit of thumbing rides along the very road we lived on. Sometimes, they—and long-haul truckers as well—had the temerity to knock on our door and ask to use the facilities. But no need to worry: as far as I know, no felon, recidivist, or mass murderer was ever allowed to plop his butt cheeks down on our toilet.

An early view of Rives Junction, Michigan.[20]

Main Street in Rives Junction—clearly destined never to become a tourist destination—was the home of Carmine's Barber Shop (only one dollar for a cut), Surbrook's Hardware, and the Rives Junction Baptist Church (Souls Saved: Hallelujah!). There might have been an actual post office in Rives Junction, too, but we would never have needed to use it, because we got our mail six days a week through the RFD delivery system.

Another measure of just how authentically rural our community was is the kind of telephone we were required to use during my childhood years: a classic, wall-mounted crank phone of the sort that had disappeared long before from more populated cities and towns. And, thanks to the party line system, we had no assurance of privacy in our phone conversations. If we stayed on the line too long, the other member of our party—a neighbor

20. "Blair Residence Rives Junction," in the digital collection *David V. Tinder Collection of Michigan Photography*, William L. Clements Library, University of Michigan Library Digital Collections, retrieved April 20, 2025 from https://quod.lib.umich.edu/t/tinder/x-28858/tinder-rppc-057715.

from just down the road—would pipe in and politely nudge us to be done with our ceaseless chatter. And when Rives Junction quietly switched to a more sophisticated system, our telephone, like those of dozens of other rural residents, was converted to a wall-mounted radio and eventually became a valuable, eagerly sought-after antique.

Now, instead of being city slickers, we'd become a quartet of wet-behind-the-ears country bumpkins crammed into a pale pink stucco-coated structure next to one other house just across the driveway, identical to ours in every way except for its nauseatingly incompatible mustard green color. So there we sat: two mismatched, garishly tinted shoebox abodes, marooned on bland patches of soil by the edge of a four-lane, semi-clogged highway which, for better or worse, was now an all-too-intimate component of our two-dwelling "neighborhood."

My guess is that the shotgun house that inspired John Mellencamp's hit song *Pink Houses* was probably even pinker than my childhood home, if that's possible. Not only did my house and the one in the song share a color, they also shared positions smack on the perimeter of their respective highways—that house in Indiana, mine in Michigan. And now I have to confess that it's heartwarming, somehow, to know that Mellencamp and I—and Indiana-born writer Kurt Vonnegut, too—share deeply imbedded Midwest, blue-collar roots—roots that have obviously made indelible marks on all three of our personal and creative lives.

Less than a mile from our new home was the Van Horn farm, where I eventually learned how to bob for apples, build a hay-bale hideaway, and turn a simple cow's teat into a deadly War-of-the-Bovines weapon. It was there that I also witnessed, for the very first time, what was for me the terrifying spectacle of an about-to-be-born animal—in this case, a calf—being pulled laboriously from its mother. Even worse, given how ignorant I was about procreation, was the fact that what I saw was a hard-to-imagine, even-harder-to-watch breech birth.

Buck's Cabins and Trailer Camp, half a mile from my childhood home.

Just up the hill from the Van Horn spread stood **Buck's Cabins and Trailer Camp** (known locally as Bucks Corner), a shabby, dumpy-looking country store where one could buy penny candy, soda pop (an endearing, enduring Midwestern term), and—not for *me*, of course—twenty-five-cent packs of Camel brand cigarettes. And just down the road from *that* was a primitive but wildly popular drive-in theater where the tickets were dirt cheap and the mosquitoes were more plentiful than popcorn.

It didn't take long for us to learn that unless one happened to be a hard-core, Bible-thumping Christian, downtown Rives wasn't exactly a high-voltage, happenin' place. And as a family, we absolutely were *not* that, which was just one of the many reasons I hardly ever spent time in the Rives Baptist Church. I chose instead to stay close to home, where I could always ride my bike, roam the nearby cornfields, or play with the neighborhood children. And if I were suddenly in the mood for a Western—nearly always starring **Gene Autry** and **Champion the Wonder Horse**, **Roy Rogers** and **Dale Evans**, or **The Lone Ranger** and **Tonto**—I knew I could always see one for nothing by climbing high up into a tree near the drive-in and, like a crow on reconnaissance for his supper, watch, undisturbed, from what was surely the Best Seat in the House.

One thing about Rives Junction that my parents must surely have loved to distraction was Vacation Bible School. It wasn't because they wanted us to be immersed in the Ways of the Lord; after all, they never talked with us about religion, and my recollection is that they'd never expressed an interest in doing so. For them, the appeal was entirely secular. Since money in our family was always hard to come by, and since VBS was free, the church was in effect a delightfully affordable summertime child-care service.

My parents quite understandably yearned for some time away from childrearing, and not surprisingly, the church had an insatiable appetite for Conversion—for adding to the Flock—so it shouldn't surprise anyone that for everyone involved, whether saints or sinners, VBS was an irresistible deal for any parent, whether saint or sinner, in search of marital bliss.

When fishing for converts, the church's strategy was anything but subtle. The moment each daily session began, an adult in charge would whip up the emotionally manipulable young attendees into a frenzy by having us sing "I've Got That Joy, Joy, Joy, Joy Down in My Heart" with thunderous, high-decibel enthusiasm. I had no idea what the song meant, but, ignorance aside, I really enjoyed the singing.

Next would come the Bible drill, an exercise in which a church deacon would shout out one small fragment of a New Testament verse, then see who in the audience would be the first to identify the chapter it came from. The prize? I don't really remember. Perhaps unconditional passage through the Gates of Heaven (to be cashed in at a more convenient time). After all, what could possibly be the hurry for children not even into adolescence?

So far, so good. But the most potent weapon of persuasion was launched when the singing was done and we were taken outside, lined up, and herded onto a bus with the words *Rives Junction*

Baptist Church haphazardly emblazoned on its rusty, faded-blue sides. The guide would then pull the bus's accordion door shut, whip out his Gideons Bible (I wonder what motel he got it from), and, with the bus windows sealed, wasps buzzing, and the sun bearing down on us, begin preaching to us. The volume of the man's voice was ear-splitting inside that tin can of a bus as he laid the groundwork for what he clearly hoped would be a mind-bending, life-changing mass conversion of Biblical proportions.

Eventually, the mood inside the bus would grow eerily silent. Then, once his arm-twisting homily had run its course, the man with his purloined Bible would begin calling out to his lassoed band of coughing, squirming sinners-in-embryo, pleading with us to come forward and give our hearts and souls to Jesus.

Lassoed? I pray you'll forgive me for the mixed metaphors, but not even one little fishy took the bait. All I remember is that on one of the days we were in attendance, I leaned across the aisle, in the throes of a major panic, and whispered to my brother, "Should I *go*? Should we do what he *says*?"

"*I'm* not goin'," he whispered back to me, "and I don't think you should go, either." And with that, another sanctimonious, in-your-face Baptist fishing expedition was over with nary a minnow in the creel.

At the time I had no idea what the man on the bus was ranting about. All I knew was that I was ever so thankful when we were sprung, finally, from his four-wheeled rotisserie and I was allowed to return to my own shameful, heathenish roots, where, according to him, I belonged until the moment I would finally heed his command. I also hoped fervently that the Guy in the Sky would forgive me for having done what made the most sense to me at the time. That, I'm proud to say, was precisely *nothing*.

* * *

My family around 1949. I'm the boy on the right.

Our life in the country was a challenging, invigorating mixture of country pleasures and self-inflicted embarrassments. Around nearly every corner were stumbling blocks that threatened to reveal our déclassé blue-collar status. Needless to say, I didn't always have that "Joy, Joy, Joy, Joy" down in my heart.

The pleasures were easily identifiable and always welcome. First and foremost were the animals—a vaudevillian slapstick menagerie of Creatures Great and Small, hungry for affection and amusingly interactive. A partial list will serve our purposes for now: Joe the duck (who loved quacking at airplanes and slept in our bathtub at night); Petunia the de-scented skunk (who took special pleasure in chasing Joe around the house and pulling the sheets off our beds to signal his need for breakfast); and Billy the parrot (seventy-five years old, and deafeningly proud of his mindless, round-the-clock ability to say "Hello Billy" as if he'd just met himself for the very first time).

Signs of our diminished status, on the other hand, weren't easy for neighbors and passersby to see. But when my childhood friends from Jackson paid a visit, the signs as I experienced them became glaringly obvious and quietly mortifying.

To begin with, *wasps*—those sinister creatures whose sole purpose in life is to sneak up and scare the crap out of little children— had absolute *carte blanche* in our unfinished attic. And since that same attic also served as my bedroom and occasional rec center, those menacing, multi-winged little shits went out of their way to spoil any overnight I'd try to have with friends.

When it came to bathing, for the first few years, at least, we were the Ma and Pa Kettles of the Lower Peninsula. A classmate and neighbor of mine dropped by one morning, and while standing outside on the front porch he heard what appeared to be a fierce bubbling sound coming from the kitchen.

"Oh, that's just my mom," I said. "She's been invited to a Tupperware party, and before she can take a bath she has to boil the water on the stove."

"No kidding!" he tittered. "I'll bet *that's* fun, dragging that big ol' bucketful o' hot water down the hall. I mean, in *our* house we just turn on the spigot, and in a few seconds we've got all the hot water we'll *ever* need!"

"Fun?" I said. "Not really." Then it was my turn to stand there, humiliated, wondering if he was watching my face as it turned red as a Michigan cherry.

And finally, a word or two about our *backyard*. While it was spacious and, thanks to a trio of highly productive, eminently climbable apple trees, a pleasant place to be, it also had one horrifically unappetizing, unceasingly odiferous blemish: an uncapped rectangular cesspool smack in the center of the only portion of the yard that was the right size for a game of softball with friends.

"What's *that*?" they'd ask, staring contemptuously down as expressions of incredulity swept across their crinkle-nosed faces.

"Somethin' creepy," I'd respond, too embarrassed to make eye contact with them. "My dad says it's got something to do with our septic system, but he doesn't have enough money to get a cover for it."

"Well, it sure does *stink*!" they'd sneer.

I decided not to tell them that just the year before, Angus, our Scottish terrier, had fallen into the pit while chasing a chipmunk.

We'd been wondering where he was—he usually ran around and around the yard, hoping we'd throw him a stick—but one day he'd inexplicably disappeared. It wasn't until we heard some whimpering that we found him paddling frantically around in the pool of muck and rescued him. He was black as a stick of licorice by then and disgustingly nauseating in smell. It took us more than a week of daily dog baths to get rid of the stench. I probably don't need to tell you that my mother was understandably pissed about the whole affair.

Looking back on those days, I have no doubt that the person in our family who had the most reason to feel blue about our fall from grace—our sudden move from city to country—was my mother. That's because when my father was away at work and we were in school, all the chores she could imagine—and even those she couldn't—landed in her lap and stayed there, without cease, eight days a week.

To cope with the daily grind, and with her deep disillusionment about her circumstances, my mother—an avid reader who graduated from high school with a 4.0 average—absorbed all of the most popular radio and television programs of the time. These included *The Arthur Godfrey Show*, Art Linkletter's *Kids Say the Darnedest*

Things, Queen for a Day, This Is Your Life, and—from the more sophisticated end of the entertainment spectrum—*Playhouse 90.* For the news, she depended on **Gabriel Heatter**, **Charles Batchelder** (no relation to us), and **Paul Harvey**.

But Sundays were the day of the week my mother most looked forward to, because she was hooked on John Lair's popular, long-running radio program *Renfro Valley Sunday Morning Gatherin'.* The show's saccharine-sweet Sunday-go-to-meetin' music, in combination with Lair's slow, mellifluous Appalachian twang and evangelical homilies, captured the unique flavor of the Kentucky foothills—and Kentucky was the state her mother had been born in.

On Sundays, any chores my mother hadn't gotten around to doing during the week would finally get done—sometimes even by her husband or her sons, all of whom were notoriously, characteristically AWOL when it came to most household chores.

But our sporadic, disingenuous gestures couldn't begin to compensate for the reality that my mother—the classic long-suffering, overburdened housewife—was exhausted, disillusioned, and increasingly angry about her barebones rural lifestyle. I should point out that, like many women of that era, my mother did not drive, which meant her isolation was unrelenting. In an attempt to rectify the situation, she began pleading, day after day, for upgrades in the home's major appliances—everything from a new washing machine to replace the archaic, malfunctioning wringer washer in our basement to a more sophisticated stove and a refrigerator that would actually cool the perishables and make them last.

Like millions of women around the country and beyond, my mother was living the very chore-choked, unglamorous existence that **Betty Friedan** and other increasingly vocal feminists were determined to transform. Women's marital servitude, by and large, was a form of indentured, blue-collar labor. And yet, little did we as a family realize that in less than a decade, from Sea to Shining Sea in America's uptight, male-dominated households, all conjugal hell was about break loose.

Look out, warned Gloria and Bella, Betty and Germaine, and a host of other justifiably angry women in a growing drumbeat of indignant screeds. But like all the other struggling nuclear families across the country—men, women, and children barricaded in their little postwar blue-collar cottages, living within a patently unfair distribution of labor—we in our little pink house on the outskirts of Rives Junction—the Bachelders—didn't collectively listen. Like the others, we were simply too busy, too distracted, too unaware, and too set in our ways to realize that a fierce, portentous, society-altering storm was looming just over the horizon.

ESSAY

MY ONE-ROOM BLUE-COLLAR EDUCATION:
Never Underestimate the Power of Country Learning

*"The more that you read,
the more things you will know.
The more that you learn,
the more places you'll go."*[21]
—Dr. Seuss

A few years after our move to the country, the time came to enroll my brother and me in school. But exactly *where*, our mother must have wondered, was *that* going to be?

Had we stayed in metropolitan Jackson instead of moving out to the boonies, she'd have undoubtedly enrolled us in one of the several standalone kindergartens within the city-wide school district. By the time we entered high school, we'd have matriculated, along with more than two thousand other students, at Jackson's one sprawling high school, which served grades nine through twelve.

But life had other plans for us, and the result was that I began my public school education in a tiny one-room brick schoolhouse. The land on which it was built had been donated to Jackson County by **Horace Gould Cole** (1808–1893), my great-great-great-grandfather, and the schoolhouse was named after him. Cole School was one of thirteen one-room schools still operating in rural Jackson

21. Dr. Seuss, *I Can Read With My Eyes Shut!*, Random House, 1978, 27.

County when I entered kindergarten in 1949, and we happened to live a short distance down the road from it.

A typical Michigan one-room schoolhouse. This one, in Grass Lake, Michigan, was built in 1878. *Photo © 2014 Mary Lea McNulty.*

In a typical calendar year, Cole School would house thirty-five to forty students ranging from kindergarten through grade twelve, all of whom learned, played, and made mischief together as a remarkably close, cheerfully interactive family. So intimate was our learning experience that, in the winter months, our teacher would often heat up homemade soup for us on a pot-bellied stove at the front of the room, next to her desk. And no matter what the weather, my brother and I would walk to school—a quarter-mile trek along a tree-lined gravel road—entirely on our own.

We'd eventually add three more one-room schools to our academic résumés: Wilbur, Morrill, and Maple Grove, each with its own unique architectural quirks, distinctive personality and unforgettable characters.

Among my classmates at one time or another from kindergarten though grade twelve were Karen Cooley (who quickly became my very first girlfriend, though I don't recall ever having told her so), Raymond "Buzzy" Swart (who struggled mightily with reading due to what we learned only years later was a serious, yet-to-be-understood case of dyslexia), and two oddly-behaved siblings, Charlie and Gracie Bloss. For some mysterious reason, Charlie and Gracie didn't appear to inhabit the same world the rest of us did. Yes, they were there in the physical sense of the word. But emotionally and intellectually, they appeared to be stranded on another planet, never really interacting with anyone except each other. Educationally, they were like a pair of abandoned rowboats carried along without benefit of oars on the towering waves of a turbulent ocean.

Some of my grade five classmates at Wilbur School in Rives Township, Michigan. Wilbur was one of four one-room schools I attended.

The highlight of the day at Wilbur, at least in the spring, was lunchtime softball, with half the school on one team, the other half on the other, and the teacher no doubt happily alone inside, thanking God for her one daily thirty-minute escape from teaching. Sometimes, after school, I'd walk a few yards left of the property and have a snack at Applegate's Restaurant, a sleepy, rundown breakfast and lunch place with tired-looking spin stools, booth-side jukeboxes, and a palpable sense of time standing still.

Perhaps the most emblematic of the problems facing a rural, one-room school system was **Mary Northrup**, a middle-aged, cartoon-like character who came across to many people in town, including her students, as the quintessential Old Maid educator. During the one merciful year she was my teacher at Morrill School, I never once saw her crack anything close to a smile. Her one and only *raison d'être* seemed to be to slump down in her chair, glare at the thirty or so children seated in front of her, and tap-tap-tap on her desktop using a dark, sinister segment of rubber hose meant to assure us that here, directly in front of us, was a woman who wasn't about to take shit of any *kind* from any*one*. She struck terror in our hearts, and because she also had a dense forest of thick, dark bristles on her chin, we privately dubbed her "Bluebeard the Pirate."

Yes, I knew our secret laughter was small compensation. But it took at least some of the sting out of being subjected, five days a week, to her skulking, dystopian demeanor. And quite honestly, I don't recall having learned one damn thing from Miss Bluebeard while under her questionable tutelage other than, perhaps, that her ham-handed theatrics would eventually prove to have been only one miserable episode in the mostly heartwarming, humanizing tale of my country-bumpkin, one-room schooling.

I finished my one-room educational odyssey at Maple Grove School, the most classically beautiful structure of the four and my hands-down favorite. Brick-walled and topped with a bright white, well-preserved belfry, it stood serenely beneath a lush canopy of towering deciduous trees that during recess protected us from blistering summer sunlight and sudden rainstorms. We were a close group there, too—so close, in fact, that when Leola Keeney's mother, Margaret, was struck and killed one day while walking to her mailbox just down the road from Maple Grove, the entire school, in an act of genuine affection and classroom solidarity, attended the funeral. In the best sense of the word, we truly were a *family*.

I knew that I was going to sorely miss my one-room school experiences, but as my sixth-grade year came to a close, I'd begun to wonder what was ahead of me and my classmates.

And then, suddenly, the growing undercurrent of rumors north of Jackson—that dramatic changes might very well be just around the corner—became cold, hard fact. All thirteen of the district's one-room schools were formally consolidated, then sold as private residences, and those of us in grades seven through twelve—more than three hundred students altogether—were united under the roof of one sprawling, aesthetically appealing structure called Northwest High School, featuring individual classrooms, a gymnasium, a workshop, a band room, a cafeteria, and even a stage for theatrical performances.

No pool, of course. A luxury like that was provided only for the big-city schools south of Rives Junction. And while moving into a much bigger, noticeably more culturally diverse community of students was at times a frightening prospect, the good news was that, like typical children in their pre-teen years, I was emotionally resilient. And because of it, I knew deep down that I was more than ready for the adventure.

Yes, I was still young and inexperienced and deeply uncertain of my abilities. But, as Napoleon Bonaparte so eloquently wrote, "Ability is of little account without opportunity." And the good news was that I could feel wonderful things coming. I knew I was about to grow intellectually—to make enormous strides in my understanding of the world—all without ever having heard or even *seen* the word *intellectual*, either at home or in school.

I also realized, pretty much intuitively, that I was about to go forth and stand on the very precipice of opportunity. And because of it, my chances of succeeding, in not one but more than one endeavor, seemed more possible than ever before in my young, yet-to-be-tested, painfully parochial existence. And so, *onward* I marched!

ESSAY 7

THE HIGH SCHOOL YEARS:

Three Parts Survival, One Part Enlightenment

*"True terror is to wake up one morning
and discover that your high school class
is running the country."[22]
—Kurt Vonnegut*

My freshman year at Northwest High School, 1959.

No longer sixth-graders and more eager than ever to learn, on day one of grade seven we quickly found out just how dramatically different life was going to be at Northwest High School, our new home.

Instead of storing our books beneath the squeaky-hinged lids of initial-scarred desks straight out of Washington Irving's *The Legend of Sleepy Hollow*, we'd be locking them inside one of dozens of numbered lockers. Instead of being bused to another school's gymnasium for once-a-week physical activity, we would have our very own beautiful, parquet-floored gymnasium featuring pull-out bleachers, a regulation basketball court, an athletic field, and spacious, state-of-the-art shower rooms.

---

22. Kurt Vonnegut, *If This Isn't Nice, What Is?: Advice to the Young*, Seven Stories Press, 2013, 88.

Now, instead of learning music once a week with an itinerant music educator—a caring, kind-hearted woman who taught us with the help of a syndicated radio program called *Today's the Time for Singing*—we'd be learning the musical ropes in purpose-built band and chorus rooms. And finally, instead of eating sack lunches at our own stained and battered desks, we'd be dining in a brightly lit high-volume cafeteria the size of at least a half dozen tennis courts.

To make sure the kids at Northwest wouldn't be tempted to turn their backs on their spiritual obligations, the school would periodically book a prominent area speaker—a Gantryesque Bible Belt evangelist appropriately named Mr. Goodwin—for an all-school assembly. It was never clear to us whether he was a minister, an enthusiastic layman, or an entertainer, because no one, either in town or on the politically conservative school board, ever bothered to tell us what Goodwin was actually up to. That, or—pardon me—where the hell he'd come from.

Goodwin looked and sounded remarkably like **Buffalo Bob Smith**, the creator and on-screen raconteur of NBC Television's *The Howdy Doody Show*. Whenever we heard over the school's intercom that "Mr. Goodwin is coming," we were beside ourselves with excitement—and a great deal of relief, too—because not only was the man genuinely entertaining, with a wealth of music, puppetry, and stage props in his biblical bag of tricks, we knew that for well over an hour, we were going to be free of any readin', writin', and 'rithmetic that wasn't either covertly or openly infused with the Word of God.

Goodwin had *carte blanche* with the school board, simply because at the time, neither the board members nor the federal government felt a need to keep the affairs of church and state separate within the public schools—as a clause in the first amendment of the United States Constitution clearly implies that it should. And unfortunately, in the real world there was also no Phineas T. Bluster to keep the locals in check. Eventually, as a compromise, the district decided to make available an after-school bible club for interested students.

Inviting a deeply religious figure like Goodwin into the school was also just fine and dandy with a small group of hardcore Baptist students whose parents and church leaders considered dancing to be a sin. But trust me: those students were no dummies. Why? Because they always managed to find ways, while on one of the area's wildly popular church-endorsed hayrides, to feed their libidinous appetites deep within layers of locally grown and harvested hay.

An upscale, multipurpose gymnasium! A cafeteria worthy of at least a small-town Midwestern college! Basketball, football, and track teams (*Go, Mounties*)! And even a traveling evangelist who served up not just the Word of the Lord but the precious gift of time away from the classroom!

All of it could feel a little overwhelming at times. But for the majority of us, it was also an exhilarating, multi-faceted adventure—a community-wide drama we'd all be appearing in, day after day, on a sophisticated stage bubbling over with big-city sensibilities. We arrived at school each day feeling miraculously reborn and—well, *some* of us, anyway—doubly committed to learning.

But few things ever really stay the same. Reality may have taken its own sweet time coming, but by late in the first semester of grade seven, it had arrived without fanfare and woven itself, incrementally, into what until then had been a decidedly more placid, more provincial existence. Suddenly, just getting from one room to another between classes had become a Herculean challenge.

Who are all these kids? I'd ask myself while elbowing my way through yet another fast-moving stream of book-laden, adolescently clumsy, appallingly impolite book warriors, all of them trying their damnedest, just like me, to get to their next class on time.

There were still many familiar faces amongst them—students like Buzzy Swart, Karen Cooley, and siblings Charlie and Gracie Bloss—all of who'd been classmates of mine in one or more of the one-room schools I'd attended. Having them there in a brand-new, unfamiliar high school, fighting the crowds alongside me, gave me a heightened, much-appreciated sense of security.

The students came in every imaginable size and shape but, as far as I could tell, only one color: the one described in textbooks of the time as *Caucasian*. Why? Because racially speaking, Jackson, Michigan, was split right down the middle. Anyone whose color wasn't like mine—i.e., lily-white—lived not way out in the country like me, but on the far side of an unofficial, unspoken inner-city color line called Franklin Street. I hardly ever saw what we now call "people of color" while in downtown Jackson, because somehow, without anyone ever needing to remind me, I knew Franklin Street was strictly off-limits for Whites. And if I did happen to see a "colored person," it was nearly always from the other side of the town's main thoroughfare, Michigan Avenue. Blacks in Jackson kept to themselves because they were seldom, if ever, allowed to feel as if they actually belonged in the city.

There were of course signs, both subtle and overt, that to anyone born without blinders should have confirmed the truth about the racial divide in Jackson. Take, for instance, the Jackson County Fairground. I'd driven by it countless times as a teenager, but it wasn't until I was nearly out of high school that, while driving around town one night and thinking more than usual about Jackson, I finally came to my senses and understood what that small sign above the entrance to the Fairground's roller rink, saying "Colored Night," actually meant.

And then there was Parkside High School, first opened in 1963. It was built to ameliorate severe overcrowding at Jackson High School—the school on Wildwood Avenue that my parents had attended in the mid-1930s.

Or *was* it only for that reason? It didn't take long for people with a longstanding distaste for non-Whites to begin calling Parkside "Darkside." Apparently, they believed—happily—that Parkside High had been created, at least in part, to serve students on the "darker" side of town.

Suddenly, Girls, Girls, Girls

The students at Northwest High were from thirteen to eighteen years old—and in a few cases even older, thanks to having been held back during their one-room-school days. But what made the wide variety of ages especially significant was the reality that while I'd just begun to knock on the door of puberty, there were suddenly *girls* everywhere around me who were much farther along in their physiological development than I was. And since so many of the girls in the school were far ahead of me in the race to bodily adulthood, I was hooked like a Michigan sunfish on the spectacle of it all.

I now had to deal with much more than mere academic issues. I began discovering, often the hard way, that in my new, much more populous school, there were kids who not only didn't *look* a lot like me, they didn't *think* a lot like me, either.

One regularly occurring, off-putting conversational theme had to do with my last name—Bachelder—which seemed somehow to be a great mystery in the minds of most of my classmates, despite their complete comfort with locally common names such as Feldpausch and Cadwallader. My guess is that because they'd never heard of the name Bachelder, I seemed to have come from some faraway place, and my name was exotic and, somehow, out of place. (In case you're wondering, I didn't just make those names up for a cheap laugh. David Feldpausch was a neighbor and classmate of mine, and Mrs. Cadwallader was one of my bus drivers.)

"*What* did you say you name is?" classmates would ask. "*Batch-lur*? Weird." (For the record, it wasn't until I moved to Maine, nearly twenty years later, that my last name finally shed its exotic, maddeningly nonplussing persona. That was because in 1632, a liberal Puritan minister (how's *that* for a contradiction?) by the name of **Stephen Bachiler** sailed across the Pond on the *William & Francis*, accompanied by some number of his children. Bachiler eventually returned to England, but his progeny stayed in New England and multiplied. The name Bachiler morphed, as names often do, into more than twenty variants, including Batchelder (common here in northern New England) and Bachelder (my own version, nearly as common).

Suddenly, up in Maine, people I'd never met were saying things like, "Bachelder? You must be related to the man who repairs my tractor. *His* name's Bachelder. Come t' think of it, I know a Bachelder up in Kennebunk, too. Ayuh, we've got a *whole lot* o' them Bachelders 'round he-ah!"

Back to Jackson: Another sure sign of a certain deeply ingrained blue-collar mentality at my new school was what my barnyard-born-and-bred male classmates would often say when they saw me heading down to the band room with a small black case tucked under my arm.

"Whatcha got in there?" they'd ask, genuinely curious about the contents.

"Oh, just my flute," I'd reply. By now I'd been conditioned to expect the worst, and they seldom disappointed me.

"A *flute*?" they'd say. "You've gotta be kidding me! Can I see it?"

"Sure," I'd meekly reply. "Why not?" And then, being generally warm and cooperative in temperament, I'd pop open the case and hold the unassembled flute up, like three silver-plated snakes in a plush-lined coffin, there for easy viewing.

"So you can really play it? Hey, I bet you play the *skin flute* real good, too!"

Blushing profusely and inwardly angry, I'd close the case, put it back under my arm, and head off to band rehearsal. And as I walked away, feeling demeaned and downtrodden, I could hear Farm Boy shouting contemptuously after me:

"Jesus," he bellowed, "where'dja *get* that thing, anyway—from a box o' *Cracker Jack*?"

To the average boy from Rives Junction, Michigan, fresh off the Back Forty, if something didn't come off the underside of a combine or the back of a hay-baler, it had no reason to exist. But not for me. I'd played a Tonette—that licorice-colored plastic training instrument that was ubiquitous in US public schools for much of the twentieth century—but my Armstrong student model flute was my very first genuine musical instrument. Lovingly handcrafted (maybe), that flute was my gateway to musical mastery and a genuine Gift from the Gods. To the Boys from the Farm, though, it seemed like no more than a useless little plaything—a cheap toy, good only for big-city twerps and babbling toddlers.

Oh, Deanna!—High-School Romance, '50s Style

While in high school, I was blessed with a gem of a girlfriend, a girl named Deanna. She lived in the nearby town of Concord, a charming farm-country village whose name was as sweet and unpretentious as she was. And, like me, she played the flute. What more could a young lad like me, deep into music and increasingly interested in the female of the species, have asked for?

Our relationship—the kind of blue-collar fairytale that was really the societal norm all across America—began as a result of our having been chosen, entirely independently of each other, to participate in a multi-district, invitation-only high school honors band.

I have no idea how I managed to introduce myself to her, but it happened, and we were soon writing to each other, not once in a while but several times a week. Dating soon followed, and since we lived less than an hour from each other, I was always more than happy to drive there. After all, we were living in a world where males did the driving and a woman's place was in the passenger seat, where she was expected to flatter her "steady," snuggle up to him, and make him feel special.

As if I didn't already feel special, and more! Why? Because, in that era, people in school and far beyond kept *telling* boys like me, in one way or another, that we were special. And as unfair as it so obviously was, when two teenagers were dating, it was nearly always the *male* who was expected to be both the driver and the striver, to be the young man-on-the-move—the one true measure of a couple's potential for success, both within and beyond marriage.

Our dates—yes, that's what everyone called them at the time— nearly always took place in one of two memorable destinations: either the spectacularly rococo **Michigan Theater**, with its majestic Barton organ that rose up from the basement on a mechanical plat- form whenever it was needed, or the world-renowned **Cascades**, a multi-tiered man-made waterfall whose ever-changing colored lights were accompanied by—what else?—a nonstop flow of sweep- ing, intensely romantic orchestral music and sugar-coated ballads like "Moon River" and "Chances Are." We were far from the only young people who enjoyed the Cascades. Only God knows how many babies have been born over the years as a result of late-night dates there, topped off by steamy backseat liaisons. Sometimes, Deanna and I found a way to enjoy both the Michigan Theater and the Cascades on the same long, idyllic day.

Our first film date was *White Christmas*, with **Bing Crosby, Rosemary Clooney, Danny Kaye, and Vera Ellen** as the featured luminaries. After having lived through the birth of the Rock era— **Bill Haley and His Comets, Gene Vincent, Elvis Presley** and the like—it's still next to impossible for me, after all these years, to imagine that we as teenagers actually found a sappy, old-fogey melodrama like *White Christmas* entertaining. But of course cinema at that time was tailored for adults, not teenagers. The teen cinema genre would not take off for another several years.

For people my age, it wasn't really the movie itself that drew teenagers to the theater. "Going to the movies" was just a bland, socially acceptable cover—a polite, presumably harmless starting point for what was bound to happen, in one form or another, that evening. Teens at the time proudly called it "messing around," and as my girlfriend and I limped through a movie we never really wanted to see, our sweaty hands locked blissfully together, I knew that *I*, at least, could hardly (sic) wait for the fun to begin.

I don't know how all those never-ending, half-fulfilled intimacies affected my girlfriend—it would have been unthinkable for the typical male of the time to even *ask*. But thanks to the sinister, omnipresent aura of sexual repression hanging over my childhood well into my teen years, I would come home from date after date after date with a serious case of *blue balls*. And since at the time I couldn't conceive—now *there's* a double entendre for the ages!—of ever finding someone I'd be comfortable talking about it with, I, like countless sexually repressed teens of that era, suffered my sexual deprivations shamefully and secretly.

It's probably a blessing that Viagra—"the blue pill"—wasn't introduced until 1998. Of course, my recollection as a teenager was that I had no trouble with erotic feelings. My only difficulty was that, socially speaking, I was scared shitless at the prospect of actually *doing* something about them.

We were taught then that the only socially acceptable way to deal with our sexual appetites was to wait until marriage. More often than not, thanks to the era's deep fear of engaging in premarital sex, that south-of-the-border Gateway to Nirvana would remain clamped shut tighter than the dark, vaulted entrance to a Transylvanian castle. And so, like tens of thousands of late-'50s couples, we did exactly that: we *waited*. And I guess I don't really need to tell you that such habitual deprivations are never physically or psychologically good for two well-meaning people who are deeply in love, in urgent need of sexual fulfillment, or both.

The irony of my "failure" to make the Big Move on my girl-friend over our four long years of dating was that, in the end, doing *nothing* about our carnal desires was the best possible thing we could have done. That's because we weren't at all ready to have children. Nor, when we finally got married, were we even ready for *marriage*. And given how little we actually knew about each other, we were most certainly not ready to spend the rest of our natural lives together. So, for those and other reasons, the marriage lasted less than a year.

Fortunately, Deanna went on to remarry and live a rewarding life with another, more suitable mate. And there can be no doubt that the two of them were far better prepared, both emotionally and practically, than she and I were. Sadly, she's gone now—she died in 2022—but at least I have the satisfaction of knowing she found happiness with another.

Can I rightfully claim to have been a *victim* of the era's confused, duplicitous, unresolved ideas about sex? Not really. Was it other people's fault that I couldn't bring myself to set sails to the wind and "do the dirty" I as a teenager wanted so desperately to do on those nights when I was so hot and bothered and burning with desire? I don't think so.

Here, as I see it, are a few of the dark forces, quietly at work, that made me as sexually inhibited as I so obviously was. Whether those forces were somehow "blue-collar" in nature is still an open question:

- **My mother and father**, who could never quite bring themselves to talk with me openly and honestly about sexual matters. They apparently had enough to do just keeping up with their *own* bedtime frolics.

- **The public schools**, which were still lightyears away from offering candid, comprehensive, constructive guidance in matters of temptation and the flesh.
- **Church leaders of every kind and denomination,** who supported the culture's code of silence around sexuality even though the congregants (and, sometimes, the clergy themselves) obviously went home and messed around at bedtime. Any mentions of sexuality in the average House of Worship were more often than not politely evasive, thoroughly whitewashed *Let's Pretend* moments, meaning that in matters of sexuality, the congregants' children in particular were left entirely in the dark and on their own.
- **The Hays Code,** which kept Hollywood in line, resulting in saccharine-sweet films such as *White Christmas* and, perhaps a little less sugary, *That Touch of Mink*.
- **Uptight television network executives,** who showed us an endless early-evening parade of squeaky-clean married couples—including **Ozzie and Harriet, Lucy and Ricky, Fred and Ethel**, and **Ward and June**, to name a few. The marriages portrayed on television were preternaturally blissful and essentially drained of anything even close to sexual honesty. The higher-ups in the television industry wouldn't even allow two married people to be seen *in the same bed* together, so fearful were they of losing their ratings by telling the truth about *amore* in their fraudulently prudish sitcoms. As for **Lois Lane**'s percolating libido, it was perpetually foiled by prissy, wimpy Clark Kent's failure to reciprocate—not to mention Superman's preoccupation with crime-fighting, which left him no time for such trifling things as sexual dalliances.
- And finally, **my very own highly culpable** self for failing to rebel, openly and in real time, while in the throes of yet another minimally lusty late-night tangle with my girlfriend.

I was just as guilty—just as responsible as anyone else—for my physical and ethical insecurities. Like so many other cautious young men of the '50s (perhaps especially those labelled "blue-collar" and raised in Michigan's Bible Belt) I might have been a Straight Shooter in my *dreams*, but fortunately, I shot only *blanks*—the *imaginary* kind—in the back seat of my Chevy, the 1950s equivalent of a motel room for unmarried couples. I simply wasn't ready to be biologically honest with myself. So instead, I did what the times demanded and my parents expected me to do: I *deprived* myself. And for some reason, when I look back on those days, the only color I can see is *blue*—the color of the collar of that segment of the population who often felt powerless, ill-informed, undervalued, uncertain of themselves, and trapped in someone else's idea of where they belonged in the hierarchy and how they should conduct themselves there.

* * *

Over the next half-dozen years—1957 to 1962—I studied hard, dreamed big (at least within my limited range of aspirations), and joined every available organization including the Future Teachers of America while earning awards, accolades, and a coveted scholarship to northern Michigan's Interlochen National Music Camp.

But at home I was given little if any active, constructive advice about how to conduct myself, how and why to make wise decisions, and how to prepare for adulthood. Nor was I regularly praised for either my basic intelligence or my many run-of-the-mill, day-to-day accomplishments.

The precious gift of praise was more frequently doled out to my brother, a science-minded, technology-loving student who went on to become a psychologist at a time when "science people" were thought to be inherently more intelligent than poets and actors, dancers and musicians. I soon learned to my chagrin and disillusionment that my parents, like countless others of the era, had bought into that presumption wholesale. And because of it, they clearly considered me to be intellectually inferior to my brother while at the same time actively struggling—more often than not without success—to hide their real feelings from me.

It was during my senior year in high school that I was offered, one sunny afternoon, the deadly Kool-Aid that was my mother's "advice" in the matter of me and higher education.

"I thought I should remind you," she said with uncharacteristic sweetness, "that just because your brother's gone off to college doesn't mean you have to. After all, maybe college just isn't right for you."

Mommie Dearest must have thought she'd delivered her poison-dart soliloquy at just the right time. After all, she knew perfectly well that I was waiting anxiously to learn whether any of the three colleges I'd applied to were going to accept me. So, once I'd absorbed her message, I was left to consider only two possible motives for what seemed to be her less-than-sincere advice. Either she was genuinely worried that rejection would have a devastating effect on me (and, of course, she would have been absolutely right about that), or she and my father were secretly, ardently hoping that, whether I liked it or not, an across-the-board rejection would be welcome salve for their chronically ailing budget.

Still—in spite of the increasing difficulty I was having living with my parents in a cramped, claustrophobic, tension-filled home—life was good. The sun nearly always seemed to be shining, at least at school. Thanks to six years of private instrumental instruction—yes, paid for by my father, to be fair—my skills as a musician had steadily improved, and I would soon be more than ready to study music at the university level.

So *why*, I often ask myself, were their expectations for me—and indeed my own expectations for myself—so low and so deeply entrenched? I would need many anxious, ill-focused, painfully underproductive years to learn the answer.

Like so many others in the post–World War II Era of Conformity, I had no one around me with intellectual drive, personal ambition, a sense of adventure, or—perhaps worst of all—any real sense of parental responsibility for my intellect. The prevailing mindset in blue-collar families was that the public schools, not the parents, were entirely responsible for the intellectual growth of children. As the parents saw it, they had enough to do in trying to put food on the table and clothes on the backs of their children. Compared to those duties, the active nurturance of anything considered intellectual, for either their children or themselves, were trivial and unimportant.

Whatever aspirations I managed to keep alive during my high school years were nearly entirely the result of a small handful of **public school educators** who labored for more than the weekly arrival of their paychecks. I owe those teachers an enormous debt and would dearly love to be able to go back and thank them, one by one, for what they gave me: a genuine sense of possibilities far beyond the painfully low horizons of the mired-in-the-past, religion-obsessed village I called home for so many years. But of course the natural passing of time has made such a reunion all but impossible.

An equally important intellectual lifeline for me throughout my junior and senior high school years was the Carnegie Library on Michigan Avenue in downtown Jackson. I remember it as an elegant, inspiring architectural wonder both inside and out. Not only did the Carnegie give me my very first dependable, in-depth immersion in the joys of reading; its second-floor art gallery was a must-see destination for me, long before I could have imagined just how important the visual arts would become for me in my later years. While the Carnegie was thirteen miles away from our home in Rives Junction, the distance didn't stop my mother—herself a passionate, intellectually curious reader—from getting us there on occasion, always chauffeured by my father, to stock up on books.

The Carnegie Library at 244 West Michigan Avenue in
downtown Jackson, Michigan.[23]

Fortunately, it seemed to me that, in the minds of nearly all
my classroom teachers, I was pretty much destined to enroll in
college and would therefore have no need of career counseling. The
decision about what colleges I might actually apply to—or in fact
whether I should go to college at all—was left either to my parents,
to particular teachers who believed in me, or to my great-aunt
Olive, who was rumored to have taken one college-level course
years before and who therefore would surely know all about higher
education and which college would be the "best fit" for me.

All this makes me think of an especially meaningful passage
from **Ayn Rand**'s best-selling 1938 novella, *Anthem*. In Rand's chill-
ing, mind-controlling dystopia, youngsters are actively discouraged
from ever thinking they are *individuals*—people who might have
thoughts, feelings, and aspirations different from those of their
classmates. In *Anthem* world, to think as an individual is strictly
forbidden, and anyone caught using the word *I* instead of *we* is

23. "Jackson District Library, Jackson MI" by Andrew Jameson (own work), CC BY-
SA-3.0 (https://creativecommons.org/licenses/by-sa/3.0), via Wikimedia Commons.
Available at https://en.m.wikipedia.org/wiki/Jackson_Carnegie_Library#/media/
File%3AJackson_District_Library_Jackson_MI.JPG.

immediately snuffed out—disposed of as worthless to the cause of what **William H. Whyte** would later call "groupthink."

When the students in *Anthem* turn fifteen, they're brought before the author's version of today's career counselor, the Council of Vocations. Each student steps before the Council and is immediately pronounced either a doctor, a carpenter, a cook, or a leader. Then the students raise their right arms and say, "The will of our brothers be done." Only the students identified as leaders are allowed to explore interests of their choosing.

Sounds a lot like *totalitarianism* to me. And indeed, there were moments in high school when, while trying to make critical decisions about my future, I might as well have been standing before Rand's Council of Vocations, waiting humbly for what was to be my lifetime "assignment."

I ended up as a freshman at **Eastern Michigan University** only because of a chance conversation with my twelfth-grade civics teacher, Mr. Stott. While demonstrating how, as the marching band's drum major, I would need to present myself, he paused and said, "By the way, Ross, where will you be going to college?"

"Actually, I haven't really thought about it all that much," I replied.

"Well, then, why don't you go to **Eastern Michigan University**," he smiled. "I went there, and I really liked it!"

"*Okay*, then!" I smiled in return. "Guess I *will!*"

And when my three college acceptances arrived in the mail, I chose EMU without even one brief consideration of either the wisdom or the foolhardiness of my choice. This, then, was parent-free, analysis-free "career counseling" as I lived it. And I suspect that thousands of high-schoolers in the Eisenhower era got their career counseling the very same way.

So now, with *that* decision off my shoulders, I could begin to plan for my future. Deep down inside, I was convinced that I'd just put my blue-collar roots behind me forever and was now securely positioned on the Conveyor Belt to Nirvana—destination, Eastern

Michigan University in Ypsilanti—where, I was certain, my mobility would be nothing but upward and my success at an endeavor of *my* choice and no one else's would be both guaranteed and truly, exhilaratingly glorious.

The one deep disappointment I experienced my senior year of high school concerned my wanting to take an introductory studio art class. I begged to be excused from band for just one day a week so I could fit the art class into my schedule—but the administrators denied my request.

Their argument—which I've always considered to be specious, ill-advised, and unforgivable—was that I owed my allegiance not to what they must have considered to be my adolescent moment of whimsy, but to the band itself. It is perhaps ironic, then, that it wasn't until many years later, when I was nearly sixty years old, that I taught myself, entirely from scratch and without any formal instruction, to be an imaginative, highly productive visual artist in several media. To this day, I continue to create and exhibit my artworks here in northern New England.

In September of 1962, I moved fifty miles east to Ypsilanti and became an EMU freshman. I left Jackson and its more plebeian municipal offshoot, Rives Junction, with my self-esteem still reasonably intact and my sense of life's possibilities blossoming like the intoxicating, many-colored flowers in a truly magical garden.

BYE-BYE, JACKSON, HELLO YPSI!

From Bumpkin to Sophisticate in One Giant Leap

"I see death by culture shock."[24]
—Woody Allen

For the record, any broad, negative assessments I make while describing my experiences at Eastern Michigan University are *in no way unique to EMU*. The internal issues facing Eastern in the 1960s—everything from student underachievement and faculty incompetence to curricular weaknesses, underfunding, and less-than-ideal facilities—were undeniably endemic to all but the most elite, most heavily endowed institutions. Colleges and universities of every kind were being profoundly negatively affected by ongoing social problems, weak governmental support, stubborn resistance to change, public misperceptions, and, all too often, a debilitating lack of imagination.

Especially problematic was Eastern's close proximity to the world-renowned University of Michigan—less than fifteen minutes away by car on a good day. That topographical reality made it next to impossible for EMU not to be branded as academically inferior, blue-collar in composition, or an unpleasant and debilitating combination of the two. And no matter how brilliant, nationally renowned, or universally respected many of the more illustrious

---

24. Woody Allen, *Whatever Works*, Sony Pictures Classics, 2009.

EMU faculty were, there was always a nagging, campus-wide undercurrent of uncertainty: *Hmm,* we often wondered, *maybe Professor Chichi is here in Ypsi because he couldn't cut it over in Ann Arbor!* And, not surprisingly, a large segment of EMU's undergraduate students—including my own chronically self-doubting self—felt the same unsettling way, at times, about *themselves.*

I suppose it's only human for some of us, on occasion, to slap derogatory, dehumanizing labels on anything or anyone who happens to be different. But it really shouldn't be necessary to point out here that some of the finest students—and *faculty,* too—in America's colleges and universities come from families who've been living the blue-collar life for generations. And regardless of their family history, they can be *damn good* at what they do in academia and beyond—in the same way that the Silver Spoon members of America's more elite institutions can be *damn bad* at what *they* do. White-collar folks have *no* monopoly on competence, creativity, reliability, or plain human decency.

It's also critically important to know, but seldom acknowledged in the media, that some of the finest imaginable students and faculty come from public, state-sponsored institutions—colleges very much like EMU—which are nonetheless generally considered to be somehow inherently inferior to the elites.

This genuinely enrages me. Have you noticed how many Ivy League graduates have been in the headlines in the last few years for High Crimes, Misdemeanors, and other very public displays of indifference to common sense, ethics, and morality? To cite just one glaring, horrific example, we in the US only recently voted Donald J. Trump—a convicted felon, unapologetic bigot, admirer of dictators, and five-star misogynist—into the White House for a *second* time. Simply put, there is no logical connection between sound moral judgment and the perceived status of the college a given person has attended. What, we must ask, did the Wharton School do to instill in the president of the Free World *any* semblance of a moral compass?

But back, now, to *my* college of choice, Eastern Michigan University.

* * *

When I first set foot on the campus of Eastern Michigan University, I fell instantly in love with the place.

There were, of course, many perfectly understandable reasons for my feelings: I was now officially a *college* student, and EMU, known proudly at the time as the Home of the Hurons, would be *my* home, too. My high-school girlfriend would be impressed, and from an admittedly inconvenient distance, I was certain she'd love me even more. And, perhaps best of all, I'd just cut the rapidly fraying umbilical cord between my parents and myself. As I saw it, I was finally *Free at Last! Free at Last! Thank God Almighty, Free at Last!*

For a very young man like me, raised on the edge of the sleepy, insular village of Rives Junction, Michigan, the city of Ypsilanti—pop. 21,000—was an exotic, breathtakingly sophisticated mini-metropolis, teeming with life and full to overflowing with yet-to-be-imagined possibilities.

It was in every respect my very own Harvard, an ivy-laced oasis of Higher Learning, resplendent with meticulously mani-cured lawns—no open cesspool here!—and handsome, historically significant buildings. One of them, hard on (sic) the edge of the campus, was Ypsilanti's world-renowned water tower—a provoc-atively penis-like structure, erected (sic) in 1890, that must surely have teased the already percolating sex drives of countless incom-ing (sic) freshmen over its more than six decades of metaphorically concupiscent existence.

And while for me, at least, the campus was Harvard-quality *all the way* because of its peaceable, contemplative elegance, it didn't stop me from being equally charmed by its decidedly blue-col-lar extremities. Along the periphery of the area I was destined to spend the most time in—the Alexander Music Building and its nearby, umbilically connected companion, Pease Auditorium—was a less-than-shimmering necklace of inelegantly designed, decidedly blue-collar buildings that had nothing directly to do with the university. Among them was one chalk-white, Lilliputian sugar cube of a place called **Roy's Grill**.

To enter Roy's, you had to squeeze through a narrow screen door at one beveled, streetside corner of the structure. Then, once inside, you could either sit on one of the half-dozen available spin stools or take your order and run—an early incarnation of today's grab-n-go style of dining.

The latter approach may have been good for others, but I always preferred the counter. It gave me a chance to study and sometimes even talk with my fellow thrown-together epicureans—a fascinating, sometimes exotic mixture of bleary-eyed students, instructors on the way to their lectures, and a steady flow of colorful, early-morning working-class characters to whom I was irresistibly drawn. Between them and Roy, the proprietor—a beefy, pie-faced curmudgeon who always made his guests feel welcome—I found myself being subconsciously tutored in the art of identifying characters worthy of populating the fiction I would eventually be writing. For me, Roy's Grill became another classroom, one for which I had an exceptionally deep and lasting affection.

* * *

I didn't just saunter effortlessly into EMU. While my brother had earned enough scholarships, two years earlier, to fund his acceptance at Michigan State University (a much larger and more prestigious university just north of us in Lansing), I hadn't quite matched his windfall. So to supplement the modest scholarships I *did* earn, I borrowed money from the Jackson-based John George Jr. Student Loan Fund—at an astonishingly low 2% interest rate—to cover at least four years of tuition.

Not surprisingly, the loan didn't even *begin* to cover all the other costs I'd be incurring. The result was that every semester during the academic year, I kept myself in school through the university's federally funded Work-Study Program. And every summer I worked full-time in a variety of Detroit area factories—most of them intimately connected to the Motor City's then-booming automotive industry.

Nor did I have the advantage of what today is called legacy admission, the still controversial practice of giving preference to applicants whose affluent parent or parents had attended the school—long before the applicant was born—and who would therefore be a "good investment," thanks to the likelihood that said parent(s) would make a generous donation to that school. Like a great many post–World War II parents, my mother and father never went beyond high school. This meant that they lacked sufficient earning power to send me off to the college of my choice, free of worry over finances.

The Work-Study Program was a very good deal. Not only did it help students afford their schooling, it often matched them with jobs remarkably relevant to their academic majors. Thanks to that program, I landed several meaningful jobs over the years. One of them was as orchestra librarian under the baton of internationally renowned conductor and composer **José Serebrie**r, who'd taken a one-year sabbatical assignment at EMU in the hope that it would give him the freedom to compose in a quiet, academically serene environment. Since I played flute in the EMU orchestra, being orchestra librarian was an especially pertinent assignment.

Earlier in my undergraduate years, I also worked as a classical music programmer for WEMU, the university's FM radio station. Later on, in graduate school, I condensed criminology articles for **R. Neil McLarty**, who at the time was the acting head of the school's Department of History and Social Sciences. Like all the jobs I held as an undergraduate, the grad school assignment was also a part of the Work-Study Program.

Whether you consider yourself blue-collar, white-collar, or, like me, an often-befuddled mixture of the two, I feel certain that as you continue reading these essays you'll see reflections not just of yourselves but of your friends, your neighbors, your co-workers, and the sometimes maddening but always exhilarating story of a multicolored America, hard at work. Because with or without labels, we know deep down that we're all in this together, trying to discover just who we are and where we belong in the human community. And what better place to do the discovering than in a college classroom?

ESSAY

MY UNDERGRADUATE INSTRUCTORS:
A Faculty Sampling

"After all manner of Professors have done their best for us [. . .] [t]he true University of these days is a Collection of Books."[25]
—Thomas Carlyle (1795-1881)

As anyone who's been a college student knows, faculty members, like students, come in a wide variety of backgrounds, appearances, personalities, academic obsessions, and teaching styles. A large portion of them seem well prepared, both academically and emotionally, to deal with students of the blue-collar kind—students who may arrive on campus with less than secure self-esteem and even less parental guidance in the shaping of their futures.

I came to higher education bursting with pride for my musical accomplishments and more than merely eager to make my mark in the classroom. But I was also a classic blue-collar specimen: emotionally insecure, intellectually shallow (thanks in part to the low standards and questionable ambitions of the people around me at home and in school), and negatively affected by what I would later learn was the suffocatingly conventional thinking in rural, overwhelmingly conservative south central Michigan, where I was raised.

---

25. Thomas Carlyle, *On Heroes, Hero-worship, and the Heroic in History: Six Lectures,* James Fraser, 1841, 262.

So it ought not to surprise anyone that the moment I walked onto a college campus for the very first time, I was ravenously hungry for meaningful role models—academics who would recognize my solid intellectual potential, my praiseworthy idealism, and my unquestionable ambitions. Even if my own mother and father thought I wasn't "college material," I was no dummy. And I had come to college determined to prove them not just wrong, but *dead* wrong.

A sampling of the academics I quickly learned to respect might help you understand just what I was looking for and which instructors were, in my opinion, the most capable of delivering the goods.

Judith Gallatin

She was an articulate, sophisticated, and ever so erudite assistant professor—so obviously learned! So worldly-wise in demeanor! And to a late teen with a natural-born appetite for both knowledge and the opposite sex (in what order yet to be determined), she was eerily, provocatively, undeniably sexy. I loved her course in adolescent psychology. It shouldn't have come as a surprise to anyone, either. After all, I still *was* an adolescent, and I had the fired-up, leaping libido to prove it.

Hayden Morgan

Morgan, at the time the chairman of the Department of Music, was the man for whom the word *avuncular* must surely have been coined. He was handsomely dressed, meticulously groomed, and academic in demeanor, yet without so much as an ounce of pretentiousness in the way he carried himself in the classroom. He was terrific as our first-year instructor in *solfège*, the art of learning to sightread music with the aid of sol-fa syllables. He was at all times warm, patient, encouraging, and tolerant of errors. And he was the only professor in the music department ever to call me into his office one day and warn me, with astonishing politeness, that smoking pipes, cigarettes, and cigars was probably not the wisest choice of indulgence for a wind instrument specialist like me.

Sadly, I wasn't mature enough at the time to take advantage of his common-sense, well-meaning advice. Was I crazy or what, sitting there sprawled out in the lobby, dragging on unfiltered Camel after Camel, in full view of an endless parade of professors? By the time I'd come to my senses and shed myself of my dirty habit, Dr. Morgan had moved on, replaced by a man every bit as sophisticated but not nearly as warm-hearted and indulgent as Morgan. The only good news about the entire affair is that it took me less than two years of huffing and puffing, as an allegedly serious student of the flute, to kick the habit.

William "Bill" Fitch

I'd already had experience with oboist Dr. William Fitch at Interlochen National Music Camp, so it was a great surprise and a genuine pleasure when, on day one at EMU, I learned that he would be my orchestra conductor, chamber music coach, and music ed trainer.

While every bit the academic, Fitch was also delightfully homespun as an instructor. Unlike many of his nose-in-the-air colleagues, he didn't appreciate being called "Doctor." The truth is that in our woodwind quintet rehearsals, I almost *wanted* us to play poorly on occasion because we would then be treated to another of his colorful, imaginative barnyard colloquialisms. Like, for instance, "My God! I could throw a handful o' corn against a barn door and sound more musical than you guys!" It was my favorite, and oddly, I couldn't quite get enough of it. Yes, Bill Fitch was stern. But he was also naturally funny and, on occasion, even playful. In short, he was *human*, and I'd had little of that in my "Don't sass me," "You'll get yours," "Put that silly book away" childhood.

Erich Goldschmidt

Erich Goldschmidt, EMU's resident organist and professor of music history, always struck me as being at least a rung or two above his colleagues on the Music Department's academic ladder. It may in part have been because of his guttural German accent, which was sometimes difficult for me to understand and caused me to see him as culturally exotic and intellectually untouchable. I had enormous, unassailable respect for the man. His dreamy yet diamond-hard Hermann Hesse expression made him seem almost biblical to me.

Goldschmidt also had a warm, sweet smile that invariably telegraphed to everyone around him that he was an innately gentle man—a man of high character, unimpeachable fairness, and nobility of purpose. But the gentleness and fairness didn't automatically translate into tolerance—especially of anyone who proved not to have been fully devoted to his studies. It explains why, at the end of the semester, he gave me a D+ in Music History and then, while smiling more sweetly than my grandmother's sugar cookies, apologized—profusely—for having needed to drop the axe on me.

But, curiously, it didn't offend me at all. I knew he had the highest imaginable standards and ethics. Oh—and I also knew without a doubt that I fully deserved the grade he gave me. That's because, at the time, I was working much harder on my social life and personal challenges than on any of my classwork. He needed only to have a second look at my pathetically inept performance on his final exam to know that by giving me the grade he did, he'd done the right thing.

He also must have been genuinely mystified at my poor performance in his class because, as he told me one day while rehearsing one of his favorite J.S. Bach organ partitas at Pease Auditorium, "The truth is that Bach is my Daily Bread. I really don't know what I would do without it."

Goldschmidt must have wondered on more than one occasion what *I* thought of his favorite composer. But unfortunately, I was far more deeply in love with the works of moderns and romantics like Mahler, Stravinsky, and Borodin to worry about Papa Bach and all the other Baroque-era luminaries, and my grade in Music History proved it.

My appreciation of Bach would come much later in my evolution as a musician, but at least it came, and I learned to love his works as much as those of any of the other Greats.

Dorothy James

Like her colleague Erich Goldschmidt, Dorothy James—the Music Department's veteran music theory guru and a nationally known choral composer—had sky-high standards. She'd been through a lot as a student of music, both in the US and abroad, and, like Goldschmidt, she had no problem giving me precisely what I deserved in her music theory class. I managed, somehow, to squeak by with a C+. (Did she like me just a tad more than Goldschmidt did? Maybe so, but I doubt it.)

The truth is that I was surprised she gave me a grade as high as she *did*. At the time, as an enthusiastic, recently-declared English minor, more in love with authors and allegories than with half-steps and harmony, I turned in a truly execrable performance as a student of music theory. So, *ouch!* I got just what Ms. James knew I deserved, proving to me that her standards were no lower than Goldschmidt's—and, who knows, maybe even higher.

I continue to have an unalterable, picture-perfect memory of James's manner of dress while lecturing: grandmotherly flower-print dresses which to me seemed straight out of 1930s British cinema. But I have an even more immoveable memory of an incident that occurred one day in her classroom—one in which I happened to be the dubious, entirely uninvited protagonist.

I'd been hanging out in the department lobby before class and killing time by, of all things, *smoking a cigar*. (My God! In Alexander Music! What would I have done had Hayden Morgan been around at the time?) I was deep in thought, puffing away, when the lobby's clock said it was class time.

I thought to myself, *Already? I can't afford to be late!*

It was still the dead of winter, so I was wearing my heaviest all-weather coat. I remember jamming the cigar against a metal door frame—how terribly uncouth of me—then cupping my hand around the stub and tucking it into my coat pocket as I dashed down the hall. *Whew!* I laughed inwardly. *Just in time. I'm sure it's out, so I'll just keep it in my coat until class is over. All Clear!*

But it *wasn't* out, and the emergency wasn't over. Somewhere in the midst of a discussion of linear progression and chord clusters, I smelled *smoke*. Then I glanced down and watched in horror as a spiral of noxious cigar fumes began rising conspicuously up from the left side of my coat. Fortunately, the room where music theory was taught faced out on a parking lot, and at the far end of the room was a door that led straight outside.

A door! Eureka! I had to make a choice, and *right away*, so instead of sitting there at my desk and allowing myself to be ritually burned to a crisp, I leapt out of my chair, dashed out the door, tossed my coat on the pavement, and over and over again stomped the life out of both the jacket and my smoldering, foul-smelling stogy.

To my astonishment, no one—not even the renowned Dorothy James—said a word as I came in, settled back into my chair, and tuned into the remainder of her lecture.

It's a wonder I got a C+. Dottie James would forever be one of my most beloved academics—a kind-hearted, very human mother figure who, with incomparable compassion, tolerated conduct which in any other classroom would have resulted in permanent dismissal.

Franklin Case

Top of the line! I couldn't have asked for a better first-ever college-level instructor, especially in the art of essay writing. Handsome and well-dressed, with state-of-the-art elbow patches and a quietly elegant tie, he was the perfect choice to help build the character and work ethic of a young, bushy-tailed, blue-collar upstart in search of the perfect role model.

Franklin Case in Ypsilanti in 2014.

Case also has the distinction of having provided me with my very first opportunity to publish as a writer—a short story, title forgotten, about a Civil War soldier—in *Cellar Roots*, the EMU literary magazine he founded and oversaw for many of his forty years as a college professor. I'll have much more to say about Mr. Case later in this book, but I mustn't forget to tell you that many years later, when visiting Case in Ypsilanti—a joyful reunion—I confessed to him that I'd needed more than a glass or two of wine to light my fire and write that story for him. The B+ he gave me was the Light of My Life as a Freshman Comp student in need of reassurance about my skills as a writer.

Wendell Harwood

Wendell Harwood, September 1967. Wendell was the custodian for the EMU music department and, though few people knew it, an outstanding pianist.

In the strict sense of the word, Wendell Harwood—the head custodian of the Department of Music—was anything but an academic. But I've given him an honored place on this list because, from the very beginning, he taught me as much about life as any tenured faculty member I interacted with while at EMU. Because of that, Wendell had—and indeed *continues* to have—a very special place in my heart. And I can promise you that Franklin Case, my Freshman Comp instructor, would have been the first person to understand why I admired Wendell so much.

What makes Harwood's influence on me so powerful—and so remarkably inspiring—is that, unlike Case, Harwood never finished high school. And yet, in his own unique way, Wendell will forever be chiseled into my personal stone tablet as every bit as intelligent, insightful, compassionate, and wise as Case—or for that matter, any other heavily credentialed academic on the campus. Why? Because he had qualities that come not from the accumulation of credentials—sheepskins from prestigious Halls of Learning—but from deep within the hallowed chambers of his very human heart.

Was Harwood proudly blue-collar? Unquestionably! Was Case emphatically, undeniably white-collar? You bet! But it is perhaps the dramatic difference in their status within the boundaries of campus life that makes the two of them the very emblem of the meaninglessness of labeling people according to how they chose to make a living and how they were formally or informally trained to succeed there. With degrees from the University of Connecticut and the University of Michigan, Case had a classically academic background. Harwood's credentials, on the other hand, came lock, stock, and barrel from the School of Life.

Remarkably, Wendell Harwood—the quiet, unassuming Department of Music custodian—became as much an inspiration for me as many of my favorite professors did as I worked my way through my first demanding year as a college student. Not only did he help make me a better learner, he made me a better *person*.

PLAIN OLD ME and the ROTC:

Not Exactly Top Gun

"War is the outcome of grown men not being able to act maturely."[26]
—Vanesa Molina

One of the wonders of my early years at EMU was how I managed to fit ROTC—the Reserve Officers' Training Corps—into my already overbooked schedule. And yet the scheduling proved to be not nearly as difficult as understanding why, in addition to my hard-earned status as a freshman music student, I suddenly had to be trained to be, of all things, a *soldier*. Indeed, other than in jingoistic films hawking patriotism and glorifying war, I'd never been able to see a connection between music and military conflict, and I still can't.

I didn't even have my first ROTC experience until several weeks into the first semester of my freshman year, and to say it caught me entirely off guard would be an understatement of epic proportions. *ROTC? Where the hell did this come from?* It was as if some tin-star, medal-blanketed general parachuted down from "Headquarters" smack into the middle of band rehearsal and ordered all musicians

---

26. Vanesa Molina, "War is dumb, it's time to grow up," Cerritos College *Talon Marks*, November 1, 2023, https://www.talonmarks.com/opinion/2023/11/01/war-is-dumb-grow-up/.

of the male persuasion to put down their instruments and "report for duty at 0700, rain or shine."

I guess I should have read the small print in my application form. But I *hadn't*, because, quite frankly, all I really cared about at the time was how I should plan to dress while on campus, how I'd ever get my head around *solfège*, how I'd be ranked in the orchestra's flute section (*Please, God, not third part!*), how to finger a high D-sharp on the flute, and whether the tip a high school friend gave me—that college girls were "hotter than hot and ready to trot"—was really true.

ROTC, it turned out, was an absolute requirement for the first two years of any male who happened to be matriculating at a land grant college. And yet I didn't learn—or even inquire into—the reasons I was being trained for military service until long after I'd finished school. The growing conflict in Southeast Asia wasn't even on my radar in 1962. All I knew was that, as an incoming freshman, I was allegedly going to be miraculously transformed from a nerdy, run-of-the-mill high school band member into an expertly trained, fully certified music educator—not into some nameless small-town grunt with an M16 on one shoulder and a saxophone on the other, all set to step in when, God forbid, there were suddenly not enough officers to do Uncle Sam's work.

It soon became clear to me that being ordered to "report for duty" was no joke. We were told we'd be in *trouble* if we didn't. And once the order came down, we'd scramble the night before to get ready for the dreaded inspection that all soldiers, even the *pretend* ones like ourselves, must face. Our scratchy olive-drab uniforms—shirts, pants, and ties—had to be crisper than a potato chip and absolutely free of either wrinkles or stains.

Uniforms, yes. Well-fitting, no. But it was the condition of our *shoes* that triggered our greatest apprehensions. While we stood inspection, would the officer in charge discover a nearly invisible scrape or smudge on one of my shoes, gleefully stomp on both of them, then order me to take them home and make them respectable again? This, I was warned, was a very real possibility.

To try our best to ward off a windstorm of demerits, we'd dash down to the nearest off-campus drugstore and buy a jar of **5 Day Deodorant Pads**, known throughout the ROTC community as the ultimate guard against shoe-based inspector rage. And the universal understanding was that if, after giving our black leather oxfords several rub-downs with these things, we couldn't see our reflections in perfect focus on the surface of our shoes, we'd receive a generous helping of humiliation, seasoned with demerits, in the near future.

Every few weeks, we were required to march together in perfect left–right cadence. Each student also had to present a perfectly cleaned and polished rifle, demonstrate how to operate it, and properly execute the ritual of "presenting arms." I've no doubt that EMU's ROTC program never had to suffer a more incompetent rifleman than Yours Truly.

For me, at least, ROTC was altogether a nightmare. I was profoundly grateful to know that after my sophomore year I would no longer be required to be a soldier-in-training as a condition of mastering the flute and, eventually, waving my baton at a band full of aspiring high school musicians. And with a little more after-the-fact research, I discovered that had I enrolled at EMU in 1968 instead of 1962, I wouldn't have needed to worry about ROTC at all. Why? Because 1968 was when, thanks to nationwide protests against the Vietnam War, the program was no longer mandatory for men at EMU. *Maybe*, I sometimes say to myself, *I should have waited until then to become an EMU student.*

As I look back on my experiences with M16 training, ill-fitting uniforms, and 5 Day Deodorant Pads, I can't help feeling that ROTC was less a golden opportunity for young men than an inefficient way for the US military to create more officers to push forward the blue-collar cannon fodder—disproportionately African-Americans—in what had become an unjust, ineptly handled, profoundly humiliating blemish on America's once-sterling reputation as a militarily superior country.

Once my freshman year, including my first year of ROTC, was out of the way, it was time for some well-deserved summer fun—but it wasn't destined to be the kind of "fun" I envisioned.

Summertime employment during college gave me my first tastes of genuine blue-collar labor, and it was seldom if ever to my liking. During my undergraduate years, I tackled a wide variety of relatively lucrative blue-collar jobs, working long, hard hours at everything from burning off the ends of rebar trapped in discarded cement barriers (one of the worst jobs I've ever had) to lifting fenders during third shift at the renowned River Rouge Auto Assembly Plant in Dearborn—at the time, the largest automobile plant of its kind in the world.

If you've ever seen **Charlie Chaplin**'s brilliant 1936 film *Modern Times*—I highly recommend it—then you have a very good idea what it was like for me at the Rouge plant my first and final night. I couldn't keep up with the frenetic pace of the assembly line. When, in desperation, I shouted to the foreman that I simply couldn't continue to do the work, he ordered me to stay right where I was. "Get back to your position!" he roared. "You ain't goin' *nowhere!*"

But guess what? I *did* go—right off that diabolical assembly line, straight out the door (muttering a fiery string of fuck-yous under whatever breath I still had left in me), and then back, that September, to what I considered to be a far more civilized kind of labor—as a hard-working, passionately devoted student in the Department of Music at EMU.

My "career" as a lifter of Ford Mustang fenders lasted, I think, around seven minutes—the most emotionally traumatic, physically demanding seven minutes of my then young, yet-to-be-fully-tested life. But the River Rouge experience proved to be a blessing in one very important way: It reignited my appetite for learning, doubling and even tripling my excitement about the reality that I was about to be a college sophomore.

MY SOPHOMORE YEAR:

Baptism By Fire

"Love is an exploding cigar which we willingly smoke."[27]
—Lynda Barry

It was the fall of 1963 now, and I was back in school again, where things were going well for me in many important ways. I'd reconnected with my Music Department friends, rekindled my work ethic as a musician, and happily immersed myself in the rigors of music theory, band and orchestra, private flute instruction, woodwind quintet, and challenging electives such as Earth Science and Introduction to Psychology (the course that introduced me to the irresistible Professor Judy Gallatin).

I'd also begun reading avidly in my spare time, and I soon fell in love with fiction. It was *Lust for Life*, **Irving Stone**'s epic novel about Vincent van Gogh, that did it. Always quick to act on impulses, I went straight to the registrar's office and proudly declared a minor in English and American literature. Soon after that, I remember spending one brief weekend strolling around campus with a straw hat on my head and a bouquet of paintbrushes in my shirt pocket, playing the role of Vincent for all it was worth.

---

27. Lynda Barry, *Big Ideas*, Real Comet Press, 1983, 66.

But I soon discovered being a sophomore was a whole lot more difficult than being a freshman. With year two came a heavier academic workload, even more daunting challenges, and entirely unexpected complications.

* * *

When not doing classwork or practicing flute and piano, I continued to read novels and short stories, but I soon discovered that balancing two deeply satisfying obsessions—in my case, music and literature—wasn't even half as manageable as I thought it would be. My English minor required a lot of reading, analysis, and writing. I was also still very much a music major, obligated to spend countless hours in rehearsal rooms to maintain my hard-earned skills as an orchestral musician. While trying to balance these two entirely different disciplines, I realized I'd bitten off more than I could chew.

Something had to go, and I decided that something should be marching band. I wanted out of the commitment for what I considered to be several entirely sensible reasons.

First, rehearsing with a marching band is exhausting and time-consuming.

Second, I found nothing at all musically rewarding about playing the flute in row one of a small army dominated by heavily orchestrated, obnoxiously loud brass instruments, all while simultaneously stomping down the field and doing my damnedest to keep my music lyre in place. This was not the modern kind of marching lyre with a molded plastic cuff that straps onto the flutist's forearm with Velcro. It was a wooden paddle, and to make it work, you had to jam it under your right armpit while marching. To me, struggling to keep that fiendishly ludicrous device in position was a maddening and humiliating exercise.

Third, the Vietnam War was well under way in 1963—my sophomore year. Like so many other peace-loving, disturbingly draftable college students across the country, I was dead set against wars of any kind and considered our involvement in the Far East to be irrational, immoral, and untenable. So for me, the marching band culture, with roots proudly and stubbornly military in nature, was the last thing I, a classical musician, wanted to be a part of.

Fourth and last, I was not a fan of conformity, and I hated uniforms.

The simple truth was that marching band and I were way out of step. And so, I went to Director of Bands **Tom Tyra** and asked to be excused from this part of the program.

I guess I shouldn't have been surprised by his answer.

"*No!*" he bellowed, his face beet red, his cheeks puffing out like a toad in heat. "You're not gonna *do* that! But if you *do* decide to quit, I can assure you that you'll lose your music scholarships."

I wasn't about to let a swaggering, self-absorbed windbag like him brush me off so rudely, so I immediately went to **Howard Rarig**, the music department chairman, and asked *him* to support my decision to leave marching band. But alas, Rarig—a well-dressed, stone-faced academic with a haircut like an airport landing strip—politely responded that he really had no choice but to leave the decision to Mr. Windbag.

Well, damn! I snorted to myself, later that morning, in the privacy of my dorm room.

I did indeed quit marching band—the very next day. Even though Tyra soon did precisely what he'd promised to do, stripping me of my two music department scholarships, I'd happily put marching band behind me—and that, as I saw it, was good news.

"Boola Boola!" I chanted up to the heavens. "And so what if I'm not a Yalie?" Then, starting that very afternoon, in a moment of triumph laced with ecstasy, I began the business of diving ever more deeply into whatever literature I could get my eager hands and growing intellect on.

Unfortunately, it turned out that having washed my hands and feet of marching band wasn't enough to quell my anger over the Hobson's choice I'd been forced to make between loyalty to the band and my deepening love affair with books. The result was that I reluctantly began to disappear down a self-excavated rabbit hole of disenchantment with the music department—and, along with that, a steady and precipitous descent into what for any self-respecting university student is a most inconvenient mood change: flat-out depression.

And then, fast on the heels of the Great Marching Band Showdown, things really began to fall apart. A series of incidents having nothing to do with my classwork came together in rapid succession and wreaked havoc with what at the time was my most urgent, most cherished ideal: academic success.

The Gonda Debacle

Her name was Karen. Karen Gonda, to be precise.

(Come to think of it, I must have had a lifelong, built-in attraction to the name Karen, because the kindergartener I fell in love with back in elementary school was *also* a Karen.)

I remember both Karens as delightful and irresistible, but the *college-age* Karen—a plump and pulchritudinous Detroit-area girl I was immediately attracted to—happened also to be one hell of a good piano player.

For me it was yet another perfect situation. Not only were the two of us more than ready for what males so disingenuously tend to call "romance"—aren't *all* boys like that at that age?—I was also a skilled and highly ambitious flute player who happened to be in dire need of a piano accompanist.

It took only **Cécile Chaminade**'s seductive *Concertino for Flute and Piano* to set our hearts on fire and seal the deal. From that moment on, we couldn't get enough of either that magnificent composition or each other.

Things were definitely heating up, but then another romantic figure—a handsome young trumpeter with an engaging personality and enough charm to melt a glacier—stepped in and stole her heart from me.

At the time, I wasn't bothered all that much by the intrusion. I was still an enthusiastic, fresh-out-of-high-school musician, and deep down, I knew that to succeed as a performer, I needed to lock myself in the nearest rehearsal room, every day, while keeping the lid on my champing-at-the-bit sexual yearnings.

And after all, Reggie—I can't remember his name, so I guess "Reggie" will have to do—was such an all-around swell fellow, beloved by everyone in the music department, that I must have considered it my sacred duty to release her into his arms and get back to work on my musicianship. Chaminade had done wonders for the two of us, but now the maestro would need to find a different pair of "Hello, Young Lovers" on whom to work her musical magic.

Fine enough, but the story was still not over. I soon learned that Karen's father, an affable fellow and a career music educator in the Detroit area, wasn't at all happy about his daughter's sudden change of heart.

He called me one day, entirely out of the blue (there's that color again!) and asked me out to lunch. And while he never actually said so during the meal we had together, it seemed obvious to me from the things he was saying that he disapproved of his daughter's new suitor. In what way? To use the socially acceptable labels of the time, I decided it must be because he was Black and she was White. And in an enterprising but appallingly inappropriate attempt to get Karen "back on track" with me, he offered to help me, once I graduated, find work as a music teacher.

Once I'd absorbed the shock of being offered career assistance from a total stranger in return for continuing to romance his daughter, I came to my senses, told him I'd "certainly think about it," then thanked him politely for the lunch—a burger and fries at a long-gone Downriver restaurant—and headed back to Ypsilanti, enveloped in a dark, poisonous cloud of confusion.

Over the next few weeks I must have appeared to others in the Music Department to have recovered nicely from my infatuation—they all knew that Reggie and Karen were now an *item* and that I was entirely out of the picture. But in reality, I was inwardly and profoundly decimated by the loss of yet another Karen—of her marvelous gifts as a piano accompanist, of our red-hot amorous inclinations, and of my precious, always fragile self-esteem.

Of Shoeless Girls and Violins

The Karen calamity was bad enough, but what came next was exponentially worse.

Beautiful moments often have an astonishing ability to revitalize a faltering psyche, and most of the time, thank goodness, they do. And yet, what in the beginning might be a genuinely idyllic experience can suddenly take an unexpected turn for the worse. Even the most subtle imaginable downward turn can become a nightmarishly self-destructive force. And if that downward turn involves two young, vulnerable college-age people, one intensely attracted to the other, the other only *maybe*, there's a very good chance the result will be anything but pretty.

For the life of me, I can't remember her first name—I probably needed to block it out after what happened between us—so let's just call her Amouretta.

I knew Amouretta was alone in a practice room because, on the night I saw her, I'd merely been acting on an innocent habit I had of peeking into the rectangular transom window at the top of each practice-room door to see who was inside diligently rehearsing instead of wasting valuable time partying the night away somewhere off campus.

She was standing at the far end of the room, playing an excerpt from what I was certain was the only violin concerto **Robert Schumann** ever composed. And no matter what instrument he'd written for, I'd always loved his works.

She had long, straight chestnut-colored hair and a pale, creamy complexion, but what I remember most about her was the heart-rending timbre of her playing and her fragile, shoeless feet.

I wanted badly to tap on that door and tell her how moved I was by her playing, but I thought better of it. After all, would she really have wanted me to interrupt her rehearsing? She seemed so serious! So instead, I just headed down the hall, slipped out through the side door, and walked back to my dormitory, feeling bad about my failure to seize the moment and, at least in my imagination, make it mine.

But no matter how hard I tried over the next few days, I couldn't erase the memory of that sound and those feet from my mind.

I vowed to keep an eye out for her, hoping against hope that if I were to see her again, I'd have the courage to approach her, politely, and say hello. And sure enough, on the very next Friday evening I saw her standing in the very same practice room, playing her violin, her feet again endearingly shoeless.

This time, I didn't fail to act. I tapped on the door, and once she'd opened it, she stood there, her violin in one hand and the doorknob in the other, and smiled politely at me.

With our awkward introduction out of the way, we spent a good ten or fifteen minutes making small talk about music.

"Oh!" I said. "So it *was* Schumann you were playing!"

This time, her smile was warmer. "Yeah," she purred, "I've always been nuts about his violin pieces. His piano music, too. Do you like his 'About Strange Lands and People'? It just sweeps me off my feet every time I hear it!"

And out of your shoes, too, I smiled to myself.

"Do I *like* it?" I frowned, then raised my eyebrows. "Not really. Fact is, I *adore* it!"

Feeling even more emboldened now, I mentioned an upcoming orchestra concert at Pease Auditorium, featuring works by Stravinsky and Hindemith, and asked her if she might wish to join me for the performance. And to my genuine shock and then elation, she said *yes*.

"Wonderful!" I said. "But tell you what: I'd better leave you to your practicing for now. Gotta do the same thing myself! Anyway, see you on the 17th, 7:30 or so, in the lobby!"

"Okay," she smiled. "I'll be there." Then she pulled the door shut and went back to work on her Schumann.

She showed up right on time on the 17th—this time wearing a leaf-green sweater, burnt-umber corduroy slacks, and an immaculate pair of charcoal-colored slip-on shoes. I thanked her for coming, told her she looked lovely, then immediately headed with her to the balcony, where both of us agreed that the acoustics would be the most favorable.

Except for a small gathering of young people to the right of us—music students on assignment, with pencils and notebooks at the ready—the balcony was nearly empty. The lack of widespread pre-concert chatter led to an eerie silence, both throughout the auditorium and between the two of us.

Things turned more companionable with the beginning of the first number—Stravinsky's *Firebird Suite*—not because there was anything heartwarming about its mournful opening measures, but because, from the look on my companion's face, I sensed that she loved the piece as much as I did.

I leaned closer to her then, wanting to feel the softness of her shoulder against mine, but instead of responding in kind, she remained aloof and continued to stare straight ahead, paying rapt attention to the sights and sounds onstage.

Then, just as the dancers were about to perform the "Ritual of Abduction," she suddenly stood up, grabbed her purse, slipped past the people seated at the end of our row, and quietly disappeared down the stairs.

Damn, I thought to myself. Then I remembered that shortly after arriving, she'd complained of having a headache. *Probably needs an aspirin. Oh, well.*

But when, during a quieter moment I realized she'd been gone quite a long time and had already missed her favorite scene—the one where the Sage comes in and kisses the earth—I began to worry in earnest. *What if it's more than a headache? What if she's really sick? Or worse, what if she's not coming back?*

Unable to concentrate on the performance, I left the balcony, went down to the lobby, and waited outside the women's restroom, hoping she'd pop out at any moment, apologize for having been gone so long, then go back upstairs with me for the rest of the performance.

But there was no Amouretta to be seen for nearly twenty minutes. *Either she's still in there,* I fretted, *or she never went in there in the first place.*

When I saw an usher standing across the lobby, flashlight in hand, I stepped up and asked her nervously if she'd seen a student with long, chestnut-colored hair, a leaf-green sweater, and corduroy slacks go into the women's room.

"I *did!*" she said. "Just ten or fifteen minutes ago. But she came out only a moment or two later, then headed straight for the exit, looking as if she were upset about something."

"Upset?" I said. "That makes *me* upset!"

"I'm so sorry!" said the usher. "But I wouldn't worry. She probably just needed to be somewhere and lost track of time."

"Maybe so," I said. But, privately, I finally admitted to myself that she hadn't needed to be *anywhere* but as far away from me as she could get.

Depressed, disillusioned, and heartbroken, I cut across the lobby and walked back to my dormitory in the midst of a warm springtime rain that under more fortunate circumstances would have lifted my spirits. But given my emotional condition at that moment, it did nothing but reinforce the feeling that I'd managed to be an abysmal failure as a companion.

Over the next few weeks I wanted badly to see her again somewhere on campus, even if only briefly and from a distance. But my wish was never granted. I finally resigned myself to the reality that I'd completely lost track of the girl named Amouretta—the shoeless mystery with the chestnut hair, pale complexion, and a violin whose sound was every bit as lovely as she was—and would most likely never see her again.

Tom Coon

The last of the three on-campus encounters that caused me so much grief and shattered my self-esteem had nothing to do with Affairs of the Heart, but *everything* to do with one young man's inexplicable, indefensible propensity for vicious, small-minded cruelty.

I remember Tom as a fellow music major, a less-than-ambitious trumpet player, and my very first college roommate. Unfortunately, I also remember him as an arrogant, abrasive, mildly misanthropic personality who kept to himself and never quite seemed to fit in with his fellow music students. Though at the time I could never have imagined it, he was destined to be forever enshrined in my memory as the one person in college who, without any apparent justification, dealt a near-fatal blow to my self-esteem at a time when I was emotionally vulnerable and could least absorb the hit.

My recollection is that, in a few fundamental ways, the two of us were typical college freshmen and typical roommates: still only half mature, only just beginning to focus productively on our academic work. And we were also struggling mightily to work around each other's annoying idiosyncrasies as roommates.

The only time I recall having shared a strong conviction with Coon was when we privately agreed that our roommate—a guy we'd dubbed "Pizza Face" because of the severity of his acne—had to go. We were no longer willing to put up with someone who clearly didn't believe in bathing, with the unfortunate result that whenever the three of us were home, our dorm room smelled so bad that no matter what the weather, we were able to coexist only with the windows wide open. We finally resolved the dilemma by having Pizza Face evicted, which meant that we now had even more time on our hands to annoy and inconvenience each other.

Sadly, not all practice-room experiences can be as positive—or sometimes even exhilarating—as the one that brought Amouretta into my life. One afternoon, while I was at Alexander rehearsing Mozart's *Flute Concerto in D Major*—I'd be playing it for my flute instructor in a few days—I heard a tap on my practice-room door.

I opened the door, and in walked my onetime roommate, Tom Coon. Then he closed the door behind him and leaned against the wall, silently smirking as usual. *That's odd,* I thought. *I've never seen him here at this time of day. Come to think of it, I haven't seen him here at all for several weeks.*

Coon was known around the department for seldom if ever putting in the countless hours of practice musicians need to maintain their level of proficiency. In short, he was an inveterate goof-off and a musical charlatan, convinced that, unlike the rest of us, he didn't need to do more than the absolute minimum as a student, not just in music but in every subject.

Before I even had a chance to ask him why he'd come here, he stepped up close to me, looked me straight in the eye, and said, "I've got something I need to say to you."

"Okay," I said, wondering what he could possibly need so urgently to say. "So go right ahead and say it."

"You're a *loser!*" he snarled. "Some friends of mine wanted me to tell you so, and I agree. They're right! The truth is that *nobody* likes you. That's because there's nothing about you to *like.*" Then, as I stood there stunned and humiliated, he spun around, walked out, and slammed the door behind him.

I'll never know why Tom Coon, the Bad Seed of the Music Department, said those things to me. After all, I was no longer his roommate, and since he was 100% brass and I was 100% woodwind, I never had reason to interact, either musically or socially, with him.

Nor would I ever learn the identity of the "friends of his" who he claimed had put him up to his vicious tirade. More importantly,

I couldn't fathom why anyone of honor and integrity would have wished to choose him, of all people, as their messenger.

A Not-So-Happy Thanksgiving

Thanksgiving 1963 was fast approaching, so whether I wanted to be with my family or not, I felt obligated to show up for Thanksgiving dinner like a *good boy* would. But I was still on campus—EMU was now on holiday break—and the relatives closest to me, my mother and father, were fifty miles away in Jackson.

Two weeks before the Big Day, I called home, assured them I was coming, and cheerfully asked them to save a place at the table for me. But to my everlasting surprise, my father had other plans.

"Listen," he said calmly and matter-of-factly. "We think it will be better for you to do Thanksgiving on your own this year. So, if it's all right with you, we're going to send you twenty dollars—enough to pay for a good meal at the restaurant of your choice right there in Ypsilanti. Okay?"

Well, it *wasn't* okay. And as I listened to him deliver his Dark Message to me, I felt as if I'd just been shoved head-first into the very cesspool our Scottish terrier, Angus, fell into when I was still living at home. In short, I felt like *shit*.

"Sure," I said, characteristically unable to tell him how shocked I was at his appalling, reprehensible callousness. "Thanks. I'll wait for the twenty dollars. But until then, *Have a Nice Thanksgiving!*" Then I politely laid the phone's receiver back in its cradle, found the Yellow Pages in the back of my Ypsilanti phone book, and began looking for a restaurant I hoped I'd like enough to help me forget I'd been told, in no uncertain terms, where I stood with the two people who had happily—I *think*—brought me into the world just twenty tumultuous years before.

When the money arrived, to my surprise it was tucked inside an elegant glass-bottomed pewter beer stein—the kind of "adult" beverage container I'd always dreamed of having.

In spite of the circumstances they'd put me in, I was deeply moved by their gesture. *My Mom and Dad!* I gushed inwardly. *They don't always know how to show it, but they really do care about me!*

On Thanksgiving Day, I proudly took the stein with me to Ypsilanti's iconic **Haab's Restaurant**. There was no finer eating establishment in Ypsi than Haab's, so to be dining there on Thanksgiving made the occasion feel even more special than it would otherwise have been.

Not surprisingly, the meal was delicious. The maître d', who was both gracious and professional, admired my stein, praised my parents for their thoughtfulness, then filled the stein to the brim with one of Haab's most popular brews, **Pfeiffer's Famous Beer**—a longtime Detroit-area favorite.

Deep inside, as I worked through my beautifully prepared, expertly cooked meal, I needed to work overtime to believe it would one day prove to be one of my most rewarding holiday meals in memory. I finished my dessert, paid my bill, thanked everyone for making my time with them so special, then drove back to my dorm room, climbed into bed, and did my best to stave off the tears gathering ominously around my disillusioned, disenchanted eyes.

Monetary Madness

A few days later, while continuing to drag myself through classes, struggling all the while to cope with the losses of Karen, then Amouretta and what was left of my crumbling self-esteem, an envelope from the Office of the Bursar arrived in my mailbox.

"Dear Mr. Bachelder," said the letter, "Your tuition for the spring semester is overdue and must be paid in full by midnight on Friday, February 15th. You may settle your account by either dropping by the Office of the Bursar during regular business hours or mailing a personal check or money order to us using the enclosed envelope. Thank you in advance for your prompt attention to this matter."

I'd entirely forgotten about both the due date of my tuition and the precariously low balance of my bank account, so the letter came down on me like Thor's hammer—at the worst imaginable time—and sent me into an emotional tailspin. *How on earth*, I asked myself, *can I possibly stay focused on my schoolwork while worrying where my next dollar's gonna come from?*

I knew the John George Jr. Scholarship Fund was highly unlikely to grant me an advance on my annual loan on such short notice. I was also much too proud to either reveal my delinquency to my parents or beg them for money. So I turned instead to a hastily compiled shortlist of possible on-campus lenders. To even *consider* such a thing, I had to be desperate.

My first candidate was Dr. William "Bill" Fitch. After all, I thought to myself, Fitch had a whole lot to do with why I chose to study music at EMU. I also happen to really like him, and he seems to like me, too!

I slept fitfully on the idea, but by the next morning I'd decided that asking Dr. Fitch—a man for whom I had enormous respect and affection—for a loan would have been a terrible mistake. Indeed, I was certain that not only would he have been terribly disappointed in me, he would also have been *angry*—insulted, really—that I'd even had the nerve to ask such a thing of him.

So I scratched Fitch's name off my list and moved to the next one down, **Mitchell Osadchuk.**

Osadchuk, EMU's lead trumpet instructor and the director of marching bands during my undergrad years, was a meticulously groomed, nattily dressed fellow—a man who never quite seemed capable of letting his guard down and becoming, even for one abbreviated moment, relaxed and fully *human*. Because of it, I should think he'd have made, *sans* trumpet, a splendid undertaker or restaurant greeter. What if Osadchuk had a secret persona as a clowning guest trumpeter on *The Pinky Lee Show* or *Lunch with Soupy Sales*? The idea gives me a chuckle, but only because it would have been so absurdly unlike the Mitchell Osadchuk I knew.

He was a more than capable trumpet instructor, though, and it's to his everlasting credit that he was so patient with me while, as a flute player, I struggled mightily to demonstrate basic brass family competency. The final exam? My performance, before a panel of judges, of a mercifully dumbed-down arrangement of variations on Niccolò Paganini's *Carnival of Venice*.

But Osadchuk apparently had an active, deeply ingrained grudge against rock, jazz, and certain other musical genres—an all-too-common nose-in-the-air attitude among classical musicians and music educators at the time. I knew this from experience, having fallen victim to his bias when he pounded on my practice-room door one day and ordered me to stop playing "that awful stuff on the piano." For the record, my recollection is that I was banging out Jerry Lee Lewis's "Great Balls of Fire" when Osadchuk caught me in the act of committing my unpardonable sin.

Mitchell Osadchuk would never have understood how it could be possible that a serious student of music could simultaneously revere **Paul Hindemith** (*Mathis der Mahler*), *Le Six* member **Darius Milhaud** (*Le bœuf sur le toit*)—and rock great **Jerry Lee Lewis** (anything of his, really) in one nifty, all-encompassing musical package. And that student was *me*.

While I'd never felt close to the man—he was emotionally distant from all of his students—I liked and respected him enough to give him a try.

I got up the next day, headed down to Alexander, saw him coming out of his trumpet studio with a stack of books under one arm, then walked cautiously up to him and asked if I could speak with him for a moment.

"Yes, of course," he said, "but I'm on the way to a meeting, so please make it quick."

"It's about money," I responded, already feeling guilty-as-charged before I'd even had a chance to present my case. "I don't have enough money to pay my monthly tuition, and because of it, I may have to—"

"Have to *what*?" he snapped. "You're asking me for *money*? I mean, look at you! Your hair is uncombed. Your shoes are filthy. And your pants aren't even pressed! You need to understand that your financial problems are yours—not mine!"

Then, his face red as a radish, he left me standing there and scurried off to his meeting, certain he'd done the only thing a person of sound mind and moral integrity could possibly have done under the circumstances. He'd delivered to me—straight up, and without even one iota of discernible compassion—a resounding, stake-in-the heart *No way, José!*

To claim his refusal to hear me out didn't upset me would be dishonest. And yet I knew I was asking for help from a man whose only obligation to me was to instruct me in matters related to music. But what was so lacerating—and so unspeakably humiliating—was the *way* he chose to refuse me. It crippled me emotionally, and I vowed never to approach him again for anything less than fully academic in nature.

Two out of three chances, down the tube.

I went to bed that night shaken to my foundations, terrified that I was about to bring my life as a college student to a screeching halt. I also knew I'd have no one but myself to blame for having squandered a golden opportunity to make something *meaningful* and *lasting* of myself.

And Then Came Franklin Case

Sometime in the middle of the night, I woke up, sweating, and realized I might actually have one more playable card in my deck, a way out of my dilemma: Franklin Case.

I was no longer one of his students—Freshman Composition was behind me now—and yet I'd never forgotten what he'd meant to me simply by being the shining example of an unpretentious, wonderfully articulate, always-nurturing intellectual. He'd done wonders to shore up my perilously fragile feelings about myself.

And even though he was only a few years older than me, I began to see him not only as an enthusiastic lover of the written word but as a badly needed father figure.

I had no idea where he lived or whether he had an office, so I found his phone number on a list of English Department faculty and called him the very next morning from a phone booth just off campus.

"Mr. Case?" I said, my voice quaking. If he'd been able to see me, he'd have realized I was also near tears and doing my best to hold them back.

"I remember you," he said. "You sound upset! What can I do for you?"

I explained the situation I was in—that I'd run out of money and was behind on my tuition. Then, ashamed of myself, I asked if there was any chance he might be able to lend me just enough money to keep me in school until summer break.

There was an uneasy silence, and then he said, "You know what? A friend of mine asked me the very same favor a few years ago—for a *loan*, I mean—but I thought better of it, and so, as gently as I could, I said no. And then, a few days later, he committed suicide. It was devastating! So right away, I promised myself that if someone in trouble ever again approached me for a loan, I wouldn't say no."

"That's awful!" I said. "I'm so sorry."

"So how much do you think you need?" he said.

"I'm not really sure. Maybe two hundred? Two-fifty? This is all so embarrassing!"

"All right," Case said. "I'll tell you what: I want you to meet me in the parking lot of Ypsilanti Savings Bank this coming Saturday morning—9:00 a.m. sharp—and then at the very same time on each of the next two Saturdays. That's when I always do my banking. And I'm going to loan you the money you need, not in one lump sum but in three equal installments. See you then. All right?"

"Yes, sir," I blubbered, feeling how a little boy must feel after realizing he'd just sent a baseball crashing through a neighbor's living-room window. "I so appreciate this! And I promise I'll pay you back in full as soon as I can."

"Of course," he said, "of course you will—but only when you're in a position to do so. And don't forget: 9:00 a.m. Saturday!"

I met Case at the bank that Saturday as instructed, right on time. He greeted me with a warm smile but had little to say. As for me, I was far too embarrassed to do anything but greet him with an awkward, half-audible attempt to express my gratitude for what was a truly magnanimous gesture.

He nodded, then pulled a cash envelope from the inside pocket of his sport coat and handed it to me. I didn't know whether to open it up on the spot or simply take it home with me and open it there. But he was gone before I even had a chance to decide what the right thing to do might be.

I got back to my dormitory a few minutes later, then stepped into my room, my heart pounding, and opened the envelope. Inside were two crisp fifty-dollar bills and a simple handwritten note saying, "See you next Saturday! Best Wishes, Franklin Case."

I showed up, of course, on the next two consecutive Saturdays, said what common sense and fundamental decency told me I *should* say, received an envelope, then went straight back to my room. And on each of the next two Saturdays, the envelope contained another pair of fifties.

Did I cry on that final Saturday? To be honest, I really can't remember. But I think it's more than likely I *did*. And why not? I'd just learned a valuable lesson about the difference between asking for help only to be shamed for having asked it and asking for help and being granted my request, paid in full, no questions asked.

The pay, of course, was more than merely monetary. I went to sleep that night thinking, *Case really is the wise and compassionate father figure I've always wanted—only much, much more than that—*and in a way, it's still hard for me, several decades later, to express my feelings about that.

I finished my sophomore year with a sense of optimism and more all-around peace of mind than I'd had in many weeks. Yes, my social life was still floundering. But I was doing well academically again, and perhaps it was my growing success in both the classroom and the practice room that amounted to fair compensation for what had become a serious lack of friendships.

Tom Hardison

The only Music Department faculty member to actually hear my pleas for help and then, entirely on his own initiative, respond actively and compassionately to them, was Juilliard-trained piano instructor Tom Hardison—fortunately for me, a recent hire at EMU. It was during a session with him at the piano that Hardison, obviously a skilled and caring listener, picked up on my insecurities and offered to go with me to **Soups**—the music students' favorite watering hole, just down the street—and talk in earnest with me about my emotional struggles.

"I don't understand," he said. "So you're not getting along with your parents! You don't like the way they treat you as if you were some kind of simpleton, incapable of thinking for yourself! But nothing is really new under the sun, is it. You see, you're hardly alone in the problems you're having with your parents!"

"I suppose so," I responded, "but . . ."

"But nothing!" he smiled. Then he leaned back in his chair, went silent, looked me straight in the eye, and brought his fist ritually down on the table.

"Now, listen!" he said. "Here's my heartfelt advice to you, Mr. Bachelder: *stop obsessing* about your home life—especially your parents—because they're not gonna change just for you. Then redirect your energies to your life here at EMU. Be a *student*, for heaven's sake!"

I blubbered to him my deep appreciation for his sage, badly needed advice and his willingness to listen, then picked up book II of Hershal Pyle's *University Piano Series*—the book Hardison had assigned me—and headed back to my dorm.

Decades later, while working on this book, I looked into Tom Hardison's life after his five-year stint as an assistant professor at EMU. I was delighted to learn that he taught piano; performed frequently as a concert pianist; became a nurse and worked with AIDS patients in North Carolina; studied Japanese; studied Zen Buddhism in Japan for seven years, after which he was ordained as a Buddhist monk; then moved back to North Carolina, where he volunteered at the Mountain View Correctional Institution in Spruce Pine, teaching meditation to the prisoners, and was honored by the state's governor for his service.

Hardison died peacefully at the age of eighty-five at his garden-surrounded home in Durham, North Carolina. I'm ever so glad I had an opportunity to know him. With no need for prompting or explaining, he just *knew*, somehow, that I'd been born blue-collar, with all the high hopes, painful frustrations, and emotional baggage that come with the label.

THE DOWNWARD SPIRAL:

I Drop Out of School

"A dysfunctional family is any family with more than one person in it."[28]
—Mary Karr

I obviously didn't listen carefully enough to Hardison, because within a matter of days, not weeks, after our conversation, I dropped out of school and went back home, there to continue my ever-growing animosity with parents who didn't seem to have even one little clue about who I was, what I was made of, or what I stood for.

Before withdrawing, I summoned whatever courage was still available to me, then went to Fitch's office and, in the throes of genuine, highly visible anguish, told him I was going to drop out of school.

"Dammit!" he roared, then hurled a snarling *"Why?"* at me.

"It's hard to explain," I said. "Problems at home, I guess."

"Well, *swell!* Just what I needed!" Then he turned away from me, clearly upset. "Listen," he said. "About that Haynes flute we lent you last year: I guess somebody else is gonna need it now. So I need you to get it back to me ASAP. Understand?"

---

28. Mary Karr, *The Liars' Club: A Memoir*, Penguin, 2005, xvi.

"Yes," I said, holding back a growing reservoir of tears. "And I really am sorry."

"Fine. *Just fine*," he said. "But y' know what? I've got a *class* to teach!" He snatched a stack of books off his desk, stepped out into the hallway, and headed off to his class, shouting, "Do me a favor and close the door behind you!" over his shoulder as he walked. Without either wishing me well or saying goodbye, he left me standing there, drowning in my very own pool of shame.

* * *

Teenagers who've lost their way, however temporarily, on the obstacle-strewn path to adulthood do not a pretty picture make.

Parents, teachers, friends—those who can plainly see them struggling and must work around them—don't have an easy task. And without either deeply embedded empathy or an active awareness of the many tools available to assist them, they can feel every bit as lost as the teenagers who are so obviously crying out for help.

And so it was with both my parents and myself.

Not long after formally withdrawing from school, I found a ride home—I cannot remember from whom—and, with a couple of favorite books and a bag of dirty laundry as my sole companions, I made my way across the lawn, stepped up onto the porch, and rang the doorbell.

I was reasonably sure I'd be greeted with a warm and welcoming hug—that and a smile or two that would amount to some small evidence that my mother and father were glad to see me again, maybe even openly eager to bring me back into the fold, unconditionally, and offer me their steadfast support.

Instead of a silk purse, I was given a sow's ear—a perfunctory, decidedly chilly acknowledgment that I really had gone and done what I'd said I was going to do: I'd come home again.

My memory of those first few days is still blurry—probably mercifully so—but my guess is that I slept a lot, not only because

I was depressed but because I wanted to have as little as possible to do with my parents. But one truth about my re-entry is undeniable: I don't recall having received even one little inkling of either warmth or empathy from either of them.

I had many reasons to feel the way I did, but one of them has been etched forever into my memory. Only seconds after my return home, I stepped into the room where my beloved upright piano was kept, and I discovered that in its place was a tiny, make-do desk belonging to my father.

"What happened to my *piano*?" I gasped.

"*Listen*," my father said. "You were up in Ypsilanti, and I needed a place to put my desk. So we got *rid* of your piano. It was only sitting there gathering dust anyway!" They never understood that I'd counted on it to be my one and only source of comfort while home again after dropping out of school.

What they'd done in my absence was just one more long, sharp knife plunged deep into the heart of me, wielded by the hands of parents who clearly never understood just how much music and musical performance had come to mean to me. "Getting rid" of my piano appeared to be their way of washing their hands of *me*—of purging the house of any reminder of my onetime, inconvenient presence there.

From that moment on, I became numb to their presence in my life. Yes, it may have been only a matter of tit-for-tat. But more likely, it was my way of beginning to rid *my* life of *them*.

My brother, Bruce, had become as fed up with them as I was. But because he was far more sure of himself—older siblings often are—he'd quickly and wisely bailed out when the going, especially with our father, began to get tough. He simply gathered up his clothes one day, moved north to East Lansing, found a job at a McDonald's, and never looked back. And within a matter of months, he was a full-time student at Michigan State University, where he eventually earned a PhD in psychology.

But back now to me and my own dilemma. As time went on, I remember getting more and more heat from "Mom and Dad" about my need to "get out of the house and find a job." What they really meant, of course, was that they wanted desperately to be *alone* again—to once again be as umbilically dependent on each other, entirely without interference, as they'd always been. But then I'd had the audacity to . . . well, you know. Just when they thought they'd finally rid themselves of any day-to-day responsibility for my well-being, I'd flown back to the nest again, settled in uninvited, and poured tub after tub of ice-cold water on their hard-earned togetherness. When the boys were away, Mom and Dad would play, and for some reason my brother and I knew it instinctively.

I also remember just how quickly I became, once again, my father's twenty-four-hour, on-demand chore slave. One of the things that had pretty much defined my father during my teen years was his intense, often blatantly insensitive focus on chores, no matter what. It affected nearly everything about our relationship as father and son. At college, I'd been thankful to be done—for good, I thought—with my non-negotiable availability for any chore, small or large, he wanted done. But now that I was home again, the old rhythm resumed. I was again at his beck and call, and *nothing*—not the morning news, not another badly needed cup of coffee, not even, say, the assassination of a president—was allowed to interfere with his chore list.

Fortunately for me, he was away at work on Friday, November 22nd, 1963, the day John F. Kennedy was struck down by Lee Harvey Oswald from high up in the Texas School Book Depository in Dallas. It meant that my father wasn't around that day to deprive me of the opportunity to watch wall-to-wall coverage of Kennedy's assassination.

I did indeed watch it—nonstop—with unprecedented numbness and righteous anger. *How can it be possible,* I raged, *that someone would want to murder a man—a public servant—as articulate and intellectually gifted as JFK?* Along with millions of people around the country, my mother was right there with me, beside herself with her own brand of profound anger and righteous indignation. And, come Monday, we both listened to the sorrowful beat of the drums and the clop-clop-clopping of horses' hooves while watching blocks-long lines of men, women, and children weep openly as the funeral cortege made its way to Arlington National Cemetery. On my lap was Kennedy's inspiring ode to high achievers, *Profiles in Courage.*

But a different reality soon resumed. It was early on the morning of Sunday, November 24. I'd have continued to watch the coverage—I wanted badly to be there, glued to the television, watching history being made—but I knew with absolute, clockwork certainty that I'd soon have the distinct displeasure of hearing my father come out from the shadows again and say, "Put that silly book away and come with me!"

Today's chore, he informed me, would be to clean out the home's leaf-choked gutters. It made sense, of course, for him to want to do so. After all, winter was coming in Michigan, and he was an all-around good caretaker who took great pleasure in performing home maintenance chores, not haphazardly but promptly and thoroughly.

And so I found myself perched precariously at the top of an extension ladder, scooping leaves out of the gutter. About three hours into the task, wouldn't you know, it began to rain. I was hungry now, too—it was already past noon—but I knew that saying so would get me nowhere with my overseer. So, like a good boy, I kept my mouth shut and continued scooping. Then suddenly, around 12:20 p.m. Eastern time, with the rain coming down heavily now, my mother came roaring around from the front of the house, her flower-print plastic apron flapping in front of her. "He's been *shot!*" she shouted.

"*Who's* been shot?" growled my father from high up on his own ladder as he continued scooping leaves. He was more than accustomed to her emotional outbursts, so another inexplicable rant wasn't about to ruffle his feathers.

"Oswald!" said my mother, now nearly in hysterics. "Lee Harvey Oswald!"

"Really!" I shouted back. I immediately scrambled down my ladder as fast as I could, the leaves I'd just scooped falling after me like rain-soaked confetti in a Thanksgiving parade. This, I knew, was one moment in history I couldn't afford to miss.

And then the axe came down along with the rain.

"You're not goin' *anywhere!*" shouted my father. "Get back up on that ladder and keep working!"

It was as if nothing in the world mattered as much as the leaves in the gutter and my obedience. I'm sure my mother felt the very same way about his insensitivity that morning.

Hearing my father react they way he did to an event as historically significant as this—the assassination of an assassin who, only two days before, had taken out one of the most important political figures in American history—brought an abrupt end to my tolerance of my father's willful ignorance and mean-spirited ways. It also added to my growing conviction that I was the unfortunate product of a stubbornly blue-collar, myopically tuned-out father. He's long gone now, but in all of the nearly five decades since Kennedy's murder, my father never once mentioned the assassination to me.

* * *

Tom Hardison had been *oh, so right* when he'd counseled me, a few days before, not to drop out of school. It was well past time for me to cut the umbilical with my parents. With so much unhappiness at home, and with Karen, the piano player, now fifty miles away and in the arms of another, I was feeling increasingly lonely and isolated. Like Jean-Paul Sartre, I needed a way out and needed it badly. So I immediately began to look for ways to escape the *little pink prison* I'd grown up in.

Finding employment wasn't going to be easy; other than my arts-related work-study experiences in college, I had no real work history to build on and didn't know where to begin to look for conventional employment. I'd also begun to miss being in school and wanted badly to kill two birds with one stone by getting the hell out of Jackson and, as soon as possible, back into school.

While I was tossing and turning one night, trying desperately to think of a way out of the mess I'd gotten myself into, memories of Deanna, my Cascades-loving high school girlfriend, returned with a vengeance. I decided to try to rekindle my relationship with her, then fell asleep, filled for the first time in months with newfound optimism.

Of course, I'd conveniently forgotten that, less than a year earlier, I'd found *another* young lass—a girl more tantalizingly big-city worldly, more musically experienced, and more conveniently located—right there on the EMU campus.

The arrogance! The hypocrisy! The preadolescent *selfishness* of it! I immediately realized that were I to reconnect with Deanna, I'd have to go out of my way to say *not one incriminating word* about my passionate, on-campus musical love affair with Karen.

Convinced I still had a fighting chance with Deanna, I rang her up. She seemed to be as happy as I was at the prospect of our pairing up again, and within a matter of days we'd joyously rekindled our relationship.

My parents were elated. Having known and interacted with her for nearly four consecutive years, they thought the world of her. And, like so many parents of the time, they were certain the two of us must surely have been meant for each other. I was elated, too—so elated, in fact, that just a few weeks later, without any objections from our relatives, we bought a cartload or two of household essentials, drove to Okemos, Michigan, found a justice of the peace, and tied the knot. No formal service necessary, we figured!

And informal it most certainly was: our witness was a man dressed in beach clothes and flip-flops who'd been called away from his swimming pool to assist.

But oh, how utterly unprepared I was for the institution of marriage! Sure, we managed to make it through the honeymoon. But the next morning, as we smiled warmly over eggs, toast, and coffee at a charming, mosquito-infested northern Michigan inn, I suddenly realized that as soon as the bloom was off the rose and we were settled into our apartment in Jackson, I'd have to find a job. *Why the hell*, I wondered, *did I not take care of that little task ahead of time?*

And so, back now in Jackson, I buckled down and found work at the Sparton Corporation as a tester of sonobuoys—underwater submarine detectors. I was one of a ten-man team, each of us side by side around a fast-moving electronic carousel, assigned to a particular series of tests. The faster we went as a team, the more money we made, so speed was of the essence and errors be damned. Understandably, any laggard on the team quickly became Public Enemy Number One, ripe for expulsion.

Mercifully, the Sparton gig lasted only two months. Next up was Aeroquip and a physically punishing job as a down-on-my-knees weaver of airplane cargo nets. And then, close on the heels of *that* job, I worked as a trimmer of excess plastic from the edges of injection-molded stereo cases at a nearby subsidiary of Phillips Petroleum.

The work at Phillips wasn't just tedious and repetitive; at certain critical moments, it could also be *dangerous*. We were warned never to jump up from our work tables if we'd left our utility knives in the back pocket of our jeans. Why? Because we'd need only one moment of forgetfulness to carve out a serious hunk of our rear ends—a guarantee that we'd more than likely spend the rest of our natural lives living up close and personal with a colostomy bag.

Sparton and Phillips were bad enough for me, but the job that probably contributed the most significantly to the eventual dissolution of my star-crossed, increasingly shaky "child marriage" was as a nurse assistant trainee at Ypsilanti State Hospital.

The job felt important. Ypsi State, in operation since 1931, had been designed by revered Detroit architect Albert Kahn, and it was imposing in part because of its sophisticated neoclassical touches. I also knew I'd be helping people with serious behavioral challenges—the Forgotten, Misunderstood, and Undervalued—and as I saw it, there was a certain nobility in work of that kind.

To make me feel welcome in my new place of employment, the ward supervisor gave me what he assured me was a plum assignment for a new recruit: a chance to be maître d' to Professor Brown—one of Ypsi State's most illustrious long-term residents. I was encouraged by the gesture. *They're gonna take good care of me!* I smiled to myself.

Off I proudly went to Professor Brown's room, balancing his tray—which held a plateful of waffles with sausage and a side order of fresh-baked peach cobbler—on one hand, just like the pros. I entered his room, smiling, then addressed him warmly. "Good morning, Professor Brown," I said, "I've come with your breakfast!"

I expected an equally warm, appreciative smile in return, but I watched in horror as he thrust one bony, hairless leg out from under his bedsheet and artfully kicked the tray and all of its contents out of my hand and straight across the floor like a large rectangular hockey puck, leaving me standing there with waffles and sausage on my shoes and cobbler smeared down the front of my freshly laundered uniform.

And that was only the beginning. My next assignment at the hospital, in concert with three other equally ill-prepared recent hires, was to hold down the thrashing, gyrating limbs of an electroshock therapy patient. By the time the dreadful zap-a-doodle session was over, I was dashing wildly down the hallway, tearing off my white coat as I ran. Anyone passing through the facility at that moment might have assumed I was just another nuthouse resident, this one in the throes of a bad hair day and eager to fly over the cuckoo's nest and out the door of Albert Kahn's masterpiece, never to return.

I can promise you that I needed weeks to get over the twin traumas I experienced while working at the mental hospital. And by that time, thanks to my and my wife's extreme emotional fragility, stress, and around-the-clock financial worries as a couple, our well-intended "child marriage" was over, having lasted about six months.

I went into another emotional tailspin and was soon back home again with my parents. It was the only place I could afford to stay until I got my financial affairs together. With no clear sense of purpose and no viable plan to regain control of my life, I struggled to find meaningful things to do with my time as the days dragged on.

* * *

After several weeks of ill-focused searching for worthwhile activities, I finally found something close to what I was looking for: a badly needed sense of *belonging*. I began attending a Unitarian Universalist Fellowship at the Hayes Hotel in downtown Jackson, and my suddenly rekindled social life seemed to please my parents as much as it pleased me. There was a difference, though: I was happy because I'd found a "family" of like-minded idealists to assist me in the mending of my postmarital wounds; *my parents* were happy because they'd now have at least their Sunday mornings entirely to themselves. The good news, for me at least, was that my mother had finally begun to get over her misguided, all-too-predictable conviction that "you really shouldn't go anywhere for a while," because, Heaven help us, "people might find out you've gotten a divorce."

But as rewarding as my involvement in the Fellowship was for me, it still wasn't enough. Then, one morning, out of the blue, Forrest "Forrie" Martin—a high school friend of mine who, like me, was a musician—rang me up. He quietly told me what he'd been doing since high school, and I responded in kind, careful to avoid any talk about either my withdrawal from school or my divorce.

When I mentioned the Fellowship I was attending, Forrie suddenly got fired up. "Unitarians? Listen: I've got a church I think you'll like even more! It's on Franklin Street—the East End—and the music's absolutely fantastic! You've gotta come with me some Sunday and hear what I'm talking about!"

He made his suggestion at the perfect time given my circumstances, and I immediately decided to go there with him the very next Sunday. My mother, who had always liked the idea of respectability, was happy to learn that I'd rekindled my friendship with Forrie and especially pleased that we were going to a church. "How nice!" she tittered. But it never dawned on me to tell her which church it was.

Sunday finally arrived, and as Forrie and I pulled into the church's parking lot that morning, I could already hear why he had wanted so badly for me to come with him. The music—unquestionably gospel, but with the hard-driving, soul-pumping exuberance of early rock and roll—poured out of the thrown-open front doors like lava from a just-erupted volcano.

For one astonishing moment, it was almost as if we, and not the Lord Jesus, were the special guests! As we walked into a packed house, wondering where we'd ever be able to sit, nearly everyone in the place turned back toward us in unison—stunned, I think, at the spectacle of two young, culturally alien White boys who by simply stepping into this church had crossed the color line of the city of Jackson.

The congregants, elegantly dressed and clearly in Seventh Heaven, were collectively *beaming* at the sight of us. And trust me, *we* were beaming right back at them. It was a moment I've never forgotten, even after all these years. I'd only been on "the Black side of town" one time, in the early '60s, to help my boss at the time—a musical instrument and small appliance repairman—fix an on-the-blink television in a private home.

We stayed long enough to hear several spirited, heartfelt paeans to the Almighty, but we lacked the maturity to stick around after the service and interact with the parishioners. I think those in attendance forgave us for our social ineptitude—after all, we were still young and oh, so green behind our lily-white ears. But in all the years since that adventure, I've continued to chastise myself for having failed to take full advantage of a most extraordinary opportunity.

I got home that day, bursting with pride because of where I'd been and what it meant to me. I started talking about it, and that's when the shit hit the fan in our cramped, pathologically angst-ridden home. Had it been a doubled fist instead of a fecal tsunami, I'd have lost all my teeth in the confrontation.

"You did *what?*" shrieked my mother.

"We went to this little church down in the East End—Franklin Street—and heard some *fantastic* music. You'd have *loved* it!"

"Oh, my *God!*" she continued. "You did this to *humiliate* us! Why? Why, in God's name, did you ever *do* such a thing?"

"Because I like music?" I muttered, wondering now why she was so upset.

"Don't you *realize?*" she raged. "Your father's going to lose his *job* over this! You ought to be *ashamed* of yourself! He's gonna be *rippin' mad* when he gets home!"

My mother had always pulled the Daddy Card—"Wait'll your *father* gets home!"—out of her always-at-the-ready Deck of Iniquities when I was a child. So I nearly burst out laughing when she flung it at me yet again, even though I was emotionally shaken out of my shoes at the time. But my more dominant emotion was genuine, down-to-the-marrow stupefaction. *So all her claims of racial tolerance,* I thought to myself—*"Some of my best friends in high school were colored!"* and *"I even took showers with 'em when others wouldn't!"—were only self-serving, sin-concealing gibberish!*

I was well beyond disillusionment by then. I was *crushed*, really, when I finally realized the depths to which she was willing to go with her nauseating hypocrisy. *How could I have missed it? I wondered. How could I have been so incredibly naive all these years?*

One of the supreme ironies of that incident—the soul-shattering revelation of her actual feelings about Blacks—was that by unintentionally revealing her deeply entrenched bigotry, my mother had given me one of the most precious gifts I've ever been given: the reinforcement of an already unshakeable belief in the equality of every man, woman, and child, no matter what their skin color, country of origin, social circumstances, religious convictions, or sexual orientation.

You hypocrite! I whispered to myself. *You bitch!* Then, painfully aware that I was still lightyears away from being ready to stand up to my parents' cultural ignorance and bullying ways, I went to bed knowing the view I'd once held of the world had been shattered. I also realized it was going to be my responsibility—and mine alone—to put the pieces back together again, no matter how many years it might take.

I tried to keep the peace within both the walls of our home and myself, but it didn't last long. I knew the arrangement was untenable, so I finally moved to Mount Clemens, Michigan, and took a well-paying job in nearby New Baltimore as, of all things, a worksite construction accountant. It doubtless looked like a normal, sane move to most, but looks can be deceptive: I must have been completely off my rocker to have taken a job so astonishingly ill-suited to a person of my tastes and temperament.

My boss, the honorable Vernon "Don't Give Me Any Crap" Buttles, was good to me. He did administer me a tongue-lashing once when I left a shitload of construction supplies languishing on a train car, creating a costly delay in his project. But for the most part we got along well. He even treated me to an afternoon at Detroit's premiere men-only cultural attraction, the Playboy Club—where I saw more décolletage in one titillating hour than the average married man sees in a year. After six months at that job, I turned in my resignation and within a matter of weeks was back on the campus of Eastern Michigan University in Ypsilanti, my recent traumas tucked nicely away in the attic of my mind.

* * *

By 1969—the year Kurt Vonnegut published *Slaughterhouse-Five* and Neil Armstrong walked on the moon—I'd finally finished my undergraduate degree in music with a performance emphasis, along with a minor in English literature. My gradual shift toward the study of literature was in some ways the inevitable result of my disaffection with the music department, coupled with my growing love affair with books and the prospect of living the Writing Life.

Marilyn and I before we were married, happily perched on our '63 Ford Galaxy while visiting her parents in Flat Rock, Michigan.

And there were other dramatic changes in my life. I'd married again, just two years before entering grad school. This time around, I had a chance to prove I was actually marriage material.

And then, *yow*—I'd also become a father! I knew right away that having a child would require a steady income, so I went to EMU's human resources center and, with the help of its affable, universally loved director, Theo Hamilton, began in earnest to look for tolerable employment.

My prospects, I figured, were grim—things had been tight for months in the local economy—and at first, Hamilton confessed he couldn't be optimistic about my chances. "Listen," he said, "I

Marilyn and I in our very first home in Ypsilanti. She made the trumpet lamp, and together we created our first area rug by patching together multicolored samples from a local carpet store, *à la* Piet Mondrian.

know it's not what you were hoping for, but why don't you run downstairs and have a look at the part-time employment board? I mean, what the heck! Even if you find a job that isn't exactly to your liking, it'll keep you financially afloat until something really *good* comes along!" Discouraged all over again, I went ahead and did as he directed. I knew he was right! I dragged myself down to the board, trying my best to be optimistic. But to my alarm, I could see right away that it was swarming with dead-end jobs like "Closer, East End McDonald's"; "Warehouse Forklift Operator, Night Shift"; and "Lawn Care Laborer: Starting Wage $3.00/hr." And yet, feeling enormous pressure to find a job—*any* job, really—I dutifully set about reading every single notice. *Not good*, I whimpered. *Not good at all!*

Then, when I'd finally made it down to the last row of postings, a yellow three-by-five card—the only one like it on the board—caught my eye. In tiny, hard-to-read type, it said:

"Available this fall: Graduate teaching fellowships in Freshman Composition. Starts in September 1969. Contact the chairman of the Department of English for application procedures."

The moment I saw the announcement, I went from deeply depressed to over-the-top ecstatic. *This is crazy!* I chanted to myself while driving home, determined to convince my wife that two impoverished grad students and a hungry toddler really could get by on $1,800 a year for two years while I earned a notoriously unemployable master of arts in English. Nonetheless, I was ecstatic. Oh, Happy Day!

Of course I knew, given the responsibilities I'd be taking on, that it was a ridiculously low salary. But I went straight home and pitched the idea to my wife, and of course, she figured I must surely have lost my mind.

"Eighteen hundred? That's all?" she wailed. "How the hell are we gonna manage *that*?"

"It's not a lot," I replied sheepishly. "I know! But between the two of us—me teaching and you working at the computer center—we could pull it off."

"Oh, *sure*," she growled. "Nice arrangement! You working part-time, telling kids how to put together a complete sentence—you, a big-shot *college instructor* in your jacket and tie—while *I* keep punching cards all day long while finishing a master's in my—*ha, ha*—spare time!"

The debate, fierce and unrelenting, dragged on for a good two weeks. In the meantime I went ahead and applied for the position, figuring that if they were to actually say yes, she'd be more likely to give me her blessing.

And then I finally received the *yes* letter I wanted so badly—
They've actually hired me! I swooned—and I was now in a position
to make what I considered to be a critically important career move.

But naturally, there was a hitch—a *condition*—and I knew I
needed to hear my conditioner out.

And then we were three. This photo is worn from years of
riding around in my wallet.

"Only as long as *you*," she shouted, "promise that after you
finish *your* master's, you'll work *full-time* while I finish mine—just
like I did for *you*!"

And so her answer was yes, and into the battle we went, armed
to the teeth with exorbitantly costly textbooks, serious parental
responsibilities, and a stubborn resolve to make the best of our
penny-poor circumstances. In less than two weeks, I'd be a teaching
fellow and she'd be up to her armpits in extended counterpoint,
four-part harmony, and endless stacks of COBOL cards.

ESSAY  13

THE GRAD SCHOOL GRIND:
My Two Years as a Graduate Teaching Fellow

"I always feel it's not wise to violate rules
until you know how to observe them."[29]
—T.S. Eliot

I was still in shock, but I can assure you it was a *happy* shock. I really *was* a graduate teaching fellow now! In the midst of my exuberance, it was hard for me to imagine how anything could possibly be more grand than this.

And yet it didn't take long for my optimism to begin to erode. I needed only a few visits to the faculty lounge, for instance, to sense that to the tenured faculty, the teaching assistants were merely briefcase-toting pretenders—men and women barely older than their students, lacking a terminal degree and therefore unworthy of acknowledgement as bona fide members of the department.

To cope with our less than rewarding place in the pecking order, we immersed ourselves deeply in our lesson plans, showed up on time, and thoroughly prepared for every session, taking care to dress in ways that might help us be taken more seriously as instructors.

Along the way, we suffered all manner of indignities at the hands of our students, our fellow TAs, and even our

---

29. Philip Gourevitch, ed., *The Paris Review Interviews, I: 16 Celebrated Interviews*, Picador, 2006, 76.

administrators—injustices that came to be seen as an inevitable part of being a teaching assistant. Now, I feel certain, is a good time for me to share a few of *mine*.

* * *

My career as a budding university instructor got off to a shaky start. Remarkably, it took only one pesky, decidedly white-collar word to at least temporarily derail what I imagined to be my guaranteed Train Ride to Tenure.

How amusing it was that I, an avid reader, constant writer, and connoisseur of words, should fall victim to just one relatively arcane nine-letter word—a word I'd never had reason to say out loud, either in public or all by my lonesome. But any amusement I feel is only in retrospect, because at the time, my collision with that word was anything *but* amusing.

Here, then, in a drab, windowless, exceedingly claustrophobic classroom on the seventh floor of the Pray-Harrold Building, is how it all happened:

"Today," I intoned, "we're going to talk about the importance of understanding *terminology* in the world of writing. To become a successful writer, one must have a thorough grasp—indeed, an intimate familiarity—with all the terms designed to help an unseasoned writer become an *expert*—a genuine Master of the Written Word."

So far, so good. But alas: the Devil had other plans for me.

"Take, for instance, the word *hyperbole*."

So much for best intentions! Because what came out of my mouth that day wasn't quite what they'd expected to hear. Instead of sounding like "high-PER-bo-lee," it came out as . . . God help me . . . "HIGH-per-bowl."

Do I really have to tell you what came next? No! But I believe it's my sacred duty to tell you anyway.

THE GRAD SCHOOL GRIND

The very *instant* I mispronounced that beastly word, I realized I'd just brought the entire house down on my shoulders. The laughs were thunderous—a choir of the flabbergasted—and I felt as if I'd just been stripped buck-naked in church, then told it was now time for me to conduct the Sunday service.

Can one mispronounced word ever stand as proof of intellectual inferiority? Of *course* not! But after mispronouncing a word as white-collar precious as *hyperbole*, I certainly did *feel* intellectually inferior that day, especially compared to the roomful of aspirants who'd come there in all good faith to *learn* from me, not teach me.

This incident may very well have marked the birth of my contempt for what I call the cult of pronunciation—a fanatical, self-appointed group of intellectual elitists who measure the intelligence of others, according to not how much people actually *know* about the world but to how they happen to pronounce the words they use to *describe* what they know about it.

Remember the celebrated author and linguist Richard Lederer? He was an ever-vigilant guardian of the written and spoken word—a world-class, over-the-top, linguistically anal purveyor of "proper" English-language expression. Thank God he wasn't in the room with me the day I committed that truly heinous atrocity! He'd have bound and gagged me, then righteously taken my place at the podium and gone on to show my students—*my students,* mind you—what a dreadful mistake they'd made when they randomly chose "R. Bachelder" from the list of purported "experts" in English Composition 101.

I've no doubt that if it hadn't been for **John Mifsud**, an international student from the island of Malta, I'd have fallen to the floor that day and, like the puddled witch in *The Wizard of Oz,* evaporated into nothingness. Mifsud, who seemed to be the only student in the room who understood my humiliation, sprang up straight as a fencepost and came gallantly to the rescue.

"It was just a *word,* and he only mispronounced it!" cried Mifsud, silencing the roomful of impudent scoffers with one dramatic sweep of his arm. "Mr. Bachelder knows what he's doing! So how about showing the man some respect?"

What a beginning *that* was! But sadly, it wouldn't be the last incident that tightened the noose on my disillusionment with the idea of Higher Education as a career choice.

* * *

Like any normal teaching fellow, I was often hungry for assurances from both students and administrators that I was performing at an acceptable level in the classroom, but praise was seldom available when I needed it most. When I felt especially underappreciated, I could always go out of my way to help struggling students with their deficiencies as writers, then bask in the sunshine of their deep appreciation for the extra help.

The majority of my encounters were polite and perfunctory—brief sessions in which the student needed an assignment clarified or a grammatical error explained. There were moments, though, when I needed to call a struggling student up to my desk and arrange for some badly needed one-on-one tutoring.

A girl with the fetching name Ernestine was among the neediest. Her essays—appallingly incoherent and nearly entirely lacking complete sentences—were riddled with enough grammatical, punctuational, and syntactical errors to stretch my supply of red pencils to the limit.

I arranged immediately to have Ernestine meet me in my office—really just one of several desks for teaching assistants, strung along a forgotten corridor of the Pray-Harrold building and far removed from the offices of the "real" instructors.

Our first meeting went well enough. Ernestine was a fragile, self-effacing young woman—like so many students at Eastern, a blue-collar fish out of water, painfully uncertain of herself.

I took her through every sentence and paragraph of her essay and showed her how she might have constructed each of them

more carefully and convincingly. She accepted my recommenda-
tions without argument, then thanked me profusely for taking the
time to help her with her writing. "I'd like to come again," she said.
"You were so helpful!"

I couldn't bring myself to say no—it would have been an unforgivable lapse in academic integrity—so I smiled, thanked her for
meeting with me, and scheduled another meeting for the middle
of the next week.

The second meeting was even more successful than the first
one. "I'm really impressed with your progress, Ernestine!" I said.
"You've clearly earned a higher grade for this assignment. But if
you run into trouble again, don't hesitate to make an appointment
with me. And don't worry, we'll get you through this course and
on to other, more exciting challenges."

Another week went by, and sure enough, Ernestine was having
trouble with the assignment to write a persuasive essay and needed
to see me again. "I've a faculty meeting tomorrow," I said, "so I
can't see you then. Would Wednesday morning at 8:00 be all right?"

Her elation was palpable. "Oh, yes!" she chirped. "I don't
know what I'd have done without your help! You've been *so, so*
good to me!"

Oddly, when I stepped into my office on Wednesday morning,
Ernestine was nowhere in sight. *Probably overslept,* I figured. *I'll just
correct some papers until she arrives.*

As I popped open my briefcase, I noticed a single sheet of note-
book paper, neatly folded and sticking out from beneath the pencil
cup. I settled into my chair and opened the letter.

October 17, 1969

Dear Mr. Bachelder,

*If you don't stop meeting with my girlfriend, I'm going to come down
to your office and beat the crap out of you! Understand?*

Sincerely,
Alvin McKindling

P.S. Have a nice day!

Ernestine continued faithfully to attend my lectures. She sat quietly in the back of the room for the rest of the semester, fiddling nervously with her textbooks while working overtime to avoid eye contact with me. She always managed to turn in her assignments—slightly more well written than in the past, but still badly in need of repair—but she never asked to meet with me again.

I figured I was a writing instructor, not a Miss Lonely Hearts, so I gave her a D+ for the course. Someone would have to deal with Alvin McKindling again—and soon—but it wasn't going to be me.

* * *

Fortunately, incidents like the one with Ernestine—and, what, her lover?—were rare. As neophyte instructors, we usually had the pleasure of a classroom full of wide-eyed freshman initiates, collectively even more eager than Ms. Eager was to be counseled in the art of writing.

Except, perhaps, for Abelard and Heloise, two students of mine who were so visibly head-over-heels in love with each other—right there in *my* classroom, on *my* teaching time—that no one else could possibly compare to them when it came to *demonstrative intensity*.

Of course, their names weren't really Abelard and Heloise, but to cope with them, that's what I decided to call them in my spare time. The actual Abelard and Heloise—two star-crossed lovers from twelfth-century Paris—were *for real*. Don't believe me? You can read all about them in any reputable library. In fact, I actually stood teary-eyed at their grave a few years ago while exploring the City of Light's world-renowned **Père Lachaise Cemetery**.

I was able to handle, for a while anyway, the fact that my two poor-excuses-for-students would incessantly hold hands across the aisle from adjacent rows, all the while pretending they weren't really in a college classroom at all. Their watery eyes never left each other, and their lips seemed to be eternally puckered up and ready at any moment for something close to wanton osculation.

I finally brought up the obvious impropriety of their conduct under the circumstances, but their hands—and not surprisingly, their *eyes*—continued to be locked together, not casually but *defiantly*—in a bond more powerful and inseparable than Krazy Glue.

Finally losing patience, I took them out into the hall with me one day (I could have sworn this was college, not junior high school) and told them that, in my class, the conduct they were engaging in was unacceptable and they needed to cut it out.

What caused me genuine alarm was that in each and every subsequent writing assignment they handed in, they implanted long, angry diatribes—entirely unrelated to the assigned topic—which, like fistfuls of poison darts, were blatantly and unapologetically directed straight toward the bleeding heart of none other than Yours Truly.

Amidst the lines of their essays were the following passionate love notes to their favorite professor: "You're a jerk! You don't know one damn thing about writing." . . . "You're unbelievably ugly!" . . . "We'll do whatever the hell we *want* to do in your class!"

I finally went straight to Dr. Foster, the chairman of the English department at the time, and asked him—*pleaded* with him, really—to grant me permission to have the two mooning miscreants removed from my class.

But the answer, delivered with all the force of a velvet sledgehammer, was: "I'm afraid not, Mr. Bachelder. The way I see it, those two are *your* problem, not the Department's problem. So you'll have to deal with them entirely on your own. All right, then?"

But it *wasn't* "all right, then." Not to me, anyway. And yet, whether I liked Foster's point of view or not, I continued to work delicately around Abelard and Heloise while lecturing.

Sadly, after the department chair's refusal to help, I carried with me always the distinct feeling that the majority of the tenured faculty at EMU considered their graduate teaching fellows to be little more than well-groomed, nattily dressed, textbook-dependent babysitters—eager, idealistic emerging academics whose sole purpose was to relieve them of the chore of having—God forbid—to teach writing to the department's incoming freshmen.

I was also eaten alive by the nagging suspicion that because Heloise happened to be White and Abelard happened to be Black, EMU's faculty and administrators—including Chairman Foster—were running scared from the many highly contentious social issues of the time, most notably, *racism*, which was alive and well and creating havoc both on and off America's college campuses. And I probably don't need to tell you that Ellie 'n' Abbey must surely have sized *me* up to be a White Honky Racist of the worst kind.

During the Long, Hot Summer of 1967, a clash between Detroit's Black residents and the city's police department—the 12th Street Riot—resulted in 43 deaths, nearly 1,200 injuries, and at least 7,200 arrests. And just two tumultuous years later, that notorious event was still very much on the minds of people in the Greater Detroit area, including Ypsilanti and well beyond.

The dominant fear among the country's academics was that classroom confrontations like the one I was dealing with—intimately related to the region's racial animosity—might very well result in negative publicity, departmental turmoil, and lowered student enrollment, leading to job insecurity and even costly litigation. So it shouldn't have surprised me that the English Department wasn't about to go to bat for me. It was easier by far for them to leave me to fend for myself while allowing the grossly misbehaving students Abelard and Heloise to insult me and make a mockery of what ought to have been my uncompromising academic integrity.

Imagine an English department chairman at any reputable university telling me that it was the absolute right of freshman composition students to say whatever they wished in their assignments—even shameless, baseless attacks on the instructor, having nothing to do with the composition's theme! That's what happened to me at EMU that semester, and it contributed significantly to my growing disillusionment with higher education. Was this the way any serious, idealistic, proudly ethical academic would wish to live his or her life?

Sadly, in some college classrooms it was the *students*, not the instructors—students aided and abetted by defensive, politically weak-kneed administrators—who were ultimately, and sometimes tragically, in charge of the marketplace of ideas. Such were the conditions, at the time, of all too many colleges and universities from Sea to Shining Sea in this, the land of Academic Integrity Gone Wobbly.

* * *

During the time I taught freshman composition at EMU, the Department of English made very little effort to monitor the appearance, textbooks, or classroom techniques of the teaching assistants under their jurisdiction. Not only was their easygoing, hands-off policy a sign of the decade we were living through, with its growing distaste for bureaucratic restrictions of any kind, it was also the result of what I came to see as departmental indifference to anything the teaching assistants did as long as it didn't interfere with the daily affairs of the department or besmirch the reputations of the intensely status-conscious professors.

It took the department chairman many weeks, for instance, to learn that one of the more free-spirited teaching assistants—a brash young Kansan I'll call Jeffrey—was teaching freshman comp without benefit of shoes and socks.

That Jeffrey preferred to teach while barefoot didn't bother me in the least. I was charmed by his intellectual integrity, his romantic ideas about the world—he was fond of calling the vast, windblown wheat fields of his Kansas childhood "the Oceans of the Midwest"—and even his brazen indifference to the commonsense rules of hygiene in a civilized society. It was the contents of his head, not the appearance of his feet, that mattered most to Jeffrey, and that alone was enough to cause me to trust him unconditionally as a colleague.

When Jeffrey approached me one morning and asked to borrow one of my dozens of 45-rpm rock singles for use in a classroom project, I didn't hesitate to comply with his request.

"Sure!" I said. "Tell you what: I'll lend you one of my favorites—Elvis Presley's 'Hound Dog.' It has 'Don't Be Cruel' on the flip side. It's the first record I ever bought. That should generate *plenty* of enthusiasm!"

"Perfect!" he said. Then he tucked the record into his briefcase, shuffled down the hall sans shoes, and waved goodbye to me as he stepped onto the elevator. "I'll have it back to you a week from today," he said. "Promise!"

Just as I expected, he showed up promptly at 5:00 p.m. the following Friday. He handed me the record neatly wrapped in the Arts and Leisure section of the *Emporia Gazette,* then said, "Thanks! Gotta run!"

Back in my office, thankful to have my record back again and proud of my trusting ways and unfailing generosity, I pulled off the tape and carefully unfolded the newspaper. Out fell the record—or, more accurately, one jagged *portion* of the record—onto my lap. The rest of what was left of it crashed down onto the floor, then wobbled into the gap between my desk and a file cabinet. So much for trusting a transplanted Kansan without shoes and socks, common sense, or respect for other people's property.

It's fair to say that, thanks to Barefoot Jeffrey, I learned my lesson in record-breaking time.

* * *

Grad school affected me in either positive ways, negative ways, or *both* ways in troubling juxtaposition.

A university campus is but a miniature version of the larger world, and in that world there will be strong differences of opinion, dramatically different temperaments, and outright clashes. No one is all hero, and no one is all villain. Like the beautiful Georgiana in Hawthorne's *The Birthmark*—whose suitor, Aylmer, saw her birthmark as an unforgivable flaw—no one can really achieve perfection. Some come remarkably close; others are bound to fall short.

First, my grad-school heroes.

David Stupple

The only academic in my college experience who influenced me as lastingly and profoundly as Franklin Case did was EMU's Dr. David Stupple. A social scientist and popular culture researcher, Stupple specialized in—can you believe it?—flying-saucer cults and Ann Landers. He came into my life at a critical moment, shortly after I'd finished grad school. And, simply by being the caring, unusually observant, fundamentally decent human being he was, he helped me navigate a tumultuous five-alarm emotional crisis and repair my broken self-esteem.

Both Stupple and Case are gone now, but, in a very real sense, the two of them have never really left me. Hardly a day goes by when they don't speak to me, counsel me, comfort me, and challenge me, in spite of my faults and limitations, to be the best person I can possibly be in every aspect of my life.

You'll hear much, much more about David Stupple in the next essay. Stay tuned. And now, back to my Roll Call of Heroes.

Olga Sirola

I'd only seen Dr. Olga Sirola, the university's health center physician, one time while an undergraduate at EMU. My recollection is that it was for a bad cold, and for the sake of everyone on campus—the virus was spreading—I was required to stay overnight in an attempt to rein it in.

It wasn't until 1970, when I was halfway through my time as a graduate teaching fellow, that I had another reason—a very good reason—to see her again.

The Vietnam War was raging. I'd already been granted immunity from the draft because of my status as a graduate student, followed by the life-saving reality that I was a *father* now. But the lottery was in full swing, and I saw little hope of adroitly but selfishly finding a way to avoid the draft. Like countless other young men—especially those who were married with children—I was more and more terrified of the prospect of being drafted into combat.

Why? For starters, I knew it would interfere with my marriage, my proud fatherhood, and the completion of the MA in English that I was so certain would lead to gainful employment. But, perhaps more salient to my state of mind, I couldn't even begin to imagine myself in a trench somewhere in Southeast Asia, pointing my M16 at human beings and then, God help me, pulling the trigger. I hadn't even half an ounce of hubris in me, so how the hell, I reasoned, could I ever be a military asset to the U. S. of A.—especially in a war as politically unnecessary and fundamentally immoral as this one was?

So, after weeks of wondering what it would be like for us to pull up anchor and move to Canada—being a draft dodger didn't strike me as the worst thing a man in the 1960s could do—I came up with the idea of hiking myself down to the university health center, removing my shoes and socks, and showing Sirola how astonishingly flat my little footsies were. And I wasn't making it up, either: my feet really are flatter than the underside of a steam iron and always have been.

Dr. Sirola clearly wasn't fond of idle chatter. In a matter of minutes, she'd quietly, confidently, and convincingly identified the peculiar configuration of my feet.

"Fallen arches," she declared. "No question about it! You can sleep well tonight, Mr. Bachelder. Because of your flat feet, you are unfit for service as far as the draft board is concerned."

I was close to tears of relief coupled with canyon-deep feelings of appreciation. I thanked Dr. Sirola profusely for her assessment, then put my shoes back on and left her alone in her office.

Hello, grad school! I thought as I skipped down the hall, exited the building, and cavorted all the way back to Married Housing with a mile-wide smile on my face. *And goodbye, boot camp!*

Notley Maddox

Notley Maddox, a professor of medieval literature in EMU's Department of English from 1947 to 1970—and the resident Chaucer expert during my time as a teaching fellow—was the very archetype of the pipe-smoking, excessively tweedy, eternally-glowering curmudgeon. Perched like Toad of Toad Hall on the desk at the front of his room high up in the Pray-Harrold Building, he would lovingly—and indeed expertly—croak out his very own rendition of how the average Englishman of the Middle Ages spoke.

Maddox—cultured, authoritative, and stentorian to a T—always came across to me as having become wrinkled and weary entirely from decades of celebrating Chaucer's linguistic gifts through the analysis of timeless works like *The Canterbury Tales* and *Troilus and Criseyde.*

He never laughed out loud, at least not while teaching. In fact, I don't think my classmates and I ever heard him let out even one tiny chuckle in our time together. And yet we all seemed, in our way, to love or at least genuinely appreciate the man.

Though at the time I didn't consider Maddox to be friendly or even approachable, I never actively disliked him. His command of Chaucerian dialogue impressed me deeply, and over time he became a formidably erudite, always-close-to-his-vest grandfather figure to me—my very own Chaucer-adoring Grampy—holding forth at the House of Higher Learning while fast approaching the end of his earthly academic tenure.

My favorite memory of Maddox was the crisp, concise critique he inscribed on a research paper he'd just returned to me. It's tucked away in a cardboard box somewhere in my home in Maine now, and I plan never to allow either myself or my surviving relatives to be separated from it. Dashed off in blood-red pencil across the top of page one, right next to the C+ (ouch!), was this straightforward, unadorned appraisal: "Too much Chaucer, not enough Bachelder." It was vintage Maddox, and inexplicably, it made me love my highly accomplished, less-than-affable, Chaucer-spewing Grampy even more. To be fair, the way he chose to disparage my sincere effort at research was one good measure of the man's plain-spoken, sophisticated sense of humor. I left his class wishing he'd shared it with us more often, but he was on the very precipice of retirement, so who could really have blamed him for being parsimonious with the one-liners while in the twilight of his career?

Notley Maddox's formidable erudition may on occasion have made me feel almost as blue-collar as a ditch digger, but from a man like him it caused no distress at all—only a quiet, non-toxic feeling of envy, tempered with genuine affection.

Wendell Harwood

Wendell Harwood was an unlikely candidate to become one of my most loyal friends and encouragers while I was an undergraduate.

When Harwood was just out of high school, his mother was in poor health. Then his father suddenly died, leaving Wendell no choice but to become the sole wage-earner in his family. He'd been studying piano privately at the time but was forced to end formal instruction. Instead, he took a position as custodian of the EMU music department. The job made him enough money to keep him and his ailing mother out of poverty, but it also kept him close to what he really loved—the piano.

Throughout his tenure as music department custodian, Wendell managed to stay in touch with his chosen instrument by finding as many moments as possible, between his never-ending custodial chores, to play the piano. His happiest musical interludes came while cleaning Pease Auditorium—rehearsal rooms, dressing rooms, bathrooms, and especially the Pease Auditorium stage, home of the university's Boston-made Aeolian-Skinner organ and a Steinway grand piano that served faculty, students, and celebrated guest artists.

Nothing pleased Harwood more than to slip up onto the stage late in the evening after completing his chores, sit down at the Steinway, and bang out the classics. He loved playing his favorite piece, the Turkish March from Beethoven's *The Ruins of Athens*—and sometimes he'd hammer at the keys with such fury that he'd draw blood from the quicks of his nails.

There was no one else on campus like Wendell Harwood, with his rare combination of musical passion, fundamental decency, rock-steady blue-collar work ethic, and unimpeachable integrity. He was one of the members of the EMU community I loved and respected most, and he's had an enormous influence on the nearly sixty years of my life since then.

*　*　*

And now, the villains of my grad-school experience.

Martin Kornbluth

Martin "Marty" Kornbluth, a World War II Marine veteran, was a tenured graduate-level English professor at EMU during my time as a teaching fellow.

Initially, Kornbluth came across to me as an ideal role model. Silly as this may sound, it was partly because of his diminutive stature, which was close to mine. He was also learned, articulate, and elegantly dressed—just the sort of Man of Experience a young, idealistic grad student like me, actively searching for a lifetime career somewhere in the beloved Halls of Ivy, was undoubtedly shopping for—at least when I wasn't writing lesson plans, correcting papers, and worrying every day about my own less-than-stylish appearance in the classroom.

Kornbluth may have lacked the radiant warmth and kindly demeanor of Franklin Case, the beloved Freshman Composition teacher from my undergraduate years, but he impressed me for having what appeared to be supreme self-confidence and a certain suit-and-tie, patched-elbow allure that must surely have impressed the average freshman girl even more than it impressed me.

I was now a recently anointed "colleague" of his, basking in the glory of his intellectuality, worshipping at the altar of his well-earned standing within the academic community. And yet the very idea that I had any professional kinship with him was pure fantasy. I knew I would never be entirely welcome in his charmed, airtight circle of academic celebrities.

But I was a glutton for punishment. I mean, who *isn't* while still in his early twenties, mucking around half the time in search of that ever-elusive Excalibur, the Meaning of Life?

So, as you can guess, I simply couldn't help myself. I remember hanging around the department water cooler some mornings, looking desperately for ways to hobnob with the Upper Crust—for even one tiny crumb of evidence that I was being actively, warmly welcomed into the department's exclusive Chamber of the Brilliants as an invaluable, card-carrying academic crony.

I did have one brief moment with Kornbluth during which I felt at least marginally accepted into his tweedy, book-heavy enclave. My recollection is that the conversation went something like this:

"So, Mr. Kornbluth—"

"*Doctor* Kornbluth. PhD, Penn State, '56."

"Oh. Sorry!" (*Another Major League faux pas*, I grimaced. *I'm so, so bad at this!*) "Anyway, I wanted to ask you: Who are some of your favorite authors? Mine are Nathaniel Hawthorne and, especially, Sherwood Anderson. I've always been absolutely *crazy* about *Winesburg, Ohio*—my all-time favorite novel."

"It's not really a *novel*, though," he purred, "now, *is* it! I mean, even the most eminent scholars of Anderson say it's little more than a thrown-together, *what's next, why that* affair—something Lucifer Butts may very well have written, had he been a writer. You *have* read the critiques, *right?*"

Damn! Kornbluth had me down for the count again, but this time I wasn't about to settle for a TKO at the hands of such a self-congratulatory hotshot as him.

"Maybe so," I said, a disingenuous smile creeping across my face. "Of course, I also enjoy reading Updike and Nabokov—writers of *that* caliber. And yet I just can't seem to find enough time to read all the writers I so badly *want* to read. Know what I mean?"

"Listen," he smirked, "when you're as old as *I* am—when you have as little time left as *I* do— *that's* when you'll finally learn what 'not having enough time' actually means!"

"Touché," I mumbled, not entirely under my breath. *A sucker punch to the kidneys!*

That was bad enough, but it was like the flutter of a butterfly's wing compared to the *next* punch Kornbluth threw at me—actually an arrow straight into my heart. It happened a few months later, and it would reinforce my growing distrust of the man's sincerity.

"Good morning!" I chirped, trying my best to sound like One of the Gang. "I know Dr. Schnitzel won't be arriving for another half-hour or more, so I wanted to ask you if you can spare moment or two with me. It's about a rather private matter, I suppose."

"Well, if it's not *too* private," he said with raised eyebrows, "then *sure*. Go right ahead."

Relieved, I settled in for what I hoped would be a good fifteen or twenty minutes of wise counsel from a Master Teacher—a man who undoubtedly had spent years in the trenches, fighting for publication in prestigious journals, before being granted the tenure he deserved.

"The problem," I said, "is that I'm only months away from finishing my fellowship, but I can't decide exactly what my next career move should be. It's embarrassing! Instead of celebrating my advance along the path to tenure, I find myself *floundering* inwardly! Should I seek a full-time teaching position, or go straight into a doctoral program? And if it's the *latter*, what university do you recommend? I mean, where do you think would be the best place for me to earn a PhD? I value your opinion!"

I must have been praying, subconsciously, that he would hear my plea, believe in me, and offer to recommend me to Penn State, the prestigious university where he'd earned *his* doctorate. *Miracles can happen*, I told myself, and suddenly my mental fingers were transformed into a tangle of sweating, wriggling earthworms.

Kornbluth pushed back a sleeve on his blazer—a high-end, Brooks Brothers "Golden Fleece"—and checked his Rolex.

"Sorry," he said, "but I'd better cut it short. I've got a class to teach. To answer your question: If I were you, I wouldn't lose any sleep worrying about where best to earn a doctorate."

"But why would I have reason to worry?" I asked him. "I don't understand."

"You needn't worry, because you're never going to get a PhD anyway."

The bastard! I mumbled under my breath as my face waxed a deep, smoldering crimson. *The peacock! The unmitigated gall of him, trying to tell me—a man reasonably in control of his own intellectual gifts—what I can or cannot accomplish!*

I nodded my deep "appreciation" for his little Moment of Enlightenment, then flashed him a meek, patently dishonest smile and left the room.

Why an otherwise intelligent, successful, generally well-thought-of college professor would say something as cruel and arrogant as that to me—a budding academic with nothing but an eagerness to please and the best of intentions—was lightyears beyond me. For some reason, he needed to put me in what he considered to be my place. Perhaps it's best that I'll never know. His answer might very well have been even more deleterious than his cold-hearted, more-than-curmudgeonly assessment of my prospects as an educator.

Joe Sobran

Michael Joseph Sobran, Jr., an extreme right-wing journalist and onetime darling of renowned conservative **William F. Buckley**, earned a BA in English and American literature from the same school I attended (Eastern Michigan University) in 1969.

It also happened that Sobran—who in time became known throughout the country not as Joseph but as Joe, perhaps to fight against his growing reputation as an appallingly stuffy, intellectually constipated ideologue—stood for everything I, as a passionate political progressive, detested.

As I see it, the world we lived in at the time, and really, today's world as well, would have been better off without pretty much everything Sobran stood for.

And yet when Buckley was invited to deliver the winter commencement address at EMU in 1971, he was so impressed with Sobran's iron-fisted conservatism that he hired him on the spot to

write for the *National Review*. Not surprisingly, the more conservative faculty members went out of their way to support Buckley's
appearance on campus in spite of the fact that the school's liberal
factions were enraged to learn that he'd been invited to speak at
all and wanted none of his ilk on their campus.

To people of my political persuasion—and at the time, in the
1960s, there were droves of us on campuses around the country,
fed up with racism, misogyny, and the war in Vietnam—Sobran's
hidebound intellectual certainties and malodorous hubris were
not only obnoxious, they were deeply offensive. As we saw it, he
and his ways of thinking were in every way contrary to what an
open-minded, inquiring, peace-loving university ought to stand for.

Was Joe Sobran just another run-of-the-mill, hard-right skep-
tic—a hellishly determined stirrer of the political pot—or was he
some kind of philosophical nutcake, entirely out to lunch in a world
whose academics take pride in rational thinking and meaningful
dialogue? The answer to this question was clear as crystal to me,
but not to many others.

What, I ask you, were we to do with a man who—in public
forums, mind you—loved to imply that World War I, slavery,
antisemitism, and the Holocaust didn't really happen the way
people claimed, when history had proven, over and over again,
that they most certainly *did* happen?

Ought there ever to have been a place at the table for Sobran at
a school like Eastern Michigan University—a school which, ever
since its founding in 1849, has taken enormous pride in both its
educational philosophy and its long, proud, ever-growing list of
accomplishments? Known in the beginning as Michigan State
Normal School, it was the very first normal school (a school for the
training of teachers) created outside the original thirteen colonies.
It didn't become Eastern Michigan University until 1959, just three
years before I began my studies there.

And yet, there Sobran was on our campus, fresh from his
fellowship in EMU's Department of English, not a newly hired

professor, yet invited by the department to hold forth in the class-room, where he relished arguing that not Shakespeare but some dude named Edward de Vere, the Earl of Oxford, was the actual author of William Shakespeare's plays. And I suppose that in Sobran's stubbornly inflexible mind, de Vere penned every one of Shakespeare's *sonnets*, too—and what next, Heinrich Kramer's *Malleus Maleficarum* (The Hammer of Witches)? Poor Heinrich!

You see, Joe Sobran wasn't satisfied to be merely a loudly pontificating, insufferably staunch far-right conservative. He also considered himself—almost as if it were little more than a trifling hobby for a "genius" like him—to be an expert on everything Shakespeare.

I suppose I ought not to have been surprised that at least some within EMU's Department of English were more than happy to bow and scrape before a young, small-town, fresh-from-the-pasture academic whose questionable accomplishments might bring notoriety to a college which, like all less-than-prestigious colleges, was hungry for regional and even nationwide respect.

But what finally drove the last nail into the coffin of any respect I had for Sobran happened not to me but to Franklin Case, the beloved instructor of English Composition 101, who in 1963 helped me stay in college by astonishingly and graciously lending me badly needed tuition money.

It wasn't until I came back to Ypsilanti nearly fifty years later for a one-on-one reunion with Case that I would learn what had happened between him and Sobran in the late 1960s while Sobran was unofficially teaching Shakespeare at EMU.

In 2014, I was close to finishing what would become my very first published book, *Happy Dawg Walks the Sad Man: The Remarkably Varied Adventures of a Confirmed Arts Multiple*. In it I'd included a long, heartfelt essay paying homage to Case for all he had done for and meant to me. I knew I needed to thank him—in person—but I also wanted badly for him to know about his honored presence in the book. It's for those two reasons that I drove the eight hundred miles from Maine to Michigan just to spend a few precious hours with him.

Our meeting—at the iconic Haab's Restaurant in downtown Ypsilanti—was for me an intense and unforgettable pleasure. We talked and talked, for nearly three hours, about Case's life after teaching, the many dramatic changes in the EMU campus since I'd last been there, and my creative work, including, of course, my writing.

We exchanged many amusing anecdotes about our EMU days, including the time in my freshman year when, while struggling to come up with a theme for one of his required theme papers (actually an attempt at a short story), I consumed the better part of a bottle of wine in search of inspiration. This and other equally colorful recollections brought mirth to an afternoon of pure joy and fond remembrance.

But one of the anecdotes he shared with me brought only anger, disgust, and disillusionment.

"What was it like for you to have Joe Sobran as one of your colleagues?" I asked him over a sumptuous feast built around Haab's most popular entree—its renowned thick-cut New York strip sirloin steaks.

"Actually," said Case, "I had nothing to do with him; our roles within the English Department never really overlapped, except perhaps at staff meetings. The best way I can think of to tell you what it was like being 'one of his colleagues' is to tell you about the exchange we had one morning in the lobby before a department meeting."

"Tell all!" I said, grinning, already deeply skeptical that there could possibly have been anything good about the exchange.

"It was strictly a low-key, purely social situation," he said. "We were waiting to be called into the meeting room, so, in an attempt to make Sobran—the newest member of the English Department faculty—feel welcome, I stepped up to him and said, 'Joe: if there's anything I can do to help you feel welcome here—information, insights, and the like—just let me know.' "

"How nice of you," I smiled. "And very professional—exactly what I would have expected from you, had I been in Sobran's shoes."

"I thought so, too," said Case. "But you know what? All Joe had to say in response was, 'Really, now! Why should I need or even want anything from you? You don't even have a PhD.' "

Do I have to tell you how disgusted I was to learn how horribly Sobran—a self-appointed big shot and intellectual *wunderkind* from blue-collar Ypsilanti—had treated a man of such high character—such fundamental decency and good intentions—as Franklin Case?

Another way for me to underscore my feelings about Sobran would be to tell you what that seething ultraconservative ideologue Ann Coulter said in October of 2010 in the *St. Augustine Record*:

"My friend Joe Sobran died last Thursday," she mourned, "and the world lost its greatest writer."

Of course, I would never begrudge Coulter's absolute right to love, and indeed miss, her friend Joe. Friendship is one of the most precious human commodities, and who we choose as friends is an intensely personal, inviolable privilege.

But really: who can take seriously Coulter's assertion that Sobran was "the world's greatest writer"? I wonder if what she really wanted to say was that Sobran was the world's greatest *thinker* because he'd once written in his syndicated column that "Martin Luther King's 'dream' has become America's nightmare" because the Civil Rights Movement had encouraged "black thugs."[30]

Many years later, when I was planning my first book, *Happy Dawg Walks the Sad Man*, I knew I had to tell the story of how Franklin Case, my all-time favorite college professor, had helped

---

30. Joe Sobran [syndicated columnist], "A Liberal Theory of Causation," *Odessa* [Texas] *American*, Monday, October 19, 1998, 4A, retrieved June 10, 2025 from NewspaperArchive.com, https://newspaperarchive.com/odessa-american-oct-19-1998-p-4/.

me with that loan of badly needed tuition money. I wrote and wrote and wrote, more passionately with each emotional paragraph, and when the book was finally done, I wrote to Case and told him I was eager to send him an autographed hardbound copy. But, to my complete shock and everlasting sadness, I learned from his wife, Dr. Mary Case, that Franklin had passed away shortly before *Happy Dawg* made it to market.

I'll never really get over that lost opportunity to express my love and respect for a one-of-a-kind teacher—a man who, out of pure compassion, kept me in school and gave me a role model I could turn to, proudly and unconditionally, for the rest of my life.

My guess is that Franklin Case would have been both proud and amused to learn that my tribute to him was a little over 1,500 words—equivalent to three of his 500-word Freshman Comp essay assignments, with a dozen or so words left over for I don't know what—good luck? Additional praise? I should think the *latter* would have been the best choice.

I'll never be able to think of Case without remembering how shabbily—*cruelly*, really—Joe Sobran treated him that day in the lobby of the English Department. But I am consoled by the simple fact that Case and I shared equal contempt for All Things Sobran. That revelation cemented our respect for each other, strengthening what to me—and I hope *him*—was a spiritual bond that could never be broken.

O. Blaine Ballard

Blaine Ballard, who began teaching at EMU in 1960 and was the chairman of choral and vocal music for seventeen years, was impressive in nearly every traditionally masculine way. You know: the chunk-o'-granite chin, the stentorian voice, the meticulously coiffed salt-and-pepper hair—an all-around commanding presence. As I saw it, he was the ultimate example of the stylishly dressed, hyper-academic professor. And yet he also came across as emotionally distant and conversationally unapproachable. *He might just be shy,* I told myself while doing my best to avoid contact with his laser-beam glances and mildly menacing glower. Yet I couldn't help but wonder whether he was hiding something.

Since Ballard was strictly choral (and a professor) and I was strictly instrumental (and a flute student), we were destined to have little to do with each other. But one day he came to me and asked me if I'd like to appear along with flutist Dorothy Youells in a performance of Johannes Brahms' *A German Requiem*—a piece Ballard loved and would soon be conducting at EMU's Pease Auditorium. I gladly accepted the invitation and was proud to know I'd be a part of the event.

The performance went well for Ballard, for the orchestra, and for me. I'd turned in what was, for me at least, a flawless performance—meaning no calamitous big-note errors—and while he must have been relieved that I'd delivered the goods, he never mentioned the performance again, either to me or to any of the other instrumentalists who'd so proudly backed up the chorus that night.

The next time I saw Ballard was several months later, when I was required to take an introductory course in choral music. I knew from personal experience that the man's rehearsal style was strictly down-to-business serious. Moreover, I was an instrumental major. So it followed that his course wasn't going to be a walk in the park for anyone in the room, including, especially, *me.*

On and on he droned while perched on his broad cherrywood desk at the front of the class, serving up a slow-moving, well-stocked conveyor belt of arcane, desert-dry information about the art of choral singing and the genre's essential literature. It didn't help that it was also summer, and yet all the windows in the room were inexplicably closed. *Does the man have allergies?* I wondered.

Everything was grinding on as planned until Ballard abruptly jumped down from his desk, made a beeline to the back row of seats, and violently kicked George Rice's folding chair out from under him, sending him, stunned and rudely awakened, onto the floor. Unknown to those of us in the front row, Rice had simply dozed off.

It could have been any of us classmates—we were all bored and listless that day—but it was George's misfortune that he fell asleep and was singled out and humiliated in front of his fellow music students.

Of course, we'll never really know why he fell asleep, will we! Was it a lingering summer cold? Had he pulled an all-nighter? Or had he been out on the town the night before? Or perhaps it was simply the logical result of a boring lecture in a stifling-hot room. Whatever the reason, Ballard's action at that moment would forever reshape my opinion of him—and not for the better.

Did the punishment for this very human episode really fit the crime? Had the incident finally laid bare the "something" I'd suspected Ballard was hiding behind his stern, off-putting demeanor? And, if my hypersensitive hunch was right, what might that something have been? Did the professor secretly dislike his job—or even, God forbid, his students? Did he secretly dislike *African-American* students? Or did he simply believe, openly and unapologetically, that his lectures were too vitally important to be slept through?

For the rest of my years at EMU and many more beyond, I wondered why a man of such privilege, accomplishment, and well-earned fame as O. Blaine Ballard had allowed himself to act in such an ugly, Dickensian way.

MY PRECIPITOUS FALL INTO ACADEMIA'S UNDERBELLY
(and How David Stupple Got Me Out)

*"'T was brillig, and the slithy toves
Did gyre and gimble in the wabe;
All mimsy were the borogoves,
And the mome raths outgrabe."[31]*
—Lewis Carroll

I'd been through so much by now: the humiliating mispronunciation of that fiendish word *hyperbole*; the ill-timed conflagration of that infamous cigar in Dorothy James's music theory class; and my supremely understandable disillusionment with Joe Sobran, Martin Kornbluth, and Blaine Ballard. Over time, my academic Garden of Eden had become a swamp of insecurity where nothing made sense.

And yet, in spite of the inevitable setbacks and disappointments that came with being a teaching fellow, I survived my journey through the educational gauntlet. Less than a week after wrapping up my fellowship, I earned my coveted MA in literature.

But later that summer came another blow to my ego. After laboring for months without success to land a teaching position at a community college, I realized I'd have to find some other means of earning a living. The truth was that I'd been so deeply immersed

---

31. Lewis Carroll, *Through the Looking-Glass and What Alice Found There*, Macmillan, 1893, 32.

in my graduate studies, my teaching, and my all-important role as a father—and so certain that I'd easily find a full-time teaching position *somewhere*—that I simply waited too long to prepare for Life After the Master's Degree.

But all hope was not lost. Once again, it was Theo Hamilton, EMU's job conjuror, who came to my rescue. In a bittersweet mood, I headed down to his office and tearfully described my circumstances to him, resigned ahead of time to another cork-board cruise for tolerable evanescent employment.

As always, Hamilton was dripping with genuine empathy and admirably eager to serve. "I'm truly sorry you haven't found a teaching position," he said. "Life can be so unfair!"

"Don't *I* know it," I whimpered, tired of his clichés and yet painfully aware of the truths lurking behind them. "And a real *bitch*, too!"

"Uh-*huh*," he said. "I suppose you're right! But y' know what? This time, you can forget the cork board. I just got word there's an opening—a *full-time* opening—for a clerk at the EMU Post Office!"

"Oh," I said, trying to hide my profound disappointment with his less-than-thrilling revelation. *"Wonderful. Can't wait!"*

"I know it's not what you're looking for," he said. "But having a steady paycheck is *bound* to beat hangin' out at Employment Security five days a week!"

Only Humpty Dumpty, I felt, was known to have taken a greater fall than the one I was about to suffer. But once again, I knew Hamilton was right. So I swallowed hard, made an appointment for that afternoon with the mail-room supervisor, Malone Hall, a man originally from Kentucky. I took the job without even bothering to ask what, beyond the obvious, the work might actually entail. *Why bother?* I grumbled. *I can't afford to say no. The pity party is over!*

I reported to work the following Monday, doing my best to keep a stiff upper lip about my new assignment. After only half a day of on-the-spot job training, I realized that the chief characteristic of my job would be maddening, soul-killing repetition—remarkably similar to working the assembly line at River Rouge, but for only one-tenth the salary.

Every Monday through Saturday, the rhythm would be pretty much the same: pour the contents of large canvas bags onto a sorting table; sort the mail into departmental exactitude; then load the truck and deliver the goods to dozens of multi-story academic buildings, along with even *more* dozens of monstrously heavy cartons full of textbooks—then come back to the P.O. around noon, thoroughly exhausted, and do it all over again, after lunch, for afternoon delivery.

In the beginning, I thought sure that in a matter of weeks, if not days, I'd be putting the job of 'mailman' behind me and would never again need make a living as a postal employee. And yet, ever the optimist, I found ways to make my work seem like more than mere labor. I'd occasionally take my daughter with me on Saturday mornings, sit her on the sorting table, give her rides on a mail cart, and generally do my best, by example, to make her feel proud of me for the work I was doing. I had no desire to turn my daughter into just one more class-conscious elitist.

As I became more and more proficient as a university postal clerk, I actually began to *like* my job. Thanks to plain old repetitive physical labor, which I performed at what the average academic would consider a maniacal pace, I lost thirty pounds by the end of my first year and felt like a million dollars physically for the first time in more than two years. I enjoyed the easygoing camaraderie with my fellow laborers, and I also met many fine people on the job, including my supervisor, Malone Hall. He was about as blue-collar in his thinking and lifestyle as anyone could be, and so it surprised me a bit—perhaps because of the way I'd been raised—that he was also quiet and accommodating, patient and supportive. I knew that when I found more rewarding work and left the post office, I'd miss him.

However, the romance of being a devoted, tireless blue-collar worker bee soon began to lose its luster. The main reason for this was the five-days-a-week feeling of self-abasement every time I had to walk into the English Department to deliver mail to people who, only a few weeks before, I had considered colleagues. That was the most painful part of the job: suddenly being Mailman to the Stars. I hadn't wanted to admit it to myself, but I perceived the job as a profound loss of status within the university community, and that was emotionally devastating.

One Tuesday morning, I came to work and learned that Malone Hall, the mail room supervisor, had hired another mail clerk—an African-American man named Jamal. (After so many years away from EMU, I've entirely forgotten his name, so I trust that for my purposes here, the name Jamal will be fine and dandy.)

Jamal appeared to be an excellent hire; he was quiet, hard-working, friendly, and fully cooperative. With the exception of a flashy, multi-sequined pendant suspended from his neck by a gold chain, he was casually but conservatively dressed—a fitting wardrobe for anyone about to do the work he'd be doing.

"What's with the pendant?" I asked him, hoping to loosen him up and make him feel welcome. "Pretty damn fancy!"

"You're right," he chuckled. "Fancy! But it also has personal meaning for me. It belonged to my Uncle Linwood—he died in a car accident last year, and it helps me remember him."

"That's really sweet of you to do that," I said. "And besides, we could *use* a little more 'fancy' around here! Just the other day, I—"

Suddenly, a sharp, authoritative knock on the door interrupted our heartwarming small talk.

"Look busy!" barked the supervisor. "It's *Hawkeye!*"

Gary Hawks, a beefy, burly, jock-like specimen stuffed into the kind of clothing usually worn by middle management at an accounting firm, wasted no time showering us with his effervescent, bombastic personality. At the time, he was EMU's Vice

President of University Relations and the administrator who oversaw the campus mail room.

"So how's your new employee doin'?" he asked, bubbling over with good intentions.

"Just fine," said Hall. "Couldn't have found a better man for the job."

"And which one *is* he?" said Hawks—who'd hired Jamal blind, entirely over the telephone, and hadn't expected him to be on the job so soon.

"That's me," chirped Jamal from across the room. "And I want to thank you personally for hiring me. I really needed this job!"

"Whatever makes you happy, Mr. . . ."

"Hebron," said Jamal. "Jamal Hebron. Just moved here from Hamtramck!"

"Hamtramck, huh?" said Hawks. "I hear it's a *nice* little town! EMU can always use another good pair o' hands. By the way, I'm kinda the Man in Charge here in the mail room. You know, the absentee manager. Malone here doesn't like to admit it, but the truth is, *he* works for me, too—just like *you*! Anyway, I guess I'll be seeing you around. Right?"

Then something brought a screeching halt to Hawks' managerial grandstanding. Around campus, they didn't call him Hawkeye for nothing: at the drop of a hat, he would turn into a one-man goon squad in a three-piece suit.

"Whoa!" he snapped. "What d' we have *here?*" He grabbed Hebron's pendant, pulled it up to get a closer look at it—he was a good ten inches taller than our new hire—and then let it slap back against Jamal's chest.

"You aren't going to wear that monstrosity—or any other junk jewelry—while you're working in the mail room," Hawks shouted. "Not while *I'm* in charge!"

"Okay," said Hebron, no doubt used to being held to a higher standard because of the color of his skin. "I'll leave it home tomorrow. *Promise.*"

"Not good enough," said Hawks. "You're not going back out on your route with that thing around your neck. I want it off—*now!*"

Hebron needed his job, and I needed mine. So, even though he'd just been humiliated in front of his new co-workers, and even though I was thoroughly disgusted with the spectacle, Jamal removed the pendant, and the two of us went back to work without uttering even one word of protest, even to each other.

Hawkeye went about his business and never came back to the mail room again during my time there—and you can bet that was fine with me. But it turned out that I'd not seen the last of Hawks. An opportunity for him to stage another tough-guy melodrama arose one morning late in August while I was in Strong Hall, the science building, preparing to drop mail off at the main office.

Thanks to Hawks, mail room employees were now wearing olive green, discreetly monogrammed work shirts. While I loathed mine—it separated me, by class, from the academics, of whom I'd recently been one—I understood why Hawks thought a uniform necessary, and I accepted it as the price I had to pay for turning in my white collar for a blue one.

Since the last time I'd seen Hawks, I'd grown a beard—a handsome, meticulously groomed, van Gogh–worthy facial accoutrement. I'd always wanted one, and I thought it looked good with my green shirt—my whiskers were somewhere between burnt orange and rich rouge red in color, and red goes well with green. I wasn't sure how Hawks would feel about the beard, but no one had told me I *couldn't* have one.

But who was I kidding? My apprehension became reality when, on this particular morning, I cut across the lobby of Strong Hall and saw the man himself standing just inside the entrance, jawing with a small circle of his administrative cronies.

The second he saw me, he broke away from his pals, came swaggering up to me with a look of rank indignation on his face, then walked me up against the wall and stood so close to me that his chin was very nearly resting on the top of my head. His breath was so close to my nose that I could have described to him every ingredient of what he'd had for lunch.

"I want that beard *off* of you before you go back to the mail room! It's unacceptable, and it makes you look *ridiculous*! Do you *understand*?"

"No, I *don't* understand," I said quietly. "It's trimmed, it's clean, it's—"

"And *now* it's gonna be *gone!*" he bellowed. "That's what *I* understand, but you don't have to!"

"First thing tomorrow," I replied, remembering what had happened to Jamal and his medallion and, more importantly, what a responsible father must do for the sake of his child.

"Not soon enough!" said Hawks. "Finish your delivery, then go straight home and *shave it off.* I'll tell Malone you'll be back in time for the afternoon shift."

I nodded grudgingly, then turned away from Hawks and headed toward the exit, seething about the degradation he'd just subjected me to. But then he called me back, and in place of his earlier look of indignation, he'd adopted an expression of what one might call locker-room conviviality.

"Listen," he said, "Everything's gonna be okay! But before you leave, there's another thing I need you to do. You need to tuck your shirt in when you come to work! You need to look professional!"

I did what he asked—right on the spot—and, as he stood there with his trademark shit-eating grin on his face watching me obey his command, he offered me a bit of friendly, well-meaning advice.

"There's a trick for keeping your shirt tucked in no matter *where* you are," he grinned. "I've been doin' it for years, and it works like a charm!"

"Really!" I said, outwardly smiling, inwardly sneering.

"When you're getting dressed in the morning, just pull your shirttails between your legs and pin 'em together, and *presto*—you'll look like a champ whenever you're out in public!"

I went straight home after delivering the mail, told my wife what had happened, and, with great reluctance, shaved off my beard, but you can bet I did *not* pin my shirttails together.

Back at work the next morning, I did my best to keep my mind off Gary Hawks and focus on the mail I'd been hired to sort and deliver. Yes, a man like Hawks could and *did* humiliate me. He also had the power to decide, unilaterally, whether to keep me—a proud, conscientious employee—in my job in the mail room or, with the snap of a finger, remove me. But ironically, instead of forcing me to compromise my values—my hard-earned sense of decency, humanity, and professionalism—he'd only strengthened them.

I suppose I ought to have found a way to thank him for his "gift." But instead, I went less-than-merrily on my way, continued to perform competently at work, and vowed to regrow my treasured Chin Music as soon as I was finally out from under Gary Hawks' righteous, self-serving surveillance.

According to his many friends from all walks of life, one of Hawks' favorite sayings was, "Everyone you see on the way up, you could possibly see on the way down—so be careful in your treatment of others." But given my memory of my encounters with him, my guess is that he didn't discover that quaint little homily until well *after* I knew him. Otherwise, why would he have handled the matter of my beard so brutishly—not to mention that of Jamal and his pendant? I can't help thinking that a more sensitive person would have laid down the law in a much more professional way.

Over time, I finally figured out that while Hawks was strictly white-collar in his vision of himself, beneath the starched shirt, cufflinks, and penny loafers he was blue-collar through and through. Gary Hawks, small-town high school sports star turned college administrator, seemed to spend his workdays laboring to be seen as deserving of his white-collar administrative role.

It's more than ironic, then, that Malone Hall, the gentle, quietly accommodating, up-from-Kentucky mail room supervisor, registered with me and pretty much everyone else on campus as far more authentic and manly than his boss. Sadly, Malone Hall died in 2000 at the age of sixty-three, after forty-one meritorious years as the mail room supervisor.

* * *

Hawks or no Hawks, I was determined to turn what had become a difficult emotional situation into a personal triumph. I dug into my mail-room duties with great energy and idealism. But the feeling that I'd failed miserably as a budding academic would not go away.

Over the next few months, I went about my affairs with a grim determination to be the best damn university mailman in the business, hoping my daughter would someday be proud of me for my stoicism and the dignity with which I approached my labors. I sorted mail with astronomical speed and astounding precision. Twice a day, I lugged countless cartons of textbooks up dozens of flights of stairs, never failing to be prompt, courteous, and accommodating. I'd become an olive-green, non-academic Santa, bearing gifts for the learned to every academic department on campus.

While barreling around campus in my post-office van, I vacillated wildly between feelings of pride in a job well done and acute embarrassment at the downward turn my life had taken. My greatest fear was that I'd encounter a student or two I'd had while a teaching fellow—maybe my very own Abelard and Heloise from the fellowship days—who'd gleefully realize, on the spot, that I'd suffered a humiliating fall from grace.

One day I'd remember Ralph Waldo Emerson's admonition to know a man not by what he *does* but by who he *is*, then rejoice in my ability to see the dignity in all labor. But, back then, I went home each night with my tail between my legs—not my shirttails with pin, I assure you—angry at the world for having orchestrated my tumble from the Halls of Academe into the bowels of servitude. I knew I'd taken the mail room job to be a responsible husband

and father, but no matter how idealistic were my motives, the bad taste in my mouth wouldn't go away.

Then, while delivering mail to the sociology department one morning, a ray of sunshine named **David Stupple** finally broke through my foul-weather, self-pitying mood.

There are rare moments in everyone's lives when a superficial, on-the-run encounter becomes a long-lasting, transformative relationship. Such was the case with Dr. Stupple and me, and it could not have occurred at a more critical moment in my life.

The sociology department was seven stories up in the Pray-Harrold Building. Ten times a week, I had to wheel stack after stack of obscenely heavy cartons full of textbooks up there on a dolly. I'd maneuver the dolly onto a crowded elevator, then burrow my way through a tweed-and-polyester labyrinth of legs belonging to nattily dressed academics on the way to their lectures. My olive-green uniform, along with the dolly I was pushing, branded me as one of the Untouchables. I was physically present, but I was for all intents and purposes the Invisible Man.

On this particular day, I wormed my way off the elevator, then headed toward the sociology department to announce my arrival and ask where to leave the boxes. The secretary was nowhere to be seen, so I flagged down the only other person in the reception room—a sandy-haired, professorial-looking man, probably in his late thirties, leaning against a chair and perusing Page One of the *New York Times*.

"May I help you?" he said warmly.

A professor of *anything*, willing to help a common laborer? It had been anything but my usual experience since becoming a university postal worker.

"Yes! I was wondering where I should leave these textbooks. Can't just drop 'em off anywhere."

He tossed his newspaper down on a nearby couch and grabbed a box off the top of the dolly. "Come with me!" he said. "I can keep them in my office until the secretary comes back. I'll give her the bill of lading then."

I thanked him profusely for helping me with the boxes.

"No big deal," he said. "Glad to help! Besides, I can use the exercise. By the way, I'm David Stupple, one of the teachers here." He smiled while giving me an industrial-strength handshake. "And you?"

I mumbled my name to him while shrinking down to nothing-ness inside my uniform. The gulf between his circumstances and mine was immense, and at that moment I didn't know if I even wanted to try to cross it.

"I've been delivering mail to make ends meet after finishing my MA," I said. "I was a teaching fellow in the English department. I had to find employment right away—I've a two-year-old daughter to support."

"Aha! *That's* where I've seen you!" said Stupple. "I have friends on the sixth floor, and when I'd go down to visit with them, I'd see you on occasion, heading down the hall with your briefcase. Thought you were a prof!"

By now my discomfort had morphed into outright distress. "Big drop in status," I said quietly, feeling more conspicuous than that odious insect in Kafka's *Metamorphosis*.

"Not necessarily," he said, smiling gently. "Not necessarily."

He went back to his newspaper, and when I was finished stack-ing the boxes, I went on my way. I hadn't consciously intended to ask for the man's pity, and yet something inside me had undoubt-edly been craving any evidence, however small, of understanding. I was at a low point in my self-esteem, hungering for any word or gesture that might offer reassurance that I hadn't failed after completing my fellowship. I didn't want to believe that this job and this uniform actually had the power to define me.

Over the next few weeks, while delivering mail to the sociology department, I'd see David on occasion, talking with colleagues or sitting quietly in the lounge. He never failed to acknowledge me, always saying, "Hello, Ross! How are things with you?"

I began to look forward to his stop on my route. Here, at last, was someone who genuinely respected me—who wasn't judging me on the basis of either my uniform or my occupation. Whenever he happened to see me, he'd invariably take a moment to engage me in conversation, asking me what I was reading and how my family was doing. He'd even talk at length about his work as teacher and researcher, making me feel almost like an equal.

Then, one day, he asked me if I'd like to come over to his house. I was thrilled, and I instantly accepted his invitation. "Next Thursday?" he said. "Bring your wife and daughter, and we'll have a meal together." I went to my next delivery humming to myself and savoring the cloudless blue sky and blazing sunlight. I'd not felt so good in weeks.

June and David Stupple at their home in Ypsilanti on one of our visiting days.

Our first visit to the Stupples' home was a revelation. To my great delight, I learned that as a sociologist he was interested in two very unusual subjects: the inner workings of flying saucer cults and the writings of advice columnist Ann Landers. Clearly, his quirky research interests fit like a glove with his own mild eccentricities.

To do his flying saucer research, Stupple would infiltrate a cult (many of them were in the Upper Peninsula of Michigan), pretend successfully to be a believer, then leave the group and publish his sociological analysis. He'd done this numerous times, and his articles appeared in a small, influential magazine called *FATE* and in other unconventional, topically relevant magazines.

I never learned why David was drawn to Ann Landers, a wildly popular advice columnist for nearly sixty years, as a subject for serious sociological research. I suspect it was not just Landers herself but the people who depended so obsequiously on her advice that drew him to study the Ann Landers phenomenon.

One night, after we shared a meal with David and his family at their home, he asked me if I'd like to come down and see his basement.

David was what doctors and most others at the time called "handicapped"—though he disapproved of the term, preferring 'physically exceptional' "—so I couldn't help wondering how easy it was going to be for him to make the descent with what were obviously severely impaired legs.

I learned later that while a teenager he'd suffered a debilitating, inexplicable illness. His parents, who were Christian Scientists, initially refused medical help because of their belief that only prayer has the power to heal the sick. David eventually got medical attention, but not soon enough to prevent permanent motor problems in his legs.

Doctors thought at first that he'd contracted polio, so they put him in an iron lung for a year. He then developed the motor problems. While his illness was never diagnosed with certainty, doctors eventually decided that viral encephalitis may have been the culprit.

Watching him walk around his home that day, I couldn't help feeling bad for him, but when he scrambled down the stairs to the basement with remarkable speed and agility, I had to wonder just how much or how little he even thought about his disability. I eventually learned that he thought a great deal about it, but never in a self-pitying way. He was passionate about the idea that the public needed to be better educated about *exceptionality*—a word that meant a lot to him because it was, he thought, a badly needed antidote to the popular notion that people like him were "cripples," unable to function successfully in normal society.

Disabled was another frequently used term in the '70s, but David thoroughly disapproved of it. I learned quickly never to use the word while in his company.

Once down the stairs, he flipped on the basement light switch. There in the center of the room, lit by a hanging lamp, was a well-worn Ping-Pong table with paddles at either end, all set for action.

I scratched my head at the sight of that table. Given what seemed to me the obvious limitations in David's mobility, I wondered how he could ever hope to play a credible game of Ping-Pong. I figured the table must be there for his children—something they could do with friends on occasion to burn off their youthful energy.

"Wanna play a game?" he said in his usual gentle, sandpapery voice. Because of his posture, his back was noticeably lower to the ground than mine as he scrambled around the far end of the table and picked up a paddle.

Why not? I figured. *It'll be good fun, and I'm pretty good at Ping-Pong.* I picked up my paddle and got into position, and before I even had time to think, the ball came roaring over the net, hot as a blowtorch and straight as a laser beam. It caught the far right corner of the table, near my right leg—a perfectly aimed volley.

"Well, that was a damn good shot!" I said, hoping it was a fluke and would be followed by something more normal—something I could actually handle.

But it was no fluke. From that point on, every one of David's deliveries was like a bolt of lightning from an angry Zeus. I quickly realized I'd be helpless to compete in any meaningful way with his killer serve and upper-body adroitness. He beat me soundly, 21–3, in that very first contest.

The truth was that I was more exhausted than embarrassed. "Where's that bathroom, again?" I panted. "I need to take a break!" (Anything to get me away from the scene of the slaughter!) "Upstairs and to the left," he said, chuckling both to himself and to the victim of his full-frontal assault. "I'll give you a couple of minutes to rest before the next set."

By now I figured that Dr. David Stupple, professor of sociology, flying saucer researcher, and Olympic-caliber Ping-Pong wizard, was quietly gloating down there in the basement. He had good reason, too. He'd just shown me by example what someone with alleged "disabilities" can actually accomplish. The man was a natural-born teacher, and I had a feeling I was going to learn a lot from him—and not just how to win at Ping-Pong.

While upstairs and heading down the hall to the bathroom, I noted that the Stupple household was not at all pretentious. In fact, it was rather average—a little frayed around the edges, with predictable '60s-vintage swivel chairs around the dining room table, Danish Modern end tables, and off-white shag carpeting. *He keeps the wild side to himself,* I thought as I reached inside the bathroom door and flipped the light switch.

When the lights came on, I felt like I'd just been blinded by the passing of a meteor sent by Otherworldly Beings from one of Stupple's flying saucer cults. The entire bathroom was lit by blacklights and pulsing with colorful psychedelic posters, glow-in-the-dark accessories, and the eerie glow and sensuous undulations of a lava lamp. David Stupple: so full of surprises, so utterly unacademic!

Over the next few months, David and I and our families became the best of friends. We nearly always got together at their home rather than ours, simply because it was more spacious and they were the ones with the Ping-Pong table. Kelly and Kyle, David's children, got along well with our daughter, Amy, and they soon became inseparable playmates.

David's wife, June, and my wife, Marilyn, were the quieter members of the foursome but no less assertive and opinionated in matters political and intellectual. Because our views on a wide range of social issues were remarkably compatible, we had many lively after-dinner discussions. The Vietnam War was coming to a close; Detroit was still trying to recover from the devastating effects of the 1967 12th Street Riot and a host of related socioeconomic ills; and the rights of Blacks, women, and physically exceptional people were being hotly debated in intellectual circles, analyzed by behavioral scientists, and confronted aggressively on the streets in the form of sometimes violent demonstrations.

David proved to be an unusually empathetic listener. When we were alone, I began to talk with him in considerable detail about my often troubled childhood: about the tensions within the walls of our tiny, claustrophobic, post–World War II home; about my struggle to be taken seriously as a unique human being with a right to my own opinions; and about my inability to penetrate the layers of emotional armor around my symbiotically connected parents. Together they were a fierce, impenetrable fortress, and as children, my brother and I were seldom if ever allowed to scale its walls and learn what was inside that the two of us might actually share with them on an equal basis.

In the course of our frequent one-on-one conversations, David taught me many things.

The first lesson—never to work from false assumptions—came over the flat green expanse of David's Ping-Pong table.

The second lesson—more nuanced and harder to learn—manifested itself in his uncanny ability to listen, fully and compassionately, to what I was telling him about myself. David had come into my life at an especially vulnerable time for me, and he quickly revealed himself as the skilled, caring listener I so badly needed. Emotionally, I was still very much a work in progress, and in his wise and unpretentious way, he went quietly about, lesson by lesson, repairing the damage to my self-esteem. His unbridled empathy—an open-door policy he maintained for friends and students alike—was one of his greatest gifts to me and, I'm certain, countless others in his life.

The third lesson—just as powerful and life-changing as the others—had to do with his rare ability, as an academic, to live and work outside the suffocating walls of ivory-tower superiority that imprison so many socially ambitious college instructors. Stupple was not a social climber; Vance Packard, author of the groundbreaking 1959 book *The Status Seekers*, would have been proud of him. The academic hierarchy might have been an unavoidable reality for David as a professor, but he never allowed it to restrict him—not in his intellectual endeavors, not in his personal relationships, and not in his inimitable way of looking at the world.

David was that rarest of breeds on campus: a man as open as a flower to the personal qualities and intellectual gifts of everyone around him, regardless of their place in the human pecking order. The characteristic humility with which he dispensed his wisdom—accompanied by his twinkling eyes and asymmetrical smile—made him seem almost Buddha-like on occasion.

The astonishing thing about David was that, unlike the pompous administrator who had a violent aversion to pendants and whiskers, and unlike the peacock professor who so arrogantly pronounced me unfit to be a true academic, David saw straight through my mail-room shirt and deep into the heart of me. To him I was an intellectual equal, and I couldn't recall ever having gotten a greater gift than that from anyone I'd known.

Examples of his egalitarian approach to thinking would show up in surprising ways. When he discovered one day that I was a prolific and competent writer—I'd shown him many of my writing samples—he didn't hesitate to make me an offer: "I've a proposal," he said. "Would you be interested in helping me edit my research articles before I submit them for publication?"

The thought that Dr. David Stupple, a well-published, highly respected academic, would ask me to help him prepare his work for submission to publishing houses astounded and then thrilled me. To him I wasn't just a lugger of boxes and sorter of junk mail. In spite of having lost my status as a member of the academic community, in his eyes I was no less a thinker and idealist than he was. Like Emerson and his fellow New England Transcendentalists, David saw no reason why working with one's hands should be incompatible with a life of the mind. As much as Emerson—and perhaps even more than him—David Stupple was *my* kind of man.

MY BUS TRIP TO DETROIT

and Our Move to New England

> *"Hey, hey, LBJ, how many kids*
> *did you kill today?"*
> *—A protest chant during the Vietnam War*

It was 1972. My fellowship was history, and it was now my responsibility—and indeed my good fortune—to stay home and take care of our daughter while my wife worked part-time and finished her MA in music theory and literature. Feminists like Steinem had really done their homework as advocates for marital overhaul, and as devoted students in her magazine-based School for Marital Fair Play, the two of us decided there would no longer be any question of a role-playing division of labor in our marriage.

Being a full-time househusband was so novel during the era of *Ms. Magazine*, Gloria Steinem, and Bella Abzug that I would eventually be asked to talk about it on television. In 1976, I appeared on stations in Boston, Bangor, and Buffalo as a part of my campaign to promote active fatherhood and the importance of sharing household chores equally.

When I wasn't showering TLC on my daughter—reading to her, building sandbox castles with her, or taking her on frequent mini adventures—I was spending my spare time sending letters of enquiry to community colleges for myself and to public schools for my wife. We'd made a pact regarding our job searches: whichever one of us found full-time, out-of-state employment first, the other would come along for the ride, no questions asked.

And then, somewhere in the midst of our relentless, quietly frantic search for employment, I got a letter from my local draft board.

It wasn't really a surprise. After all, the draft lottery was in full swing at the time. I'd already been deferred from the draft—first because of my enrollment as a grad school student, then because of my status as a married man with a child, and, finally, because of my flatter-than-flat feet. But now I was scared shitless. Would even those statuses now be taken from me?

I've never been temperamentally inclined to pick up a gun, point it at someone, and pull the trigger, unless, of course, I and others were in immediate danger and I needed to defend us. (Remember the presidential debate in 1988 when Michael Dukakis was asked whether, if his wife were raped and murdered, he would favor the death penalty for the killer? He failed to give the tough-guy answer, and it cost him the presidency.)

Indeed, I've never wanted even to *own* a gun. I'd allegedly been trained to be a soldier with the help of EMU's ROTC requirement, and, as I saw it, that experience offered irrefutable evidence that I'd have made a lousy combatant.

Nor did I have any desire to be called to fight in a war I considered unnecessary, unjust, and morally indefensible. I had a bumper sticker on my car saying "War is Not Healthy for Children & Other Living Things" for a reason: unless a threat to our national security were as serious as Hitler and the Nazis, I wanted no part of military action of any kind, and even if I did, I didn't think military action was justifiable under the circumstances. I would like to think, however, that if we as a nation had been seeing evidence of yet another Holocaust in the making, I'd have reported for duty, scared shitless or not.

And yet here I was now, bouncing down I-94 in a beat-up bus (was it sunflower yellow or jungle-fatigues green? I can't remember) on the way to a pre-induction center somewhere on the outskirts of Detroit.

Other than being in a state of deep insecurity and palpable fear, all I remember about that trip was my fellow passengers. The vast majority of them were Black. Why, I asked myself, was that the case? Why were there so few "honkies"—Black Power militants' preferred term for Whites at the time—on that bus?

I knew the answer, but I tried not to think about it. Emotionally, it hit much too close to home. That there were so few Whites on our bus, but a large number of Blacks—men who, from all appearances, were clearly not the products of white-collar privilege—meant that Blacks were being drafted way out of proportion to Whites in this, the Land of Milk and Honey.

And of course that meant that as a White male, I had a much greater chance than the Blacks did of being rejected for military duty, then sent home to live my life.

It was not fun standing buck-naked in a roomful of buck-naked strangers. It was humiliating hearing the Man Behind the Screen break out laughing when, as he poked me sharply in the testicles, I squealed with pain. I finally learned, a few weeks later, that I'd failed my pre-induction physical and wouldn't be heading to boot camp after all.

Enormously relieved but riddled with guilt, I became convinced that it was my Whiteness alone that had virtually guaranteed me an unspoken, unwritten Ticket to Freedom from racial discrimination. And as the seemingly endless Vietnam War ground on, the ugly reality of White Privilege would continue to haunt me while I watched, night after night, as anchorman Walter Cronkite glumly, angrily oversaw the suppertime March of the Coffins on *CBS Evening News*.

Ugly though it can be—and often *is*—life must go on.

* * *

My friendship with David Stupple had shored up the greater portion of my sagging self-esteem. But I was still a young man, just out of grad school and in search of occupational fulfillment. No matter how much I tried to idealize my work as mail room clerk, I knew it was only temporary. It wasn't where I belonged. Something would have to change.

At home, my wife and I put our heads together and made a pact: whichever one of us found a professional position with a livable wage first, the other would follow unconditionally, without complaint. There was no time to waste, and we got to work right away.

We began applying for jobs all over the northeastern quadrant of the US. Continuing to live in southern Michigan would have allowed both of us to be in regular contact with our families. But while that would have been good for Marilyn, who'd always had a solid, loving relationship with her parents, it would have spelled continuing trouble for me, thanks to the increasingly fractious relationship I had with mine.

I labored mightily to find employment as a community college writing instructor, sending out hundreds of letters of inquiry that landed me interviews at a half-dozen colleges in the Southeast. Meanwhile, I also applied to doctoral programs in English literature and was accepted for doctoral work at three universities: the University of Michigan, Wayne State University, and the University of Toledo.

At the same time, Marilyn, who had just finished a Master of Arts in music theory and literature, began looking aggressively for work as an instrumental music teacher. To help her with her search, I composed, typed, and sent out hundreds of her letters of inquiry in addition to my own.

Marilyn got there first. After driving alone for two weeks around the eastern US to interview with the superintendents of eight school systems from New York State to northern New England, she finally landed a teaching position in the tiny southern-Maine town of Berwick. Our dream of a new and exciting adventure had become a reality, and within the month we began planning and packing for our journey to the Pine Tree State.

I knew I would miss a great many of the personalities who'd enriched my life at EMU, including of course custodian and pianist Wendell Harwood. My unlikely friendship with him had grown and grown, and as I saw it, nothing, not even geographic distance, would ever diminish our remarkable unspoken devotion to each other.

Then one morning in August 1974, as we were preparing to move to New England, Wendell came running up to me with a smile big as a banana on his face.

"Guess what!" he gushed. "My Uncle Ted passed away last week up in Minnesota. I went to the reading of his will, and to my shock I learned he'd left me a sizable chunk of money. So of course I went out right away and bought myself a baby grand! Then, when I realized I wouldn't be needing my old upright anymore, I figured, 'Why not give it to Ross? He can take it to Maine with him and play it up there!'"

Needless to say, I was thrilled. I immediately arranged to have the piano delivered to the local U-Haul, where it would then be added to the haphazard accumulation of goods we'd be taking with us to Maine.

A week or so before our departure, I chased Wendell down at the Alexander Music Building—he was down on his knees in the basement, cleaning toilets, the very chore he was performing when I first met him—then thanked him all over again, effusively, for giving me his upright. I wished him well, delivered a tearful goodbye, then headed back upstairs, knowing I'd likely never see him again.

But Wendell wasn't done. A few days later, he chased me up the staircase, again at Alex, stood there catching his breath, and then made another astonishing announcement. "I've just found out I have cancer," he said. "I've been told it'll finally get me, so

I'm going to get in touch with my lawyer and arrange to have my baby grand donated to you after I'm gone—if you want it, that is."

Of course, I accepted his offer. The sad news of his illness was tempered somewhat in my mind by the understated humor with which he made the offer, as well as by the warmth of that final gesture. Even when he faced the end of his life, he was focused on passing on a torch to those he cared about, and I felt honored to be one of them.

* * *

We also had to break the news to David and June Stupple that we'd found a chance for another, more productive life in a distant state.

It happened on our very next get-together. "I've something difficult to tell you," I said after yet another epic, gladiatorial contest of Ping-Pong—a game in which David soundly thrashed me for what seemed like the three-hundredth time.

"All right," he said. "But it can't be as bad as what I heard at the faculty meeting last night. Seems like we've got budget problems. They're talking staff reductions again."

"Maybe worse!" I said. "Marilyn has finally found a job. We're moving to Maine in just a few weeks."

David paused, his back toward me as he hung the paddles up on the pegboard near the table, ready for his next inevitable conquest.

"Ah, yes!" he said quietly. "New England—the land of the cultural overlay!"

I didn't fully understand—something about the migration of modern-day Midwesterners to old New England, he said, followed by their slow but inevitable assimilation into the centuries-old local culture. The scholarly David was always just beneath the surface of his more playful self, waiting to be engaged.

"This wasn't an easy decision," I told him almost pleadingly. "I couldn't go on being a postal worker, and Marilyn needs to find her footing as an educator."

"I understand!" he said gently. "We had to make the same sort of decision when we moved from Missouri to Michigan. But sometimes the hardest decisions prove to be the wisest. I'm sure you'll do just fine up there in Maine."

Marilyn and I spent the better part of a month packing our belongings, then arranged for one last get-together with the Stupples. This time, instead of having dinner in their home, we picnicked on the living room floor of our empty apartment. It was a sad, emotionally awkward afternoon. The children played in a distant corner of the apartment while we made small talk together, pretending we weren't about to say goodbye to what had become an enormously rewarding friendship.

* * *

A week later, we were in New England, cheering wildly as we drove over the Piscataqua River Bridge between Portsmouth, New Hampshire, and Kittery, Maine. With our rented U-Haul crammed to the ceiling with everything from boxsprings to bicycles, we worked our way eighteen additional miles to the village of Berwick.

Two weeks after our arrival, Marilyn began the first of what became thirty-eight years as a gifted, highly motivated, and universally loved music educator. I stayed home with Amy, got her enrolled in kindergarten in the same school system where Marilyn worked, then began seeking freelance assignments as a writer and musician.

Once we as a family had settled into our new community (my wife into her new job, our daughter into kindergarten, and me into childcare and a search for employment), I waited for any sign—letter, phone call, or carrier pigeon—that Wendell had indeed bequeathed his baby grand to me. I felt guilty for wanting so badly to know, but my eagerness had less to do with being given another piano than it was about having such a meaningful gift from a man I'd come to deeply respect every bit as much as any white-collar member of the EMU community I could think of.

Wendell died about a month later. I eventually contacted someone to inquire about the piano, only to be informed by mail, politely and matter-of-factly, that there was no mention of me in the will.

I felt no bitterness about the omission. Wendell Harwood would never have needed to give me material things to prove his regard for me. My greatest reward came from simply knowing the man—his humility, his superior work ethic, his unshakeable loyalty as a friend, his unimpeachable character.

The moment I finished the letter, I tossed it away, then went straight over and sat down at the upright piano, which, in spite of its scarred-and-faded exterior, could still make music fit for kings, queens, and authentic blue-collars everywhere.

I would have preferred, for old times' sake, to play Wendell's favorite piece, Beethoven's "Turkish March" from *The Ruins of Athens*. How I loved hearing him play that piece! But my skills at the piano weren't—and still aren't—anywhere near as strong as Wendell's were. So I just called up my resolve and fumbled through Bent Fabric's '60s musical chestnut, "Alley Cat," a song I knew I could handle. I've no doubt Wendell would have been fine with that, too. There was nothing in him that would ever have allowed him to feel superior to me—or anyone else—in any way.

* * *

In the excitement that inevitably came with moving to a new and unfamiliar place, my memories of David Stupple had begun to recede. Then, sometime in October, when the leaves were starting to reveal their spectacular fall colors, the reality of what I'd left behind—a fine young friendship with an extraordinary man—finally set in.

Awake at night in our sparsely appointed apartment, blanketed against the invigorating chill of a New England autumn, I realized I missed the Stupples—and especially David—more than I ever could have imagined. In the name of financial stability and self-renewal, I'd forfeited our hard-won camaraderie, and I felt as if I'd committed an inexcusable act of betrayal.

By midwinter, feeling increasingly guilty for having left David behind, I sat down and wrote my first letter to him, lamenting that I'd not seen him in several months. Then, with what I hoped were carefully chosen words, I gently chastised him for having expressed little interest in coming to Maine for a visit. He wrote back soon afterward, reminding me unequivocally of what I ought to have known: that he had professional obligations as a university professor, and that because of his mobility issues, travel wasn't always easy for him.

It was a foolish accusation, born of what were then my own persistent insecurities, and I was immediately ashamed for having made it. Not surprisingly, our correspondence came to an abrupt halt, and I had only myself to blame for it.

Many months later, a letter arrived in our mailbox, not from David but from his wife, June. *How good of her to write to us!* I thought. *David must be too busy at school to stop and write.*

I eagerly tore open the letter and, in the very first sentence, learned what no friend wants to hear: David had been hospitalized for surgery to remove a tumor on his back but had contracted pneumonia and died unexpectedly in the hospital on the very weekend of his admittance.

In the letter, June was very matter-of-fact about the situation. "Would you like to claim his research papers," she wrote, "then compile and edit them for possible publication? I think he would have liked that."

If I'd been less preoccupied with my own affairs—more mature, more compassionate, and more certain of my abilities—I would undoubtedly have jumped at the chance to edit those papers. But

I didn't, and now, nearly four decades after his passing, I continue to harbor equal amounts of guilt and regret for having failed to take on the project. I'd let David down yet again, and I doubt that I'll ever completely forgive myself for my behavior.

Many years later, while visiting relatives in Michigan, I looked up June's new street address in Ypsilanti, then knocked on her door, hoping to stand before her and apologize for my transgressions. Unfortunately, she wasn't home. Once back in Maine, I wrote a note explaining that I'd tried to visit her. I got no response until many years later, long after her husband's passing. Eventually I visited her and her grown children, Kelly and Kyle, in Ann Arbor, but it was painful to think that David couldn't be part of the reunion.

What was it about David Stupple that influenced me in such a lasting way? It was not one thing but many. The best things in life are never simple, either in their appearance or in the depth and breadth of their influence. His gentle demeanor; the deceptively casual way in which he interacted with others, taking a genuine interest in their lives; his complete lack of interest in social status and material things; and the wise, unpretentious way he shared his observations of the world—all were woven unselfconsciously into the fabric of the man, and a beautiful fabric it was.

More than once, when he heard me saying things about myself that laid bare the insecurities that plagued me, David would smile in his distinctive way, then offer up some sage advice from his treasure chest of Truths Only David Knows. It was pretty much the same familiar litany each time, delivered with a certain musical lilt that reached inevitably into the heart of me, and I never really tired of hearing it:

"Ross!" he'd say to me right after whipping me at yet another hour-long Ping-Pong extravaganza. "There's no need for you to be so hard on yourself! I want you to get up every morning, stand in front of your mirror, and say to yourself, 'I am beautiful! I am somebody! And I'm making a lasting difference in the world!' "

I could have said it over and over to him, too, but David didn't really need his own advice. He was already somebody, he was already a beautiful human being, and he'd already made a lasting difference in the lives of countless people, including me, just by being David.

I've come to believe that the best teachers, whether in or out of the classroom, never really stop teaching. They just teach by example, and their own hard-earned lessons, in partnership with their fundamental decency, are tailor-made to last a lifetime. David Stupple was a teacher's teacher, and even after all these years, his influence has continued to make all the difference in my life.

MY VERY OWN OCCUPATIONAL HISTORY:

White-Collar, Blue-Collar, and Not-Sure-Which-Collar

*"Working is always a wonderful thing, and
there is something good in all labour."[32]
—Vincent van Gogh*

The blue-collar world and the white-collar world: like a great many free-spirited, free-thinking creatives, I've spent a whole lot of time in both, doing everything from mowing lawns, sitting babies, hanging soap samples on doorknobs, assembling bicycles, and weaving airplane cargo nets to teaching writing to college freshmen, running a theatre company (and writing the plays it performed), founding an abstract artists' group, exhibiting my own multimedia artworks, performing solo recitals as a university-trained musician, and writing books. I've worn so many wildly different hats over the years that I can no longer remember which one seemed to fit me best—as if I could ever actually *know* such a thing.

And yet, for so many years I have felt quietly, unfairly labeled by so many people as "blue-collar" in origin. They've never needed to *say* it, because, without any effort at all, I can still *feel* it. I can feel their judgment, but there's never an easy way to defend myself against it.

---

32. Vincent van Gogh, "108 To Theo van Gogh. Dordrecht, Friday, 16 March 1877", Van Gogh Museum, retrieved June 10, 2025 from https://vangoghletters.org/vg/letters/let108/letter.html.

Labels! They can be so terribly unfair—so restrictive, so suffocating, so maddeningly irrational, so fundamentally unjust—unless, of course, one finds a way to know just the right people and learns to play the game of climbing, occupationally, up the social hierarchy.

I've never really stopped wondering why we as a society need these kinds of labels at all. Did I not simply choose, entirely free of outside influence, to do the things I've done over the years? Was anyone holding a gun to my head when I made my choices? And could any one of the many jobs I've held rightfully claim to have been inherently superior to the others?

Work! On the bad days it's more a dirty word than a challenging opportunity. And to say the least, its rewards are highly subjective: nothing more and nothing less than a matter of intensely personal opinion. After all, if one thoroughly enjoys weaving airplane cargo nets—if, in the matter of job satisfaction, no other work than weaving cargo nets can possibly compare—then weaving those damned nets until your knees are cramped and your fingers are bleeding is bound to be the number one choice, and any other possibilities be damned.

And yet, in all honesty, I really do know, deep down inside me, which labels I preferred along the way. To deny such a thing—to deny that, for as long as I can remember, I've yearned to be seen as white-collar—would be shamefully dishonest of me. To make my point, I'd like to share with you some of my more memorable real-life examples.

* * *

My very first fully "adult" job after dropping out of college at age nineteen and getting married to my first wife was as a tester of Sonobuoy underwater submarine detectors at the Sparton Corporation in Jackson, Michigan, my hometown. Why? Because the day after I tied the knot, I suddenly realized I was automatically, unavoidably in hot financial water. *Wait a minute,* I must have lamented to myself the very next morning, lying there next to my bride. *I'm married now! And that means I need money!*

So, I went straight to the *Jackson Citizen Patriot* want ads and pounced on the very first job with enough compensation to keep our just-launched marital ship above water. And I can say with absolute certainty that sitting with a team of scruffy misfits—guys just like me—on a fast-moving electrical merry-go-round, test-test-testing eight hours a day, was anything but white-collar. I needed only a few arduous, time-card-punching weeks to learn my lesson: testing underwater submarine detectors was clearly not meant to be a fail-proof career choice for me. It was a *job,* and nothing more than that.

Less than a year later, after my ill-planned, star-crossed "child marriage" mercifully ended in divorce, I was happily back in school, where I ought to have stayed in the first place. To pay for my coursework, I took many work-study assignments, every one of them meaningful and occupationally relevant. But the one I remember with the most affection was as the orchestra librarian for **José Serebrier**, an internationally known Uruguayan composer and conductor who'd come to EMU for one brief season to conduct while continuing to compose in his spare time. I felt like a million dollars while serving such a gifted, world-renowned maestro, but I also worried, privately, that working for a white-collar superstar wasn't guaranteed to turn my *blue* collar *white.* And my hunch was a good one, because it didn't. Not right away, at least.

But sure enough, a year or two after that, after earning my bachelor's degree in music with a performance emphasis at EMU, I became a graduate teaching fellow in English literature at the very same institution.

Finally! I laughed. *From now on, when I look in the mirror, I'll see not even one little patch of blue on my collar—only the whitest of whites!*

I was sure I'd finally arrived.

But of course I really hadn't. The painful truth was that, like all the other teaching fellows, I was only a shockingly under-compensated substitute teacher for tenured faculty who, in general, weren't about to dirty their hands and tarnish their résumés with the likes of the one course in the catalogue no one wanted either to take or to teach: freshman comp.

I worked—assiduously—through the ups and downs of playing professor, then walked off the EMU campus two years later with my coveted Master of Arts in English. By this time I had married again and had a daughter, and my wife and I knew it was time to move on, so move on we did. And not long after arriving in New England, I snagged what appeared to be a plum assignment as the director of publicity for one summer season at Ogunquit Playhouse, known around the country by its motto, "Maine's Foremost Summer Theater."

Anyone who labors on the business side of the performing arts would have said that here was an ideal assignment with more than enough room for growth into even more prestigious work. I thought so, too. But by the time I'd promoted my last show there— *The Impossible Dream*, with Richard Kiley in the prized role of Don Quixote—I realized that my own dream of having landed in the perfect white-collar universe had become little more than a colorful but half-baked, inherently subservient meet-the-stars fantasy. *White-collar, my ass*, I whimpered while cleaning out my desk—I was fed up with the job and more than ready to bail out—then got into my car and drove off, pondering how I might next attempt to climb a rung or two up the long and wobbly ladder to white-collar fulfillment.

* * *

I spent months searching, without success, for relevant work. Growing desperate—I'd had it with superficial, dead-end interviews—I turned instead to a Portsmouth-based headhunter service, the very last business I'd ever wanted to dirty my mental hands with. They *specialists,* me *not.*

So after several weeks of garbled, ill-focused consultations with my very own High Mucky-Muck Headhunter (Mr. Remington Danforth III, if I remember correctly)—a period in which I tried but failed miserably to explain to him how I think, what I'd accomplished in my life, and what I wanted him to do for me—he was so fed up with what he considered to be my "inability to make up my mind" that he urgently recommended a battery of tests guaranteed, he said, to pin down the one profession I was clearly born to be in.

I reluctantly forked over the $1,200 fee—a hell of a lot of money in the '80s for someone living in the midst of a nationwide job slump. Then, in spite of serious misgivings, I took the test.

And the *result,* two weeks later? Why, *Flower Arranger*—of *course*! How could I possibly have failed to know, intuitively, my one true vocation—my occupational calling? *Me dumb*! I raged. *Me blind! Me up the river without a friggin' paddle!*

I listened stoically to Danforth as he delivered what to him was the good news, then quietly told him that the test he'd recommended for me had been a complete waste of time.

"A fucking *flower arranger*?" I fumed. "Are you *shitting* me?" (Of course, I didn't really use those terms, but from the tone of my delivery, he knew exactly what I meant.)

So by now, exceedingly exasperated, he pulled down what he must have considered to be the last, best weapon from his consultational gun rack.

"Listen, Mr. Bachelder," he snarled. "My best advice to you is this: either *shit* or *get off the pot!*"

In case I haven't already made it clear for you, the problem we had, together, is that while he wanted, in good faith, to identify the one-and-only profession that he and the Almighty had set aside for me, I just wanted to find well-paid employment that actually fit my temperament. But it didn't happen, because, like so many other consultants and know-it-alls in the Age of Specialization, he couldn't imagine that some people really aren't born to specialize. I just needed a damn job—a job that actually *fit* me.

Welcome to the inner sanctum of a multidisciplinary Arty Guy—a bona fide Juggler-in-Chief—doing his best to survive in a specialization-obsessed universe.

* * *

After several painful, crapshoot attempts to find ideal employment in seacoast New Hampshire and southern Maine—including seven mixed-bag years as an elementary school music educator and seasonal stints as the publicist for several area playhouses—I found, in the most unlikely of places, work much more suited to my tastes and temperament. I spent the next twenty of my midlife years as a picture framer, first in a shopping mall and then in a stand-alone art and craft supply store. To sweeten the occupational pot when things began to go sour, I turned one wall of the frame shop into a thumbnail gallery that soon proved itself, happily, to be The Little Gallery That Could.

But thanks to society's stubborn, deeply ingrained ideas about where a picture framer belongs in the occupational hierarchy, I was forced to contend on an almost daily basis with two rather distinct audiences: those who considered me a genuine artist and craftsman—a born creative who clearly knew how to add luster to artworks from the magnificent to the aesthetically challenged—and those who could only see me as just another underachieving middle-aged male scraping by as a low-paid, unfulfilled blue-collar lackey.

In the minds of the latter, I was just one more generic cog in a vast, ill-conceived and poorly managed machine, and my sole purpose was to obsequiously serve the middle and upper classes. And even worse, they seemed maddeningly incapable of seeing that *all blue-collar laborers are not the same*—that to a person, they bring their very own unique skills, passions, and personalities to their work and often love it to distraction.

I was in retail now, working five and six days a week in an unpretentious, rough-around-the-edges craft store that sold everything from paints and knitting supplies to artificial flowers and model car kits. And I had no argument, initially, with the popular notion that being "stuck in retail" is about as low as anyone in need of employment can go. Like my epic, overnight tumble from graduate teaching fellow to university mailman, my snap-of-the-finger move from onstage/offstage work in summer stock theatre—work I dearly loved—to retail framing was a truly precipitous fall from grace.

But to my grudging surprise, I discovered I was much happier standing in the back of a craft store beautifying other people's artworks than I'd ever been while standing in front of a classroom. In the frame shop, people wanted and expected me to perform magic on the works they brought to me. And because I nearly always delivered, I had a good, solid reputation as a designer.

Framing certainly made me happier than being a graduate teaching fellow. There, I'd dealt with all too many truculent freshmen who wanted only to *survive* a course they thought was being shoved down their throats whether they needed it or not. And of course, a great many of them were certain they *didn't*. Why? Because, without any verifiable evidence, they wanted desperately to believe they were already skilled writers. "I don't need a writing teacher!" they must have whined to their dorm mates in the evenings. "I can *already* write! What do they think I am—*stupid?*" Sometimes, after critiquing an especially sloppy, thrown-together essay from yet another reluctant learner, I most certainly did think so. I soon learned to be profoundly grateful to find a handful of students who respected their teacher and were more than eager to improve their skills as writers.

In the frame shop, I was occasionally forced to endure questions like "How'd a guy like you ever end up in *retail*?" from well-meaning customers. They assumed I was down on my luck, and they viewed me as unusually articulate and self-possessed for a guy toiling in the trenches. But what they didn't understand—unless, out of frustration, I decided to explain it to them—was that I didn't think for one second that I was actually *in* retail. They also didn't know that I considered *retail* to be a term inflicted on a vast and disparate group of employees by well-intended MBAs who are trained to categorize the masses, apparently hell-bent on telling them precisely where they, at least as retailers, "belong."

So it is perhaps more than a little ironic that, in spite of the public's irrationally bifurcated perception of me, I soon came to consider my woefully under-compensated work as a picture framer to be infinitely more white-collar—and even more decidedly prestigious—than my time as an instructor of freshman comp at a respected university.

Decades later, I still have people come up to me on the street or in stores to praise me for the work I did to enhance and enliven their artworks. To them, whether my collar was white or blue, I seemed to know what I was doing, and that was really all that mattered to them.

Affirmation was much harder to come by in the college class-room. Like any teacher of freshman comp, I yearned every day to be seen, in the eyes of my cynical, rebellious, ever-so-adolescent learners, as a skilled and highly literate champion of the written word—a dependable resource, always available and eager to assist.

I also hoped, fervently, they would eventually realize that no matter how odious freshman composition might have seemed to them at the time, it really had contributed, in at least some small but lasting way, to their success in their chosen professions and life in general.

So why, I frequently ask myself, wasn't teaching writing every bit as white-collar as restoring, designing, and choosing frames and mats for artworks? In fact, why did either my writing students or my frame shop customers need to label me at all? Why, oh why the ceaseless labeling! If you're good at one particular endeavor, then you'll be appreciated for your work. If you're not, then justice is shrewd. Justice is dependable. And *justice will finally be done.* Just ask a politician. Or, for that matter, a blue-collar worker!

To begin to understand why I've all-too-often cared way too much about what others think of my position within the employment hierarchy, have a close look at the work of **Vance Packard**, author of *The Status Seekers, The Hidden Persuaders,* and other thoughtful, painstakingly researched bestsellers. As I see it, Packard just *knew,* somehow, why people like me care as much as we do about the public's perception of our social status.

Humans are climbers—natural-born status seekers. And whether we like it or not, many people—people from all walks of life—continue to behave as if we live in a social Darwinist world. It follows, then, that in the minds of many corporate executives, human resource professionals, social scientists, and academicians, the color of our collars is a convenient way for them to sift through, thin out, and reorganize the occupational herd—to minimize people's differences in ability by forcing them into what they imagine to be their rightful place within the occupational hierarchy.

PART III

My Ways of Thinking

THE NEW ENGLAND TRANSCENDENTALISTS:
My Sentimental, Transcendental Journey

> *"There is no wholly masculine man,*
> *no purely feminine woman."[33]*
> *—Margaret Fuller*

Because my post–World War II, financially strapped parents considered vacationing in faraway places to be a frivolous pastime and an inexcusable waste of money, during childhood I seldom traveled beyond the southernmost region of Michigan's lower peninsula.

Then I went away to college. I was nineteen years old, full of energy, eager to learn, and—though I couldn't really see it that way at the time—intellectually blossoming. That is when I was first exposed to the writings of the New England Transcendentalists, and it was just the right time. I imagined these high-minded men and women—adherents to a philosophy of self-reliance, intuition, and the supremacy of the individual—gathering in Ralph Waldo Emerson's home in Concord, Massachusetts, to discuss important issues of the day, and I was intoxicated. The Transcendentalist mystique appealed enormously to me.

The New England Transcendentalist movement—an outgrowth of America's refusal to kowtow to the whims of the British monarchs—had deep philosophical roots ranging from

---

33. Margaret Fuller, *Woman in the Nineteenth Century*, Greeley & McElrath, 1845, 103.

Hinduism's ancient Upanishads to Poland, Transylvania, European Romanticism, and, eventually, American Unitarianism. Along the way, people including Immanuel Kant, Emanuel Swedenborg, and a long list of Boston Brahmins—New England's famed nineteenth-century intellectual elites—have been intimately associated with the origins and evolution of the movement.

By the time I'd finished my undergraduate work in music and become a graduate student in English and American literature, I'd begun to read extensively from the works of Transcendentalist authors like **Ralph Waldo Emerson**, **Henry David Thoreau**, **Bronson Alcott**, **Nathaniel Hawthorne**, and **Margaret Fuller**. (Fuller was the great-aunt of renowned inventor and philosopher **R. Buckminster Fuller**, whom I had the immense privilege of interviewing in Philadelphia in the 1970s—an inspiring, unforgettable, life-changing experience.)

I'd also branched out into other arts-related areas of intense interest, most notably the works of composer, actuary scientist, and insurance executive **Charles Ives**. While thoroughly grounded in traditional music theory and harmony, for a man of his time he was extraordinarily innovative in his approach to music, experimenting with everything from rooftop antiphony and "marching band" effects to tone clusters, aleatory ("chance") music, quarter tones, and polyphony.

So enthralled was I with the astonishing depth, breath, and originality of Ives's creative work that I wrote an ambitious analytical paper about his four-movement Piano Sonata No. 2 (*Concord, Mass., 1840–60*), known as the *Concord* sonata. The four movements are named after and pay homage to New England Transcendentalists Ralph Waldo Emerson, Nathaniel Hawthorne, the Alcotts, and Henry David Thoreau.

Compared to the typical classical music of the time, the *Concord* sonata was so daring, so indifferent to centuries-old European expectations for "serious" music, that it was nearly unintelligible to the average listener—including the majority of composers and musicologists of the period. In his own unique way, Ives was a harbinger of things to come, including Igor Stravinsky's *Rite of Spring*—a work whose primitive, sky-high energy and wildly unconventional compositional approaches nearly brought the house down when it was first performed in Paris in 1913 with Sergei Diaghilev's *Ballets Russes*. Although the *Concord* sonata was not published until 1919, its composition started seven years prior to that of *Rite of Spring*.

Ives's *Three Places in New England* and *The Unanswered Question* are to me hauntingly beautiful works of art—perfect musical companions to my longtime love affair with literary works like "Self-Reliance" (Emerson), "The Artist of the Beautiful" (Hawthorne), and *Leaves of Grass* (Walt Whitman).

Was Charles Ives a New England Transcendentalist? Historically speaking, perhaps not. But, like composers **Edward MacDowell** (*Woodland Sketches*) and **Charles Griffes** (*The Pleasure-Dome of Kubla Khan*), Ives embodied, in one way or another, virtually every major tenet of New England Transcendentalist thinking and will forever be associated, at least in spirit, with the movement.

Why? Because, even though Ives was from an elite family and became an enormously wealthy businessman, he and his music championed the dignity of work, the wisdom and fundamental decency of the Common Man, and the right of the latter to be taken as seriously as any more privileged, more highly credentialed man or woman.

And if those aren't blue-collar values, then what else could be?

In a similar vein, though Ives could not have rightfully claimed to be a blue-collar figure, he most certainly could have claimed to be a fervent blue-collar *advocate*—this in spite of the fact that the term *blue-collar* wasn't coined until 1924, when Ives was already fifty years old. My guess is that he was far too busy composing brilliant, yet-to-be-discovered music and managing his insurance company, Ives and Myrick, to worry about the color of his or anyone else's collar.

FOCUS POCUS:

The Pressure to Specialize

"Specialization is for insects."[34]
—Robert Heinlein

Specialize (verb, intransitive): "To become distinct or separate from what is common"; particularly, "to focus one's study upon a particular skill, field, topic, or genre," or "to focus one's business upon a particular item or service."[35]

We've all seen, heard of, and even benefited from examples of specialization. Go to any hospital, for instance, and both inside and outside—well beyond the walls of the actual facility—you'll see signs telling you, in no uncertain terms, who's specializing and what they're specializing in: Otolaryngology (Eye, Ear, Nose, and Throat); Ophthalmology; Obstetrics and Gynecology; Radiology.

And within each one of these specialties, like zits on an adolescent's forehead, the sub-specialties abound. Within otolaryngology, for example, one can find neurology-related inner ear concerns, including skull base tumors, implantable hearing devices like cochlear implants, bone conduction hearing aids, and balance disorders. Within ophthalmology, you can choose between ocular

---

34. Robert A. Heinlein, *Time Enough for Love*, Berkley/Penguin Random House, 1973, 255–256.

35. Various contributors, "Specialize," Wiktionary, https://en.wiktionary.org/wiki/specialize.

oncology, ophthalmic plastic and reconstructive surgery, or even vitreoretinal disease.

Had enough? I know I have! And yet to make my point, I need to finish my list of obscure examples from within the world of medical specialization.

Within obstetrics and gynecology, help yourself to female pelvic medicine and reconstructive surgery, maternal–fetal medicine, or reproductive endocrinology and infertility. And finally, within radiology, there's an absolute embarrassment of riches: cardiothoracic radiology, endovascular surgical neuroradiology, and musculoskeletal radiology, to name only a few.

Oh, my God!

And have I forgotten Subcutaneous Left-Nostril Irregularities? Or Geriatric Wandering Penis Syndrome? I didn't *mean* to. You see, I have only so much space here for stuff that arcane.

But of course, it has not been my intent, here, to condemn medical specialization. On the contrary, it has surely saved tens of thousands of lives, including, perhaps, even *yours*. The only problem I see with medical specialization is that specialists may become so astoundingly focused on one, small part of the human anatomy that they lose sight of the larger picture. After all, bodily functions are hardly isolated from each other. Right? Indeed, they're remarkably, elaborately interwoven, like an orchestral composition or the intricate parts of a space station module. And together, day in and day out, they perform biological miracles to keep you alive and kicking and available for a hot date, a round of golf, or maybe just some well-deserved time alone over a good book.

So Viva La Medical Specialization!

Now, I could talk about specialization as it exists in other societal arenas—car industry mass production, for example, or—don't worry, I *won't*—the meat industry. To immerse yourself in the latter, just pick up a copy of Upton Sinclair's *The Jungle*, and when you're done with it, you will have become an expert in How to Turn Live Animals into Sunday Dinner.

Instead, I'm going to turn the one arena in which the pressure to specialize has affected me the most perniciously over the years: the fine and performing arts.

One would like to think that the fine and performing arts offer the best possible safe haven from the pressure to specialize. But even *there*—where I live and work—life is far from perfect. While I've many examples to choose from, the following sample should help you appreciate where, in the matter of specialization, I'm coming from.

Every year, the Barn Gallery—the exhibit venue of Maine's Ogunquit Art Association (OAA)—invites artists to submit works in hopes of being juried into the group as full-fledged members in good standing.

Aspiring members are required to submit ten works, all of them from just *one* of the following four categories: painting, graphics, sculpture, or photography.

The requirement immediately flashed me a blindingly red warning light, simply because, as an artist who works in not one but several media and disciplines—an arts multiple, not a specialist—I absolutely did *not* want to be restricted to just one category while submitting.

That I work in not one but several media is at the very heart and soul of who I am as a creative.

So, aesthetically speaking, I was now in one hell of a pickle. (And for the record, I happen to detest pickles of *any* kind. Just ask my friends!)

What to do? I asked myself, suddenly all in a panic. After all, I really did want to be a part of OAA, with all of the perks, privileges, and prestige it so proudly confers on its members.

But my problem was even more fraught with dilemmas than one might think. Why? Because I'm also active—in fact, *very* active—as a writer and musician. So, needless to say, my creative time in any one discipline is necessarily stretched thinner than the eyelid of a gnat.

Had I been allowed to submit, simultaneously, ten works from *several* media, there would have been no problem at all. OAA would have been able to see the full range of my creative work at one glance, and I'd have been able share with the jurors what is probably the best thing about me as an artist: my remarkable diversity and the energy it nearly always generates when I simultaneously exhibit works in several media.

And so, feeling dissed, defeated, and misunderstood, I went ahead and submitted several *photographs*, simply because I had more ready-to-hang works in that medium than in any other.

I also knew that submitting only photos created yet another problem for me. That's because artists everywhere continue to harbor an unspoken, often ill-informed conviction that photography is not really a fully legitimate art form—that it is a mere stepchild to the plastic arts and therefore aesthetically suspect as a medium. So I knew that even if my photographs were dazzlingly creative, I had little if any chance of being taken seriously as an artist.

So thanks a lot, Mr. Ford, for your mass-production, assembly-line, One-Fender-at-a-Time way of thinking. I love your cars—they really are works of art—but your formula, when applied to the fine and performing arts, doesn't fit me. Never has and never will.

ESSAY

WIKIPEDIA:

The Resource Academics Love to Hate

"Imagine a world in which every single
person on the planet is given free access to
the sum of all human knowledge. That's
what we're doing."[36]
—Jimmy Wales, cofounder of Wikipedia

I don't know about you, but to me there's something both darkly
humorous and—dare I say it?—remarkably sagacious about my
decision to begin this commentary about **Wikipedia** with what
one might consider a longwinded, academically uptight series of
straight-from-the-source quotations from—where else?—Wikipedia.
(The footnotes will show you the way to the articles I've quoted,
and the articles themselves contain more footnotes for the sources
cited within them.)

> Wikipedia co-founder **Jimmy Wales** [emphasis mine] said that
> the concept of Wikipedia came when he was a graduate student
> at Indiana University, where he was impressed with the successes
> of the open-source movement and found Richard Stallman's
> Emacs Manifesto promoting free software and a sharing econ-
> omy interesting. Wales also credits Austrian School economist

---

36. Roblimo, "Wikipedia Founder Jimmy Wales Responds," Slashdot.org, July 28, 2004,
https://slashdot.org/story/04/07/28/1351230/wikipedia-founder-jimmy-wales-responds/.

Friedrich Hayek's essay "The Use of Knowledge in Society," which he read as an undergraduate, as "central" to his thinking about "how to manage the Wikipedia project."[37]

In an interview with *New Scientist* on January 31, 2007, Wales said:

The idea [behind Wikipedia] was to have thousands of volunteers writing articles for an online encyclopedia in all languages. Initially, we found ourselves organizing the work in a very top-down, structured, academic, old-fashioned way. It was no fun for the volunteer writers because we had a lot of academic peer review committees who would criticize articles and give feedback. It was like handing in an essay at grad school, and basically intimidating to participate in.[38]

From there, Wikipedia grew rapidly.

[Wikipedia is] a global project in hundreds of languages. [. . .] In 2005, Wikipedia became the most popular reference website on the Internet, according to Hitwise, with English Wikipedia alone exceeding 750,000 articles.[39]

Long-winded? Perhaps! But hey: I didn't write it. Wikipedia contributors did! And now, *curtain up* again!

The free online encyclopedia Wikipedia has been criticized since its creation in 2001. [. . .] Critics have questioned its factual

---

37. Various contributors, "History of Wikipedia," Wikimedia Foundation, retrieved May 11, 2025 from https://en.wikipedia.org/wiki/History_of_Wikipedia.

38. Various contributors, "Jimmy Wales," Wikimedia Foundation, https://en.wikipedia.org/wiki/Jimmy_Wales.

39. Various contributors, "History of Wikipedia," Wikimedia Foundation, https://en.wikipedia.org/wiki/History_of_Wikipedia.

reliability, the readability and organization of its articles, the lack of methodical fact-checking, and its political bias.

Concerns have also been raised about systemic bias along gender, racial, political, corporate, institutional, and national lines. Conflicts of interest arising from corporate campaigns to influence content have also been highlighted. Further concerns include the vandalism and partisanship facilitated by anonymous editing, clique behavior (from contributors as well as administrators and other top figures), social stratification between a guardian class and newer users, excessive rule-making, edit warring, and uneven policy application.[40]

A few more simple but salient facts about Wikipedia, also straight from the horse's mouth, should be helpful. I mean, *who knows?*

Wikipedia has been hosted since 2003 by the Wikimedia Foundation, an American nonprofit organization funded mainly by donations from readers. Wikipedia is the largest and most-read reference work in history.[41]

Enough already!

As I've looked more and more closely into the story of Wikipedia—its origins, its literary audacity, its remarkable ability to withstand the relentless, often vitriolic attacks on its worth to the world—I've decided there's something fundamentally, smugly hypocritical about academia's assumptions about Wikipedia.

---

40. Various contributors, "Criticism of Wikipedia," Wikimedia Foundation, https://en.wikipedia.org/wiki/Criticism_of_Wikipedia.

41. Various contributors, "Wikipedia," Wikimedia Foundation, https://en.wikipedia.org/wiki/Wikipedia.

Let's have a look at a few of them:

Assumption One: Wikipedia's contributors can't possibly produce well-written, reliable information, simply because they're not tenured, thoroughly trained, *college-based* writers—the exalted men and women whose calling as academics is to conceive, create, and monitor the "top-quality" materials that . . . you know . . . we poor *non*-academics must rely on.

Assumption Two: Academics were obviously *born* to write; otherwise, why would they have been granted tenure in the first place? For them, writing is as natural as rain. Wikipedia's contributors, on the other hand, are only marginally literate. Wikipedians are mere dreamers—a tool bucket without the tools. And because of it, their only real choice is to just *play* at being writers.

Assumption Three: It's absurd to think that a sprawling, loosely connected global network of *regular people*—most of them without hard-earned academic credentials from the finest (sic) colleges and universities—can be counted on to provide accurate information.

The most laughable and damning truth about the shitstorm of criticisms leveled at Wikipedia is that the crimes of ineptitude they've allegedly committed are the very same crimes—small, large, and in every imaginable configuration—that humankind, in all its flawed and unpredictable majesty, commit every single day. And since academics, as far as I know, also belong to humankind, *their* work is every bit as flawed and unreliable as that of anyone connected with Wikipedia.

Now, lest you hasten to brand me as hopelessly naive, I want to assure you that I *know* Wikipedia has serious vulnerabilities as an informational resource.

To begin with, I'm entirely in league with anyone who thinks all those lying, cheating high school and college students ought to be *ashamed* of themselves for pilfering, like pigeons in a pastry shop, from writing done in good faith by people other than themselves. I honestly don't know how teachers in *any* classroom are able to tolerate the fact that a certain etched-in-stone percentage of their students' assignments have no genuine originality in either their content or the minds of students who claim to have written them.

One solution to the epidemic of plagiarism is for the teacher in charge to require at least one major pop-up writing assignment per semester, to be completed under supervision and sans cell phone, sans laptop, sans books and backpack, sans ink-on-the-forearm, sans anything that could compromise the authenticity of the student's writing sample.

Listen! I mean, if students can fight dirty, then, in an honest, firm-handed way, so can the Teach.

I also think it's more than fair to say that when, in 2001, Wikipedia propelled itself into the vast public forum of ideas, it opened an enormous can of spot-checking informational worms. They should have known that trouble was coming, and it's more than likely they *did*. But it really doesn't bother me. Not at all!

Why? Because, as with humankind's relentless struggle to conquer outer space and the medical profession's determination to triumph over disease, Wikipedia saw an opportunity, risked the very real possibility of abject failure, then forged ahead anyway.

Now *that's* courage! Self-Determination with a capital S and a capital D! And really, is it not every bit as courageous of the Wikimedia Foundation to *continue*, against the most formidable odds, to do the work it does? After all, when it comes to human endeavor of every kind, permanent success is never, ever guaranteed. So it follows that no matter how successful Wikipedia becomes, they could still make a poor decision and suddenly fall on their faces.

The truth is that I'm *madly in love* with Wikipedia and have been since the very first time when, in the middle of the night, when my local library was closed, I needed to confirm something of critical importance to my writing. And I needed that something *fast* because I was writing on deadline and badly needed the parsimonious but important check I'd be getting for my labors.

I'm even more passionately in love with Wikipedia because I see it as triumphantly *egalitarian* in a world overwhelmed with corporate greed and sneaky, white-collar, under-the-table shenanigans. As much as I revere my local library, and indeed all libraries, I don't always *need* to go there to get information. And I have services like my own home library—and especially Wikipedia—to thank for that.

And finally, I love Wikipedia because, unlike so many blatantly narcissistic, self-proclaimed "top-tier" academic institutions, it isn't bound suffocatingly tight by procedure, precedent, and an exaggerated sense of either its infallibility or its worth to the world. Wikipedia is going out of its way both to *allow* criticism and to react constructively *to* it.

The people at Wikipedia seem to believe in the better instincts of the average citizen enough to *trust* us to provide, entirely on our own initiative, the majority of the operating funds they need if they're going to continue to serve us.

To me, Wikipedia has, deep within itself, the very same values that made New England Transcendentalism such a force for good in the world: respect for the wisdom and judgment of the average person, hand in hand with a determination to make information of any kind available to all of us regardless of our background, our social status, our credentials, or our lack of any credentials at all.

Remember your neighborhood's onetime mom-and-pop grocery store? That's what Wikipedia is to me: a friendly, welcoming place where I can just drop by, unannounced, and—without the torture of prerecorded, multilayered barriers to access—see what they just might have that I'd be ever so thankful to get. And at *my* convenience, not theirs, thank you.

ESSAY  20

THE CREDENTIALS REQUIREMENT:
Who Sez, and Why?

"The truth is I have absolutely no professional credentials—literally, which is why I'm teaching at MIT."[42]
—Noam Chomsky

Come with me now to the world of *credentials*—of documents, résumés, sheepskins, and curriculum vitae. Call 'em what you will, but first, we need a simple, workable definition. So here we go!

Wiktionary.org defines *credential* as "documentary or electronic evidence that a person has certain status or privileges."[43]

Oh, that! Well, I've had a few credentials in my day. But I seldom if ever mention them in person because, to me, flashing one's credentials around in casual conversation is a sign of self-aggrandizement, deep insecurity, braggadocio, or all of the above.

Now, I'd have to be just plain *dumb* not to demand evidence of credentials while shopping for certain services. A given credential may not amount to incontestable proof of competence, but it at least gives one *hope* that competence will be found. Would you hire

---

42. Noam Chomsky, "World Premier of IS THE MAN WHO IS TALL HAPPY? with Michel Gondry and Noam Chomsky at DOC NYC 2013," @DocNYCfest, November 24, 2013, https://youtu.be/BxQZzTJd9KE, time stamp 5:50.

43. Various contributors, "Credential," Wiktionary: The Free Dictionary, March 15, 2025, https://en.wiktionary.org/wiki/credential.

an electrician, a flight instructor, or a heart surgeon who couldn't supply you with verifiable credentials? I sure as hell wouldn't!

But there are areas of human endeavor in which credentials alone are not—and never will be—proof of competence in a given discipline. And intimately related to credentials are two questions: Who issues the credential? And what's required to earn it?

But it only gets messier, doesn't it! I mean, is the credential that someone just waved in your face actually up to date? And are the criteria for earning that credential rational and sufficient as proof of mastery? Altogether, these are crucial questions, and you, as a consumer, deserve trustworthy answers.

Take, for example, the Master of Fine Arts in Creative Writing degree. There must surely have been a time in recorded history when one didn't need a degree in creative writing to whip up what might just become a best-selling novel. In fact, the idea that one can't have a successful career as a fiction writer *without* one is, if not downright preposterous, just plain silly.

Confession: for several years, I assumed that the MFA in creative writing was only a recent invention—fifteen or twenty years old at most. But with a little digging, I discovered that the degree and its origins have a surprisingly long history.

Indiana University was among the first North American universities to grant an MA degree in creative writing, awarding its first graduate creative writing degree in 1949 to poet and novelist David Wagoner.

David *who*? Sorry, Mr. Wagoner; no grand tintinnabulations in *this* ear; only a faint tinkle or two. I can take some comfort, though, in knowing that a graduate degree in creative writing doesn't automatically guarantee its holder lifetime membership in the Great American Novelists' Hall of Fame.

It wasn't until 1980 that IU began granting the more rigorous, more prestigious Master of Fine Arts in creative writing. So one has to wonder: what on earth did America's more serious, more ambitious writers *do* until that priceless, *gotta-have-it* degree was conceived and implemented? I mean, where have all the hardworking, pre-MFA darlings of the literary world gone? Let's face it: in most cases, we'll never know. Ironically, the same is true for most writers who *do* have that degree.

It's perhaps worth mentioning that if I were a young, energetic aspiring fiction writer in search of a reputable MFA program for creative writing, I'd want to know, well ahead of time, what has happened to the majority of the *graduates* of that program.

Does the typical creative writing degree live up to its promise, i.e., *to turn its graduates into creative, productive, successful writers*? To take the pulse of the typical creative writing graduate student, I turned to Reddit. There, in the r/writers subreddit, user CircularBrick asked, "What are some of the problems you've faced in learning creative writing in an academic setting?"[44] Here are some of the replies.

"If you want to write for money, stop school now. MFA is only useful if you want to be an adjunct professor. There is no tenure track for the work because there's too much competition." —u/Ander_Kurtsveil

"Absolutely not worth it if it's not a fully funded program with a good stipend. The real benefit of an MFA is time to write without having to stress about money. There can be other benefits like making connections and meeting the bare minimum for a university position (which you are not at all likely to get unless you publish a successful book), but those are not guarantees." —u/manganzonaso

---

44. u/CircularBrick, "Problems in Creative Writing Degrees BAs and MFAs?", r/writing, July 22, 2021, https://www.reddit.com/r/writing/comments/opg65z/problems_in_creative_writing_degrees_bas_and_mfas/.

"An MFA won't get you a job, a good portfolio will. [. . .] Focus on generating works and projects. At least that's what all my friends who write for TV/Netflix advocate for." —u/_Takub_

"I got a BFA in creative writing and it kind of killed my confidence and joy with writing. The literary snobbishness, the focus on style over story, the endless nitpicking critiques . . . I might have learned something but I haven't written much fiction in years." —u/spruceofthemist

"For me, the whole point of an MFA is that you get to carve out a few years of your life to just focus on writing and hone your craft. The quality of my writing has increased exponentially since I've been in my program; I've gotten several pieces published and built some momentum in achieving my career goals, and I don't know if I ever would have accomplished this without the space, focus, and push the program has given my writing." —u/maybesortakinda

From this admittedly small sampling, I conclude that a creative writing degree is a credential with more pitfalls than benefits. But *don't give up*, wordsmiths. An MFA in creative writing still exists at Indiana University! That means *you, too,* can try to qualify! As of this writing, IU boasts that its "award-winning faculty works hands-on with candidates throughout a three-year program focused on the learning, application, and integration of craft concepts and the generation and workshopping of original student poetry and fiction."[45]

---

45. Indiana University, "Master of Fine Arts degree in Creative Writing," retrieved May 11, 2025 from https://english.indiana.edu/graduate/master-of-fine-arts-degree.

Well, now. I suppose I just can't help it, but there's something about that kind of pretentious online palaver that just gets *deep down under my skin.*

Whatever happened to those breathtaking moments in history when unknown writers like **Grace Metalious** and **Thomas Wolfe** could crawl down from their self-made garrets after years of mind-numbing candlelight labor, put their five-hundred-page manuscripts in the mail, then learn within a matter of months that they'd become overnight sensations? Call me reprehensible—call me indefensible—but I still believe a writer with serious chops, an unimpeachable work ethic, and *no sheepskin at all* can come up with a novel that, for all the right reasons, has worldwide appeal.

Okay, then. So one doesn't really need an advanced degree in creative writing to be a best-selling author. What rock have I been living under? I mean, I never imagined such a thing was possible!

And yet there must be *some* reason that so many US colleges—nearly three hundred, according to the MFA Programs Database—offer MFA programs in creative writing. In each case, one could ask what the program *is*—what function keeps it in existence. Is it a source of prestige for the institution? A necessary degree offering to achieve a certain stratum in college rankings? Someone's pet project, begun long ago, that refuses to die? Or, God forbid, a straight-out, unvarnished *money magnet*?

Among the many ways that colleges aggressively recruit students—the beauty of their campuses, the notoriety and intellectual sophistication of their tenured faculty, the reputations of their sports teams, the hyped-up sophistication of their dining halls and exercise facilities—is *the depth and breadth of their degree programs.*

Any program whose *title alone* provokes wonder and no small amount of very human ambition to be involved with anything described as "creative"—for example, creative writing—will draw aspiring writers like ants to a fresh-baked pie. And that translates into tuition money, which leads to operating revenue, more commonly referred to in the business world as *Profit* with a capital P.

Of course, some MFA programs in creative writing are more prestigious, and therefore more sought-after, than others. Among the most prominent and attention-grabbing ones are the Iowa Writers' Workshop, the University of Chicago's program in creative writing, and Brown University's Literary Arts MFA program.

But what about similar programs at lesser-known schools?

Let's start with **Lindenwood University** in St. Charles, Missouri. Its award-winning creative writing program is known as one of the best and most affordable online, low-residency writing programs in the country.

And then there's Michigan's **Alma College**, a private Presbyterian liberal arts college less than an hour north of Lansing. Alma's MFA in creative writing program, billed as "Writing for the 21st Century," features "a strong, literature-based curriculum and offers inspirational and exploratory residency experiences designed to develop your ability to read and think critically and to write with a high level of artistic proficiency."[46]

And finally, why not have a look at **Naropa University** in Boulder, Colorado? Its Jack Kerouac School of Disembodied Poetics, purported to be "unlike any other creative writing program in the world,"[47] was founded in 1974 by Allen Ginsberg and Anne Waldman.[48] The school "values the craft and spirit of writing," and its MFA students "work at the cutting edge [please: not *that* cliché again!] of contemporary, experimental forms alongside the traditions of letterpress printing, book arts, and small press publishing," whereupon they "enter the world ready to take their work to the next level [*another* cliché, goddammit!] from academia

---

46. Alma College, "MFA in Creative Writing," retrieved May 20, 2025 from https://www.alma.edu/academics/programs/mfa-in-creative-writing/.

47. Naropa University, hover text for "MFA in Creative Writing & Poetics", retrieved May 20, 2025 from https://www.naropa.edu/academics/.

48. Naropa University, "About the Jack Kerouac School of Disembodied Poetics," retrieved May 20, 2025 from https://www.naropa.edu/academics/schools-centers/jack-kerouac-school-of-disembodied-poetics/about/.

to publishing, performance, and community building."[49] Whoa! I mean, why look anywhere else?

So what's all of this self-congratulatory crowing really all about?

Many things, of course. But no matter how they might wish to represent themselves, schools like Lindenwood, Alma, and Naropa are only human: they want desperately to have climbed the ladder from runt-of-the-litter, blue-collar relative anonymity to emphatically elitist, white-collar notoriety. In short, they want their hard-earned piece of the action: nationwide respect, unqualified admiration, and a whole lot more cash in the kitty than schools like theirs are accustomed to having.

The MFA in Creative Writing! A feather in the cap of those who yearn for basic respect and fair compensation for their writing. It's a credential you can hang on your wall, parade in your query letters, and mention, whether quietly or noisily, at the water cooler where you actually, regularly get paid for your services.

* * *

In every field of endeavor, there are credentials that exist not as signed-and-sealed documents on paper but entirely in the minds of the people who decide whether to take you seriously as an applicant. Do you fit nicely into their idea of who fits in the role? Are you a man or woman? Are you White, African-American, or AAPI? Hispanic or not Hispanic? Straight or gay? Blue-collar or white-collar?

---

49. Naropa University, "MFA in Creative Writing & Poetics," retrieved May 20, 2025 from https://www.naropa.edu/programs/graduate-academics/mfa-creative-writing-poetics/.

All of us are one age or another, so we must learn to live, for better or worse, with the age we happen to be at any given moment. But for those of us who've been arbitrarily declared "old," the door is opened for both spoken and unspoken discrimination in every area of our life. Many people cannot fathom the value of age and experience. But does it really make sense for us to lament the accumulation of our years? No! It only makes sense to be *proud* of it and then work around it while fully embracing it.

But of course, it's not always easy to do that.

A decade or so ago—when I was either already seventy years old or fast approaching it—I saw an advertisement for a call for art at an up-and-coming (aren't they all?) gallery in trendy Portsmouth, New Hampshire.

"Are you an emerging artist?" said a playful, well-designed message on the wall just inside the gallery. The rest went something like this: "If so, we'd love to have you submit three framed 2D artworks to our annual, professionally juried exhibit, 'Art Is For Everyone.' To qualify, email us with your name, address, and phone number; high-quality digital images of the three works you're submitting; and the medium, dimensions, and asking price for each work. The deadline for submissions is midnight on August 30. Notifications will be emailed to successful entrants on September 23."

Well, I'm an emerging artist, I thought to myself. *I mean, whoever isn't an emerging artist?* Every day I emerge from my bed, thinking, I want not just to be an artist, but a *damn good* artist! (Between you and me, I wanna be *done* with this "emerging" thing.)

A no-brainer, right? So I stepped up to the young woman at the counter.

"Good morning!" I chirped. "I'd like to submit works to the annual Art Is For Everyone exhibit. Where do I begin?" (I knew all about the sign; I was just making small talk.)

Up went her sleek, tanning-boothed arm, waving flippantly to the right of her. "The sign over there tells you what to do." She disappeared into her iPhone for a moment, then turned abruptly around and said, "But I'm not sure you understand. This project is for *emerging* artists."

"But I *am* an emerging artist," I purred. "What artist isn't? Every day, day after day, I actively, enthusiastically emerge. That's what an artist does. Right?"

"What I guess I'm trying to say," she smirked, "is that this project, Art Is For Everyone, is for . . . you know . . . *young* artists. Artists just starting out."

"Then you're talkin' about *me*," I simpered. "Young at heart, young in spirit, constantly emerging. I mean, you should *know* this. After all, you're an artist, too, aren't you?"

"Not really," she snarled, her eyes aggressively rolling. "Listen: If you have other questions, feel free to talk with the manager. She'll be back tomorrow."

I trust you've gotten my drift by now, Dear Readers. Age, an inevitable physical reality, is merely a variation on the theme of that big red letter on Hester Prynne's bodice. But wait. Oh, my God! You mean you thought the A was for Adultery? Sorry to disappoint you. It's actually A for *Ancient*! If that scarlet A has been pinned on you, keep doing what you want to do. Remember that youth is not really a credential; it's a circumstance. Even *Methuselah* did a whole lot of emerging—he had to, or he couldn't have grown so old.

The moral of the story? People are only human, and because of it they'll *always* try to label you. They simply can't help themselves! So my advice to you is to be always *on guard*. Don't allow others to slap a negative label on you *under* any circumstance, for any reason. Wear who you are, what you have, and what you look like with *pride*, not shame.

Being arbitrarily labeled "old"—and especially as "*too* old"—is bad enough. But being just as arbitrarily labeled "jack of all trades and master of none" is even more odious. The world is roughly divided between specialists (who often have and indeed *should* have credentials) and generalists (who may have no formal credentials at all). Both kinds of people have critically important roles to play and invaluable services to provide in the greater scheme of things. If you're a specialist, *be proud*. If, on the other hand, you're a born generalist—like me—be every bit as proud of your gifts and the accomplishments that are bound to come from them.

WINNING AT ANY COST:

America's Obsession with Sports

"My ruthless desire to win at all costs served
me well on the bike, but the level it went to,
for whatever reason, is a flaw. That desire, that
attitude, that arrogance."[50]
—Lance Armstrong

"Successful competitors want to win. Head cases
want to win at all costs."[51]
—Nancy Lopez

"Winning isn't everything, but in my book it's a
close second to breathing."[52]
—George Steinbrenner

Why is it that more men than women seem to be obsessed
with sports? Psychologist **Robert Deaner** of Grand Valley State

---

50. Lance Armstrong, "Transcript: Lance Armstrong admits to doping and
bullying," BikeBiz, January 18, 2013, https://bikebiz.com/transcript-lance-
armstrong-admits-to-doping-and-bullying/.

51. Nancy Lopez and Don Wade, *Nancy Lopez's The Complete Golfer*, Contemporary
Books, 1989, page 169.

52. Bob Barnet, "Yankee Pride, and American Pride," *The Star Press* (Muncie,
Indiana), Sunday, May 11, 1980, 10.

University in Allendale, Michigan, sought to answer that question in a scholarly article titled "Sex Differences in Sports Interest and Motivation: An Evolutionary Perspective."[53] As you might have guessed from that title, Deaner and his co-authors come down on the side of evolution.

That dense scholarly review, which boasts no fewer than 182 references, taught me a new word: *lek*. A lek is the space where males of a species—birds, for example—gather to display their plumage and/or skills so that females can select mates and other males can assess their competition. The parallels to human sporting events are evident. It's worth noting that lek behavior is sometimes called "arena behavior." (And by the way, arena behavior sounds an awful lot like courtship behavior to me.)

Thank you, Professor! Since I have very little to do anymore with sports as either a participant or a spectator, I needed someone like you to give me a little clear-eyed perspective—a dose of scholarly *heft* in the matter of why it is that so many male sports enthusiasts, clearly obsessed with *winning*, appear to approach *politics* with pretty much the very same below-the-belt, win-at-all-costs urgency. Violate their own personal ethics? No problem! Lose their once-unimpeachable integrity? Big deal! Degrade, humiliate, and endanger the lives of others on the way to political victory? The price of competition! Nobody loves a loser!

I don't really know if I should, but when I see men well into their sixties walking around in sports jerseys bearing the names and numbers of their favorite players, I feel sad for them. I feel *sorry* for them. *Why don't they just go outside and play catch with their grandchildren?* I wonder. *Don't they have a hobby? Couldn't they just play a sport because it would help them take the "droop" out of their waistlines?*

---

53. Grand Valley State University Department of Psychology, "Robert Deaner," Grand Valley State University, July 14, 2023, https://www.gvsu.edu/psychology/deaner-robert-16.htm.

And then I can't help thinking that these balding, potbellied, long-ago competitors still want desperately to *win*. Perhaps they harbor a deep-seated resentment for having failed to go farther than they did as athletes while they were younger and up to the challenge. And now, well past their prime, they realize the thrill of winning—especially in a blaze of glory—is pretty much over for them.

Of course, all of these old farts—the ones with someone else's number on their backs (and fronts and shoulders and car bumpers and mailboxes)—were once as young as *we* were and even *younger*. But, as much as I want to, I'm going to resist going on and on about what today's "adults" are doing in the bleachers as they scream their kids on to questionable victory while simultaneously condemning and belittling the losers, the referees and umps, and each other.

Oh, well. Back now to the allegedly "mature" set: the still vigorous *grownups*. What better placebo can there be than *politics* as a substitute for raw, on-field competition? A remarkably high number of modern-day politicians—especially men—have had long, illustrious careers in sports, and they often use their fame as athletes to earn votes and get elected to everything from dogcatcher to state rep. (Sorry about the redundancy; I mean, it's all the same when competition is king.)

It makes a person wonder what some of the more prominent "tough guy" politicians say in public, whether they're athletes or not, about their win-at-all-costs mentality. Fasten your seatbelts, idealists! If you're eating, these comments may spoil your supper. If you're on the toilet, you won't even need to push to do your business.

Once-again, wanna-be jock **President Donald Trump** on what he considered the "problem" with his nephew Fred's developmentally disabled son, William: "Those people . . . the shape they're in, all the expenses, maybe those kinds of people should just die."[54] (Anything to save a buck, Donald.)

For the record, Trump was a three-sport athlete while at New York Military Academy. That was all about *sportsmanship*, wasn't it? But my guess is that whether young Carrot Top was on or off the field, he played dirty and lost infantly *then*, too. (That word, *infantly*, is obsolete according to Wiktionary,[55] but it works for me, so it stays.)

Peter Navarro said regarding winning at all costs: "It's that evil twin part of me that always comes out at the absolute wrong political moment, like a demon possessing my soul; it exhibits itself as an arrogance or disdain or obnoxiousness or meanness or anger or pettiness—all of them traits that are lethal in politics."[56]

And the result of his conduct? Navarro, a former White House aide during President Trump's first term, went to federal prison in March 2024 for refusing to answer a subpoena from the House Select Committee that investigated the January 6, 2021, attack on the US Capitol. He thus became the first White House official to be imprisoned for contempt of Congress.[57]

Politician Navarro stated in his 1999 autobiography, "I don't have any concern at all about making stuff up about my opponent that isn't exactly true," prompting *Los Angeles Times* columnist Mark Z. Barabak to refer to Navarro as self-avowedly "ruthless,

54. Fred C. Trump, "My Uncle Donald Trump Told Me Disabled Americans Like My Son 'Should Just Die,' " Time.com, July 24, 2024, https://time.com/7002003/donald-trump-disabled-americans-all-in-the-family/.

55. "Infantly," Wiktionary, retrieved May 21, 2025 from https://en.wiktionary.org/wiki/infantly.

56. Peter Navarro, "Al Gore's Love Handles and Other Tales From the Political Crypt," San Diego Reader, May 7, 1998, https://www.sandiegoreader.com/news/1998/may/07/cover-al-gores-love-handles-and-other-tales-from/.

57. Tierney Sneed and Katelyn Polantz, "Ex-Trump aide Peter Navarro begins serving prison sentence after historic contempt prosecution," CNN Politics, March 19, 2024, https://www.cnn.com/2024/03/19/politics/peter-navarro-jail-contempt-of-congress.

unscrupulous and a liar."[58] And of course Navarro's political woes seem to confirm the validity of those assertions. Although I tried and failed to find evidence that he played sports in either high school or college—maybe he did, maybe he didn't—I should think the lack of scruples he professed in politics would have made him a lethal contender in football, kickboxing, or mixed martial arts. Or at least a wildly enthusiastic spectator at cockfights. Do they have jerseys for *that* sport? He could have worn his to political rallies (but not to the prison mess hall).

Stephen Miller—President Trump's official deputy chief of staff for policy and unofficial deporter-in-chief—once told an interviewer, "I like to think of myself as a genuinely good person."[59]

An example of his "goodness"? Miller reportedly said: "I would be happy if not a single refugee foot ever again touched American soil."[60]

And another, remembered by a high-school classmate: "Students shouldn't pick up their own trash; that's why we have janitors."[61]

And still another, if you think you can stomach it: "Everything that is wrong with this country today, the people who are opposed to Donald Trump are responsible for!"[62]

Nice guy! Heart of gold! Another minor-league, tin-horn dictator-in-embryo! And who'll be next on my list? Here's my pick:

58. Mark Z. Barabak, "The weird saga of Peter Navarro, from California environmentalist to Trump henchman," *Los Angeles Times*, June 16, 2022, https://www.latimes.com/politics/story/2022-06-16/peter-navarro-trump-henchman-jan-6-committee-hearings.

59. Julia Ioffe, "The Believer: How Stephen Miller went from obscure Capitol Hill staffer to Donald Trump's warm-up act—and resident ideologue.", Politico, June 27, 2016, https://www.politico.com/magazine/story/2016/06/stephen-miller-donald-trump-2016-policy-adviser-jeff-sessions-213992/.

60. AP News staff, "Book says Trump adviser spoke dismissively about refugees," Associated Press, January 28, 2019, https://apnews.com/article/698d532f5f424dd3a807340af2259cd8.

61. Laurie Winer, "Trump Advisor Stephen Miller Has Always Been This Way," Los Angeles Magazine, October 30, 2018, https://archive.ph/phq6n.

62. See note 58.

Steve Bannon, an extreme right-wing blowhard who's proud to have said: "Darkness is good. Dick Cheney. Darth Vader. Satan. That's power."[63] He called for the firing of Christopher Wray and Anthony Fauci, adding that he wanted to "go a step farther" and "put the heads on pikes [. . .] as a warning to federal bureaucrats."[64] And, during his time as executive chairman of Breitbart.com, the site featured headlines including "Would You Rather Your Child Had Feminism or Cancer?," "Birth Control Makes Women Unattractive and Crazy," and "There's No Hiring Bias Against Women in Tech, They Just Suck at Interviews."[65]

The word *disgusting* doesn't even begin to express my disdain for this quartet of twisted white-collar demagogues.

For men like Trump, Navarro, Miller, and Bannon, politics is a *blood sport*, and winning at all costs is all that really matters. They speak with their testicles! Good and decent human beings don't adopt methods and attitudes like theirs. Bullies, racists, and misogynists—men deeply insecure about their masculinity—do.

And the result of Bannon's win-at-all-costs thinking? On February 10, 2025, he pleaded guilty to felony fraud for helping to defraud donors to an effort to build a wall along the US–Mexico border.[66] He avoided prison time in that plea deal, but his tarnished reputation will surely cut into his future earnings.

63. Michael Wolff, "Ringside With Steve Bannon at Trump Tower at Trump Tower as the President-Elect's Strategist Plots 'An Entirely New Political Movement' (Exclusive)", The Hollywood Reporter, November 18, 2016, https://www.hollywood reporter.com/news/general-news/steve-bannon-trump-tower-interview-trumps-strategist-plots-new-political-movement-948747/.

64. Madison Dapcevich, "Did Bannon Say He'd Put Fauci's and FBI Director Wray's 'Heads on Pikes'?", Snopes.com, November 6, 2020, https://www.snopes.com/fact-check/bannon-fauci-wray-head-pikes/.

65. Lucy Clarke-Billings, "Donald Trump's Right-Hand Man Steve Bannon and His History of Attacks Against Women," Newsweek, November 15, 2016, https://www.newsweek.com/donald-trumps-chief-strategist-steve-bannon-and-his-history-attacks-against-521240.

66. Hurubie Meko and Jonah E. Bromwich, "Bannon Pleads Guilty to Fraud in Border Wall Case but Will Serve No Time," The New York Times, February 11, 2025, https://www.nytimes.com/2025/02/11/nyregion/steve-bannon-guilty-plea.html.

Now, call me intellectually naive or mentally deficient, but there *just might be* a pinch or two of rampantly hubristic, testosterone-fueled misogyny in comments like those of these men. Which, of course, should surprise no one who's in touch with reality.

But back now to "arena behavior." When a typical twenty-first-century NFL player makes it into the end zone, then does a backflip, makes lewd gestures, or, in the case of Randy Moss, proudly pretends to *moon* the crowd, how does that make you feel?

Of course, I can't possibly know how Moss's gesture would have made you feel. However, having turned on my TV during a few NFL games, I can objectively report back to you how fans *in general* nearly always react to such infantile, made-for-TV hijinks. Can you say "wildly histrionic bleacher madness"? Or perhaps "textbook frat-house fanaticism"?

But things can turn a whole lot more sinister, can't they. In September 2023, a fight broke out in the stands at a game between the New England Patriots and the Miami Dolphins, resulting in the death of fifty-three-year-old Dale Mooney, a New Hampshire resident and a New England Patriots supporter.[67] In October 2023, two female fans at a Raiders vs. Chargers game got into a fistfight, and at the same game, a Raiders fan was punched and thrown down the stairs by a Chargers supporter.[68]

But that doesn't appear to have changed the average NFL fan's mind about the entertainment value of gratuitous violence, whether on or off the field. Indeed, such violence may very well be one of the things fans like *most* about professional football. If it sells tickets, then why bother working to bring it to a halt?

---

67. WBZ-News Staff, "Gillette Stadium officials 'heartbroken' by death of Patriots fan Dale Mooney," September 19, 2023, https://www.cbsnews.com/boston/news/new-england-patriots-fan-death-dale-mooney-gillette-stadium/.

68. TMZ, "Raiders Vs. Chargers: Violent Fistfight At Game . . . Women Tee Off!", TMZ.com, October 3, 2023, https://www.tmz.com/2023/10/03/two-women-get-in-violent-fistfight-in-stands-at-raiders-game/.

A 2025 poll by Sportsbook Review found that nearly 40 percent of NFL fans have witnessed criminality at or around an NFL stadium, and 7.2 percent have themselves been victims of such crime. But nowhere have more fans (63 percent) witnessed crimes than those at Lincoln Financial Field, the home of the Philadelphia Eagles. The most common crime witnessed? Physical violence.

Kinda leaves a blemish on the idea of football as a noble, character-building endeavor, doesn't it.

At the start of this essay I quoted George Steinbrenner, who was fond of saying that winning isn't everything; it's second to breathing. Many of today's man-boy players—in multiple sports—who revel in grandstanding, feuding, fouling, and other obnoxious behavior on and off the field seem to be of the same mind. We live in a 24/7 "look-at-me" era. Disgraceful antics get attention, and so they continue.

Seriously now! Whatever has happened to *humility*—that onetime common, high-character penchant for winning without shameless grandstanding? When I see players doing these things, I don't see a group of serious competitors; I see a playpen full of adult-size toddlers with looks of brazen self-promotion smeared across their faces. And then I wonder where their *coaches*—those over-compensated exemplars of professionalism—have gone.

Winning may be everything for some, but to me it will always be no more and no less than the fortunate result of a sincere effort to succeed, fairly, skillfully, and humbly, in any given endeavor. And that includes America's particular obsession, football.

* * *

Poor sportsmanship has spilled over, with ever-greater intensity, into the political arena. Every day in America, a disturbing number of politicians—both male and female—are showing us, through their harsh rhetoric, their intellectual inadequacy, and their mean-spirited actions, that they're high on power and low on the very quality that was once so prevalent and so admired in our nation's public servants: plain, old-fashioned, unassailable integrity.

Only one critically important question remains for me, at least in *this* forum: is the hyper-aggressive, narcissistic behavior of athletes and politicians uniquely blue-collar in its origins and influences?

I don't really think so! But until we have a working definition of *blue-collar*, we can't really speculate about its origins with any credibility. So here, for what they're worth, are my very own highly speculative ideas about the true meaning of the blue-collar label.

Americans by and large seem to agree that blue-collar laborers are people who work with their hands on essential, nuts-and-bolts projects—everything from roofing, road maintenance, and landscaping to construction, transportation, and trash removal.

We also seem to agree that white-collar laborers—yes, *laborers!*—work more with their minds than their hands. At a moment like this, one is tempted to consider the brain every bit as much a muscle as any of the more than six hundred muscles in the human body. For some, that particular muscle is well maintained; for others it's the forgotten stepchild, prematurely withered and knocking on Death's door.

The biggest problem with trying to divide America's workforce into two distinct camps, blue-collar and white-collar, is that today, more than ever before, blue-collar jobs require a great deal of technical expertise—essential skills in mathematics, computer literacy, and problem-solving.

From here we need to go *back*, now, to the issue of whether aggressive, male-dominated behavior in both sports and politics is decidedly blue-collar in its origins.

I may very well be about to muddy the waters all over again, but integrity requires that I confess my own longstanding inability to tell what counts as blue-collar or white-collar. The topic engenders a flash flood of speculations in this, my always overworked, hyper-analytical mind:

Are teachers white-color or blue-collar? And within that wide-ranging profession, are college teachers more white-collar than public school teachers? Is a nurse more blue-collar than a doctor? And is a computer salesperson more white-collar than a computer repair technician? Is an artist blue-collar but a writer white-collar? A composer white-collar but a musician blue-collar? A car designer white-collar but an ace mechanic blue-collar?

There'll never be clear-cut answers to these questions, simply because the very idea of what constitutes a blue-collar or white-collar profession—and a white-collar or blue-collar mentality—is profoundly up for grabs and always *will* be.

All these speculations of mine lead to an even more all-encompassing question: Why do these labels exist *at all*, and have we as a society ever really *needed* them?

Question: Do blue-collar workers yearn to escape into the white-collar universe? And conversely, are there white-collar figures who want desperately to get off their treadmills and become strictly, purely blue-collar in their orientation?

Answer: Yes and yes! People in blue-collar occupations can feel the way they're sometimes perceived—as people who've settled for less in matters of status, compensation, and upward mobility—and some of them see white-collar occupations as their ticket out. And yet, ironically, many people in white-collar jobs get fed up with office politics or being stuck behind a desk and turn instead to a simpler, more serene, more nuts-and-bolts way of making a living—one that lets them work with their hands instead of jobbing out physical labor to the blue-collars.

Status-seeking—a white-collar obsession—can be both physically exhausting and emotionally stressful. Some undeniably intelligent people would rather be tucked into the cab of a state-of-the-art long-haul sixteen-wheeler than trapped in the suffocating confines of a Wall Street cubicle. And how we choose to make a living is not always just a matter of personal taste, either; it can also be a matter of our physical and emotional health and how we can best preserve the two.

Aggressive, narcissistic behavior—acting out in the workplace—happens in every profession from NFL coaching to library science. Whether that sort of behavior is more blue-collar than white—or more white-collar than blue—will always be an unsolvable mystery. In short, to think that blue-collar workers and white-collar workers have nothing in common amounts to a clear and consequential misunderstanding of the nature of work itself. Physical or mental? Strenuous or contemplative? Good taste, good manners, and good judgment do not belong exclusively to *either* camp. And it just may be that burning calories through a harmonious, productive combination of mind-work *and* hand-work is the best approach of all.

LOWBROW, HIGHBROW, NOTHING-BROW:
Aren't We All Really Status Seekers?

"To understand bad taste one must have very good taste. Good bad taste can be creatively nauseating but must, at the same time, appeal to the especially twisted sense of humor, which is anything but universal."[69]
—John Waters

It's ever so tempting to think *blue-collar* when reflecting on things we view as "lowbrow." And of course, people are just as tempted to think *white-collar* when posing the question, "What, exactly, is highbrow?"

But things like this are never cut and dry. Take country music, for example. There's "modern country," and then there's "classic country." Is one really more lowbrow or highbrow than the other? More white-collar than blue-collar? Can anyone convince me that one is superior to the other?

And to muddy the waters of classification—of labeling—even more, people within the classical music crowd tend to think of *all* country music as inherently inferior to everything from symphonies, tone poems, and string quartets to cantatas, oratorios, and grand opera.

---

69. John Waters, *Shock Value: A Tasteful Book About Bad Taste*, Thunder's Mouth Press, 1981, 2.

My God! I could go on and on *here*, too! But for now, just a few more teasers to enrich the debate. Is the modern American-born *musical* inferior to the classic European-born *grand opera*? Is the chamber music repertoire superior to the orchestral repertoire? And is there *any* rock music that can possibly compete with classical in the matter of complexity, profundity, and popular appeal?

Well, yes, there *is*. You can mark my words about that. Look at orchestral-composer-turned-rock-guitarist **Frank Zappa**! Or orchestral-cellist-turned-heavy-metal-cellist **Tina Gao**! But those are stories for another day.

Inwardly at least, I'm laughing uncontrollably as I run down the list of "rankings" within the world of the fine and performing arts. Are short stories inferior to full-blown novels? (There's always the novelette for those who just can't quite make up their minds.) Is poetry superior to prose fiction?

And let's not forget the epic multimedia distinction between *soft* porn and *hardcore* porn! From the menu of sexual indulgences, do you lean toward the polite and easygoing missionary meal—or a down-and-dirty, all-positions-possible, multi-orifice entree?

Here's what I personally think—and what most people *know*— is going on in the worldwide highbrow-vs.-lowbrow competition. One might call it *mix-'n'-match*, or maybe *anything goes*. You can be crazy about **Philip Glass**'s monumental, cutting-edge opera, *Akhnaten*—so crazy that you and your honey watch it on video while sprawled out together on your heart-shaped, disco-balled revolving bed, engaging in "reverse Asian cowboy" or maybe "bent supine rimjob."

I've no idea what they're talking about here—trust me!—but I say *each to their own*, whether in darkness or, within the bounds of good taste, light. But of course, taste is a highly subjective matter. For some of us—no, not me!—the badder the taste, the better the experience. **John Waters**, creator of the astoundingly raunchy *Pink Flamingos*, knows.

You can be wild about art-house-influenced films like *Eternal Sunshine of the Spotless Mind* while simultaneously getting off on "lowbrow" rock groups like Motörhead.

Have an appetite for exquisitely sensitive poems like **Mary Oliver**'s "The Summer Day"? Well, you *go*, girl! But don't forget to leave room for the *smutty* stuff—like Jiffy Kate's beefcake romp *Stud Muffin*, or hot-'n'-steamy bodice-rippers like Johanna Lindsey's *Prisoner of My Desire* and Rosemary Rogers's *Sweet Savage Love*. Now *there's* a little *Night Music* that would be the perfect match for a book titled *The Secret Life of a Lady Lecher*. But as far as I know, a book with that title doesn't exist—*yet*.

All that mix-'n'-match stuff is nice. And within commonsense limits, I suppose it's perfectly respectable. *Do What You Will*, wrote **Aldous Huxley**, who by any reckoning was anything but blue-collar.

But now it's time for us to explore the idea of "lowbrow" as a distinctly all-American media phenomenon.

Perhaps the best way to sample lowbrow culture here in the USA is to settle into your Barcalounger, fire up your "smart" TV, and experience today's "entertainment." But first, it's important to understand that most of the time, what purports to be *highbrow* culture on television is actually *lowbrow culture* masquerading as highbrow.

On TV, clothing is flamboyantly designed and outrageously expensive; complexions are dishonestly wrinkle-free and yet coated with more goo than a mud hut; teeth are whiter than the whitest imaginable snow; lashes look like miniature lawn rakes; fingernails would make nice post-hole diggers; and makeup is applied to "surgically improved" facial terrain with all the blue-collar grace of a garden trowel.

Am I making my point? *Nothing* on television is really what it so determinedly, calculatingly *pretends* to be. One is tempted to label this kind of mindless cultural legerdemain as *Mar-a-Lago Gone Wild*. Subterfuges like this have become the order of the day in real life, with the result that any woman who dares to go without the required head-to-toe beauty aids is branded as somehow *less than feminine*. In the antediluvian mind of the average TV producer, nothing *natural* qualifies as *beautiful*.

Side by side with these faux philosophical concoctions is the attitude that to be beautiful is to be *highbrow*, while to be less than beautiful—what people used to call "homely"—means that in the mind of the average citizen, you're more than likely going to be relegated to the *lowbrow* universe.

How unproductive—how patently ridiculous—how deeply insulting all of this labeling is!

And by the way, whatever has happened to humane, values-based *intelligence* and priceless *wisdom*—the only true and indisputable measures of beauty worth having?

Don't give up, idealists! Those qualities are still around, but in this country's current political climate, they appear to be less admired and less sought-after than raw power, craven one-up-manship, and a pathological need to do whatever is necessary, no matter how unethical and immoral it might be, to *win*. But what a shameful, profoundly Pyrrhic victory that turns out to be! And what self-respecting athlete, politician, or run-of-the-mill human being is okay with a victory that hollow—that appallingly bereft of fundamental decency?

In my value system, hard-won, honestly-acquired *decency* is indisputably highbrow, and effortlessly or dishonestly earned *indecency* is about as low—and *lowbrow*—as one can go.

Still, one truth here should be more than merely self-evident: *highbrow* thinking isn't the exclusive property of white-collar people, and *lowbrow* thinking isn't the exclusive property of blue-collar people. Labels like these are—and indeed *should be*—not only virtually interchangeable because of their obvious subjectivity, but entirely irrelevant as measures of human character.

WHAT MEN OWE WOMEN:
A List of IOUs for the Uninformed

*"If there is a God, it has to be a man.
No woman could or would ever fuck
things up like this."[70]
—George Carlin*

This (I'm gonna go *big* on this one, right from the get-go) is what men owe women:

1. The inalienable right to their own biological destiny.

"Overturning Roe," writes an online presence by the name of **Robert Veitch**, "requires another law be passed that ensures men bear equal responsibility for pregnancies."[71]

Now *this* dude is really onto something, isn't he! It ought to be crystal clear that the first and foremost thing men owe women is *their inviolable right to control their own biological destinies* without the interference of any righteous, misogynistic, medically clueless do-gooders who think only *they* know best what a woman needs in any part of her life.

---

70. George Carlin, "Religion & There Is No God | George Carlin | You Are All Diseased (1999)," @OfficialGeorgeCarlin, https://youtu.be/_BFIRgn9OLI, time stamp 3:03.

71. Veitch, Robert, "Equal Responsibility For Pregnancies Act," June 25, 2022, https://www.change.org/p/equal-responsibility-for-pregnancies.

"Call it the 'Personal Responsibility Act,'" Veitch continues. "Using DNA as verification, paternity for every embryo should be established and the male responsible obliged by law to support the woman and the child through the child's majority, including medical costs, living costs, education—all the costs a father normally assumes for his child. In addition, the child should have a full share of this father's estate if and when the father dies.

"If women cannot decide whether or not [to] carry a child, fathers should not be able to decide whether or not to support the woman and the child. It's about time men assumed responsibility for the consequences of their pleasure."

Remember, those were *Veitch's* words, not mine. But I see no reason—*no reason at all*—to complain about them. In fact, I kind o' *like* them! We might even call 'em "Veitch's Virtues"! As I see it, they make the perfect launch pad for another *Ross's Rant*—my blog post title of choice when I need to drive home commonsense points about fair play and equal opportunity in the never-ending battle for marital equality.

I'm calling that first IOU—a woman's inalienable right to her very own biological destiny—***Mind Your Own Damn Business!*** A very special thanks to Governor Tim Walz of Minnesota for *that* one. What a breath of fresh air *he* has been, for years and years, when it comes to women's rights!

2. Sharing, rather than division, of labor in and outside the home.

For thousands of years, in cultures from within nearly every nook and cranny of the known universe, men have enjoyed the privilege—indeed, the obscene *luxury*—of constant encouragement in the matter of their intellectual and professional aspirations, however shallow and ill-conceived they might be. They're painted, irrationally, as natural-born accomplishers—men whose *sexual equipment alone*—their down-south family jewels—automatically grants their rights and aspirations an almost *sacred* precedence over those of women.

What justification can there possibly be for assigning matters of intellectual growth to *one* spouse and household labor to the *other*?

Where, in the Bible, in your marital contract, or on the door of your refrigerator does it say that cleaning pots and pans, knives and forks, sinks and toilets is the exclusive province of females? How nurturing are those chores compared to the intellectual growth one gets from a well-produced film, a compelling work of art, a damn good book, or the caring support of a devoted partner? And in what way do any domestic chores you can think of put you on the path to cognitive Nirvana?

Yes, home maintenance is work. And necessary work of any kind must finally be done. But *the nurturing of the intellect* is work, too. And one moment of loving nurturance is worth a dozen sinks full of dirty dishes.

Sadly, once the marital knot has been tied, countless men conveniently forget their prenuptial promise to share everything in the relationship equally, then dive headlong into their self-serving careers and leave the dishes and diapers to their spouses, treating them as if they're the Less-Than-Significant Other. And as all too many marital partners discover, far too late to do anything about it, these deeply ingrained presumptions are notoriously difficult to remove from the marital contract. The only good news I can think of here is *viva the availability of divorce.* Why? Because common sense should tell us that it's often the best of all possible outcomes in a deeply troubled marriage.

It ought not to be necessary to remind people that the mind of a woman is no less hungry for intellectual nourishment than the mind of a man. So it should stand to reason that at the very top of the list of things a man can do to prove he truly loves his life-mate should be to *nurture, nurture, nurture* her—to take her thoughts and yearnings as seriously as if they were his very own. The same goes for same-sex partnerships, of course.

Lofty thoughts and lowly duties: one is not innately superior to the other! And in a balanced, well-rounded relationship, both parties take good care of *all* of the other's needs, not just a select few.

The idea of two people *equally sharing* matters of mind and body in a relationship is perhaps no better illustrated than in the issue of childrearing. Can it make any sense at all to assign the intellectual development of a child to one parent but the bodily maintenance chores—food, clothing, and shelter—to the other?

We've all had to watch this irrational, self-serving division of labor play itself out in male-dominated families, whether as casual observers or reluctant participants. In masculocentric families like this, young George is actively groomed for the role of Sole Breadwinner, while his kid sister, Georgina, gets the short end of the stick as the In-House Specialist in Childcare. All too often, she ends up mothering not just her children but her husband as well.

And guess what! In an out-of-balance family dynamic like that, it is nearly always the mother who suffers the greatest losses: the loss of time to think independently; the loss of active support in matters of the intellect; and a festering, ever-growing inability to realize her fondest dreams.

I've no doubt some of you reading this will think that, for me at least, division of labor is a dogwhistle for blue-collar values. And you wouldn't be entirely off the mark, either. In the classic blue-collar household where I grew up, Daddy went to work every day (though I really had no idea where the work *was* and what he actually *did* there), while Mommy—entirely housebound and unable (by choice, to be honest) to drive—cooked the meals, mopped the floors, scrubbed the toilets, and washed and hung the laundry. And me? I spent my summers watching her make the house acceptable for her husband while simultaneously wondering what she meant when, with alarming frequency, she would shout, "Wait 'til your *father* comes home!"

Now, this is probably an ideal time for me to assure you that I also have no doubt that the classic division of labor exists in many white-collar families, too. And I believe that, perhaps especially in dual-career marriages, there can be a sincere, rock-solid commitment to as much *role sharing* as possible, both within and beyond the home. But as I look back on my childhood, the gender-based division of labor we lived under will always be strictly blue-collar to me.

3. A healthier, more constructive attitude toward masculinity.

Now it's time for me to ask men everywhere—and women, too—to rethink what it means for someone to be "masculine."

First, the definition. According to Oxford Languages, *masculine* means "having qualities or an appearance traditionally associated with men or boys."[72]

Works fine for me, but only up to a point. I can live with it for now. But I especially enjoyed their list of synonyms, which begins: *virile, macho, manly, all-male, red-blooded, laddish, muscular,* and *muscly.* What a parade of labels!

But on second thought, what is this, a *test?* Okay, it's a test. So I think I'll take it! And if I pass, will it mean I'm certifiably masculine—that I'm truly a "manly man"? One can always hope. So here I go:

a. Am I *virile?* Well, I suppose I was at one time. Otherwise, why do I have a daughter whose very existence was at least partially my doing?
b. Am I *macho?* No way!
c. *Manly?* Hope so!
d. *All-male?* The last time I checked!
e. *Red-blooded?* Hey: it ain't green, and it ain't yellow.
f. *Laddish?* That's just a little too British for me, thank you.
g. *Muscular?* From the neck up, very!

---

72. "Masculine," Oxford Languages, retrieved May 20, 2025 from https://www.google.com/search?q=masculine.

h. And finally, am I *muscly*? Not Popeye muscly, but muscly enough to haul a bag of cement or push a stalled Mini Cooper.

Well, now. Here's what I think: in some respects I passed with flying colors, while in other respects, it's safe to say I failed abysmally. But whether I passed or failed, I learned a valuable lesson as a result of taking this little testicular exam: that for me personally, the idea of masculinity has much more to do with *attitude*—a particular, always-evolving protection-and-nurturance frame of mind—than anything about my physical appearance.

So if physical appearance alone doesn't determine masculinity, what qualities *do*? I've identified four non-physical determinants for you:

Integrity! Integrity is not the exclusive property of women. Hardly! But given the appallingly high number of men who think women shouldn't have control over their own bodies, it's been more than tempting for some of them to think so! A man who thinks he knows more about a woman's needs than she does is to me in no way a "man of integrity"—or in fact a man at *all*. So to me, the more integrity of *every* kind a man has, the more inherently, joyfully masculine he is.

Humility! Any man who thinks he's "head of the house"—intellectually superior to women and naturally "in control"—is not only Biblically brainwashed, he's a pathological narcissist and a rabid, red-meat misogynist. "Toughness" may come in handy when defending someone in danger, but when it's employed in the service of dominance, it's just *bullying*, pure and simple.

Gentleness! Cambridge Dictionary defines it as "the quality of being calm, kind, or soft," or "the quality of not being violent, severe, or strong."[73] Their sample sentences include "He was a man of kindness and extreme gentleness" and "He was overwhelmed by the gentleness of the air and the scent of flowers."

I actually burst out laughing while reading those sentences. Why? Because the qualities alluded to are the very *last* qualities Republicans Donald Trump and J.D. Vance—who are now the president and vice president of the United States—would want attached to their profiles, and yet I can imagine the abject terror "tough guys" like them would experience upon being called *gentle*. At the same time, the aforementioned qualities seem like ones Democrats Kamala Harris and Tim Walz—who together lost the 2024 presidential election—would be more than happy to embrace.

True masculinity has plenty of room for gentleness, even when the gentleman in question also happens to be blessed with impressive physical strength, bulging biceps, and washboard abs. A fellow like that might very well be more than capable of violence, but *only* if it were absolutely necessary while confronting an aggressor.

Coach Walz—a born sportsman and an authentic blue-collar Midwesterner with a heart of gold and a genuine affection for children—would understand this. But Donald Trump, a phony-baloney blue-collar pretender with prepaid Ivy League degrees, would emphatically not. In his rhetoric, he glorifies and even advocates violence while scoffing at weakness. If he were still a child, I could forgive him for having acquired these views, as by all accounts they were drummed into him early on by his father. But a grown man—which, appearances to the contrary, Trump undeniably is—bears the responsibility for his

---

73. "Gentleness," Cambridge Dictionary, retrieved May 20, 2025 from https://dictionary.cambridge.org/dictionary/english/gentleness.

own ideas, and Trump's ideas about strength and weakness repulse me.

Sensitivity! Remember Roosevelt "Rosey" Grier, the former NFL tackle who loved knitting? In the 1970s, he published a book called *Needlepoint for Men*. Not only could Grier flatten an opponent with one lightning-fast rush of his 6' 9", 284-pound frame, he could knit a pair of socks or decorate a couch pillow worth dying for. Now *there's* sensitivity!

In addition to his pro football career, Grier has been an actor, a singer, and a Protestant minister. He cofounded American Neighborhood Enterprises, an organization that works to help disadvantaged city dwellers buy homes and receive vocational training. As of this writing, he is 92 and still traveling the nation, spreading his Good Seed masculinity to the masses.

In my book, a man can rightfully claim to be fully "masculine" only if he has *at least* as much integrity, humility, and sensitivity as he does bulk, muscularity, and testosterone. And just as importantly, he must *never, ever* strike a woman, unless perhaps in the unlikely event that she has a build like an NFL tackle and is in the process of attacking either his wife, his children, a bystander, or his own sorry self.

Do I really have to mention this? Spousal abuse by men, whether physical or emotional, is not a "masculine" trait. It's the entirely uncalled-for behavior of a self-righteous, hubristic bully, and no truly masculine male would ever need to engage in such behavior.

ESSAY

FLAG MANIA:

Overdoing the Red, White, and Blue

"Jingoism is an avoidance of realism. You can simultaneously love and be disappointed in the object of your love, wanting it to be better than it is. In fact, that is a measure of love. Honest critique is a pillar of patriotism."[74]
—Charles M. Blow

Not long ago, while driving down to Boston on I-95, trapped in dense early-morning commuter traffic, I found myself behind an old Harley-Davidson with not one but *three* gigantic flags mounted on the back of it, like the tail feathers of a peacock—a trio of Old Glories so big that, had a sudden gust of wind come along, the bike—and its rider, too—might very well have been swept right off the expressway and into the nearest river. The flags were so big, and the support poles so tall, they dwarfed the cycle, making it look more like a child's wind-up toy than a bona fide hog.

But on the rear end of a chopper is only one place among hundreds where people love to display Betsy's Beloved, whether small or large; freshly minted or torn and tattered; right side up or upside down; or shamelessly, contentiously altered to address

---

74. Charles M. Blow, "Who Loves America?", *The New York Times*, February 23, 2015, https://www.nytimes.com/2015/02/23/opinion/charles-blow-who-loves-america.html.

a particular self-serving passion. Here are just a few of the many displays I've seen:

From the top of a crane. At the apex of a water tower. On people's mailboxes. From tree limbs and lampposts. On the tailgate of a pickup, the bumper of a car, the rear end of a John Deere tractor. On motorcycle helmets. On wacky, ridiculously oversized hats. In front yards. On paper plates and napkins, tombstones and coffins. On condoms—male *and* female! (Not really; just making sure you're paying attention.) Along city streets and country roads. In parades, on lapels, and at military ceremonies. On toilet paper and shower curtains. On the sides of barns, the lids of toilets, and the T-shirts and board shorts of petulant xenophobes in rally crowds.

I could go on and on. Couldn't you?

For me at least, the lingering mystery—the great unanswered question—is *why*? (Side note: *The Unanswered Question* is the title of a composition by Charles Ives. Now *there* was a true blue American patriot, disguised as a composer!)

As I was saying: Why are US flags seemingly everywhere and on everything? Why the need for this never-ending visual fidelity to the Red, White and Blue?

One powerful force at work in this phenomenon is, I feel certain, the very human propensity for lock-step, no-questions-asked *conformity*. Have you ever noticed that while some neighborhoods in your region of the country are overflowing with flags more plentiful than dandelions and crabgrass, others are nearly entirely, inexplicably flag-free?

One reason for the difference could be that flags and other aggressively marketed patriotic accoutrements cost *money*. So when it comes to love of country, the more affluent is the community, the more elaborate and pretentious are the displays.

To observe that difference, visit Berwick, Maine (where I proudly live), then head northwest into New Hampshire and spend some time in and near the town of Wolfeboro, less than an hour away. Yes, Berwick—an unpretentious, decidedly blue-collar town—exhibits flag mania here and there. Sure! But Wolfeboro, a decidedly white-collar community, is oozing with old money—the result of at least four centuries of White male privilege—and around patriotic holidays, its streets overflow with ostentatious displays of patriotic fervor.

Interesting, I suppose. Big flags, little flags, or *no* flags, life in both towns marches on. But I still have questions:

1. What happens if you live in a flag-happy community but have no flags anywhere on your property?

You can bet that when your lawn is the only lawn on your street that's not swarming with *Look-at-Me, I Love America!* paraphernalia, you've automatically become a prime suspect—a neighbor whose patriotism is either entirely nonexistent or disturbingly insufficient. You could be among the nicest people in your community, but people secretly fear that you may be harboring either decidedly left-wing or—God help you—*socialist* sympathies. It may very well explain why, when neighbors are gathered together at the annual block party, even the most lightweight political discourse is more rare than clog dancers in a funeral parlor.

2. Are Republicans more flag-happy than Democrats?

I think 'Pubs are more demonstratively noisy about their patriotism than Dems. The best way I know of to validate my contention is to watch—or better yet, *attend*—both a Democratic convention and a Republican convention.

In general, Dems are remarkably restrained about their political costumery. But the Republicans? Anything but! And anything goes! At the RNC convention in Milwaukee in 2024, brick-patterned "Build the Wall" suits for men and ersatz van Gogh–like ear bandages commemorating Donald Trump's near-death encounter were all the rage. Is it possible to be too, too silly about something? By and large, Republicans seem to think it most certainly *isn't*.

The finest expression of heartfelt political conviction I've ever seen happened to me in the UK in 1997, when I traveled from London to Inverness to tour a series of small-venue play companies. I'd been invited to stay with Mickey and Barbara Wilson, two passionate theatre producers, at their modest home in Eastbourne, south of London.

After landing at Heathrow Airport, I'd taken a train to Eastbourne Station, where I was to meet Barbara. "I'll be in the main concourse," she said, "and I'll be sure to keep an eye out for you!"

Eastbourne Station was a sprawling, architecturally sophisticated transportation hub with one main corridor, several tributaries, and all the amenities a traveler could need. I stood entirely alone in the concourse that night—it was actually almost three in the morning—and looked eagerly around to find my host. Then, at the far end of the corridor, I heard a voice with a distinctly feminine, thoroughly British accent calling me.

"Is that *you*, Ross?" she shouted, then began vigorously waving what at first appeared to be a couch throw or tablecloth. But it turned out to be a large, brand-spanking-new American flag. "It's *me!*" roared Barbara. And then, when we shook hands, she said: "I brought this flag with me as a way to thank you for what you did for us in London during the War!"

Can you imagine a more pure gesture of patriotic warmth than the one she shared with me that morning? I know *I* can't.

The point I'm making here is that while the majority of displays of patriotism are heartfelt, well-informed, and historically justifiable, others are trite, jingoistic, and embarrassingly self-congratulatory—ultra-materialistic attempts to prove that *my* patriotism is greater than *yours*. Patriotic zealots seem to think they love their country more than their neighbors do. "Where are your flags?" I can almost hear them saying. "What are you—a USA-hating, immigrant-loving twenty-first-century Commie?"

As I see it, the best possible way for us to express genuine patriotism is to pay our taxes, vote, support our public schools, drive safely, be good to our and our neighbors' children, learn from history, be kind to everyone around us, give *and accept* constructive criticism, and finally, *cease* with the endlessly deafening drumbeat of tasteless, chest-thumping, love-it-or-leave-it clown shows purported to be "proof of patriotism." *Enough, already!*

ESSAY  25

GUNS AND VIOLENCE:
America's Two-Pronged Dilemma

"It takes a monster to kill children.
But to watch monsters kill children again
and again and do nothing isn't just insanity—
it's inhumanity."[75]
—Amanda Gorman

"Democracy don't rule the world / You'd better
get that in your head / This world is
ruled by violence / But I guess that's better
left unsaid."[76]
—Bob Dylan

"I keep hearing this [expletive] thing that
guns don't kill people, but people kill people.
If that's the case, why do we give people
guns when they go to war? Why not just
send the people?"
—Ozzy Osbourne[77]

75. Amanda Gorman, "It takes a monster [. . .]," @TheAmandaGorman, May 24, 2022, https://x.com/TheAmandaGorman/status/1529221064835772416.

76. Bob Dylan, "Union Sundown" (lyrics), Special Rider Music, 1983, https://www.bobdylan.com/songs/union-sundown/.

77. Staff writer(s), *New York Times Magazine*, "Questions For: Ozzy Osbourne," Sunday, June 28, 1998, sec. 6, p. 8.

First, let's talk about guns. Mass killings? You bet! A whole lot of them, one by one, all over the place. Bullets—and the guns that propel them—are more plentiful in gun-happy America than houseflies, flu germs, and irresponsible drivers. Guns have always been deeply imbedded in America's history and popular culture. Today's America is more a rules-free shooting gallery than a peace-loving community.

It's next to impossible to separate talk of guns from talk of violence in America, because statistics in general confirm that this country has more guns per capita than in any other developed country.

Let's begin with gun violence statistics from just *one* deadly year, 2023.

According to the Gun Violence Archive, 43,282 people died from gun-related injuries in the United States in 2023. That averages out to 118 shooting deaths per day. Of those dead, 1,713 were children or adolescents.[78]

Next, let's look at two types of shooting incidents that are becoming real-life, another-day-in-your-neighborhood features of American life: mass shootings and school shootings.

In the US in 2023, according to Wikipedia, there were 596 mass shootings (defined as incidents in which four or more people are injured or killed by gun violence), which killed a total of 774 people and injured 2,436 more.[79]

According to *Education Week*, there were 38 school shooting incidents across the country in 2023, which killed 21 people and injured 42 more.

* * *

---

78. "Past Summary Ledgers," The Gun Violence Archive, March 13, 2025, https://www.gunviolencearchive.org/past-tolls.

79. Various contributors, "List of mass shootings in the United States in 2023," Wikipedia, March 13, 2025, https://en.wikipedia.org/w/index.php?title=List_of_mass_shootings_in_the_United_States_in_2023.

All right, then. *Enough* gun violence statistics. It's time to talk about violence *in general,* and with it, the public's perception of who's committing the crimes.

Is violence in the Land of the Free and the Brave—with or without guns—overwhelmingly perpetrated by blue-collar people, or is it divided equally between the "blues" and the "whites"?

According to a web page at FBI.gov, examples of white-collar crime include IP theft, money laundering, embezzlement, and fraud of every sort, from corporate and financial to insurance, health care, and housing. White-collar crimes "are not violent," the page says, and indeed, you won't find any mention of knives or guns here. Rather, the tools of white-collar crime are usually intangible: false accounting, stolen passwords, inflated or deflated valuations.[80]

Some would argue that blue-collar crimes are nearly always committed against either one or a handful of individuals, while white-collar crimes are often committed against much larger groups of people—sometimes thousands or millions—and that because of that, it's a lot harder to pin down just what the crimes actually *were,* legally speaking, and who was actually, seriously *affected* by them.

And how right they are in their assertions! In the heat of the 2024 presidential race, then-former-president **Donald Trump**—ever the arsenic-tongued racist, among his long, long list of bigotries—ranted over and over again that immigrants, whom he has gleefully

---

80. Federal Bureau of Investigation, "White-Collar Crime," United States Government, retrieved June 6, 2025 from https://www.fbi.gov/investigate/white-collar-crime.

described as "animals,"[81] are murderers, drug dealers, and rapists[82] who are "poisoning the blood of America."[83]

Did you think the Donald was talking about *all kinds of immigrants* or maybe just *blue-collar* immigrants? I mean, what about the *white-collar* immigrants? Trump, and the legions of immigrant bashers who share his values, conveniently avoid mentioning white-collar crime. And why? Because they don't really consider their day-to-day, individual and corporate self-indulgences to be crimes at all. For them, it's just *doin' business*.

Take, for instance, New Jersey Democratic senator **Bob Menendez**, a son of Cuban immigrants, who in the summer of 2024 was convicted of sixteen white-collar crimes including bribery, fraud, acting as a foreign agent, and obstruction of justice.[84] While searching his home, investigators armed with a warrant found more than $480,000 in cash "hidden in clothing, closets, and a safe." Oh, and *gold bars*, too![85] Not exactly the kind of piggy-bank booty one finds in the average dwelling, I should think.

Or Georgia-born **Supreme Court Justice Clarence Thomas**. In 2024, a House resolution was introduced to impeach Democrat-turned-Republican Thomas for, among other things, failing to

81. Kaia Hubbard, Jacob Rosen, and Caitlin Huey-Burns, "Trump's anti-immigrant, domestic 'enemy' rhetoric in focus in final stretch to Election Day," CBS News, October 14, 2024, https://www.cbsnews.com/news/donald-trump-rhetoric-enemy-anti-immigrant/.

82. Joseph Neff, "Fact check: Trump relies on emotionally powerful anecdotes to portray an alleged crime wave by undocumented immigrants," The Marshall Project, October 21, 2024, https://www.themarshallproject.org/2024/10/21/fact-check-12000-trump-statements-immigrants/individual_murder_victims#individual_murder_victims/.

83. Jonathan Karl, "Donald Trump's history with Adolf Hitler and his Nazi writings: Analysis," ABC News, December 20, 2023, https://abcnews.go.com/Politics/donald-trumps-history-adolf-hitler-nazi-writings-analysis/story?id=105810745/.

84. Aaron Katersky and Meredith Deliso, "Sen. Bob Menendez found guilty on all counts, including acting as foreign agent, in federal corruption trial," ABC News, July 16, 2024, https://abcnews.go.com/US/sen-bob-menendez-federal-corruption-trial-verdict/story?id=111295557/.

85. U.S. Attorney's Office, Southern District of New York, "U.S. Senator Robert Menendez, His Wife, And Three New Jersey Businessmen Charged With Bribery Offenses," September 22, 2023, https://www.justice.gov/usao-sdny/pr/us-senator-robert-menendez-his-wife-and-three-new-jersey-businessmen-charged-bribery/.

disclose numerous gifts of luxury vacations and travel, one of which was valued at half a million dollars.[86]

Apparently, people like Menendez and Thomas consider their well-documented indulgences to be the absolute right and sacred privilege of anyone who wears not a *blue* collar but a *white* collar. To them, if there's a gun involved, the crime is blue-collar. If, on the other hand, there's no gun involved, then their violations are explained as an unavoidable part of the day-to-day, nine-to-five affairs of America's college-educated "leaders."

It seems, to the average person watching the news, that only a tiny fraction of this country's more prominent white-collar felons ever end up spending time in jail. Thank God for prominent, profit-hungry lawyers—and the serious cabbage needed to hire them. Right?

As I see it, a crime doesn't really need to be labelled according to the color of the collar of the person who committed the crime. Shoot someone to death? You've just committed a serious crime! Screw someone out of his lifetime savings for personal gain? You've just committed an equally serious crime!

So labeling crimes as blue-collar or white-collar may be helpful to economists and statisticians, but it's also a convenient way for those with their hands on the reins of power to whitewash their own crimes by blaming crime in general on blue-collar workers. And as of this writing, in America—at least among President Donald Trump and his sycophants—blaming crimes on *immigrant workers in particular* is all the rage. Immigrants in Springfield, Ohio, eating people's *pets*? Really, now! The Haitian community, who are helping to bring a struggling city back to life, would beg to differ.

When lower-income (i.e., blue-collar) people use guns to commit crimes, many people assume, entirely without evidence, that they're inherently violent people, utterly lacking in ambition, worthless

---

86. Impeaching Clarence Thomas, Associate Justice of the Supreme Court of the United States, for high crimes and misdemeanors, H.R. 1353, 118th Cong. (2024) (introduced), https://www.congress.gov/bill/118th-congress/house-resolution/1353/.

to society, and best locked away in prisons. And more often than not—surprise, surprise—the prison-bound defendants we're talking about are *Black males.*

But when *white-collar* people use guns to commit a crime—perhaps especially murder—there nearly always seems to be an available excuse or an argument, perhaps specious, that the alleged crime occurred because of an unfortunate failure of judgment, workplace pressures, personal difficulties, temporary insanity, or emotional trauma. No surprise *there*, either.

When it comes to weaseling out of consequences for one's actions, if you're a white-collar criminal with a fat billfold and advantageous legal connections, *anything goes.* The better your lawyer, the shorter your cage time. And more often than not, you can plan on getting sprung out of Con College a hell of a lot sooner than the average blue-collar felon does. Such are the cruel and lamentable injustices from the Purple Mountains to the Fruited Plains of gun-happy, violence-prone America.

EMBRACING TRUMPISM:

A Sure Path to Moral, Ethical,

and Intellectual Hell and Gone

"You know, it doesn't really matter what [the media] write as long as you've got a young and beautiful piece of ass."[87]
—Donald J. Trump

Donald J. Trump is the first convicted felon in the history of the United States to have served as president. That is an objective fact. More subjectively, he seems to me to be the most self-obsessed, unempathetic, emotionally disturbed, and morally bankrupt president we have ever had.

He wouldn't even be *mentioned* in this book if not for the deleterious effect he has had on this country's once-constructive debate of the issues, his obsessive denial of his well-documented statements and felonious conduct, his outright contempt for the Constitution and the rule of law, and the serious damage he's done to both my morale and my hopes that we as a country will eventually reject political spin as entertainment and agree on what's fact and what is fiction.

---

87. Alan Rappeport, "Donald Trump's Trail of Comments About Women," *The New York Times*, March 25, 2016, https://www.nytimes.com/2016/03/26/us/politics/donald-trump-women.html.

At first, I assumed his reprehensible conduct would only strengthen my resolve to believe in the goodness of America, but, to my everlasting misfortune and profound disgust, he has weakened that resolve.

I and my progressive-thinking friends thought we were finally *done* with Trump after his loss to Joe Biden in 2020, but this time around, we miscalculated Big Time, didn't we! And now The Donald is back in the White House, bringing even *more* shame to everything and everyone around him, including the Capitol Building he persuaded his thrown-together goon squad to attack and trash in January 2021. Some of the Capitol police who were defending the People's House actually died as a result of the violence they were subjected to.

As a part of the merriment, some of the attackers even *shat on desks*—surely the highest imaginable form of artistic expression they were capable of. And when they were finished doing their (stinking) business, they looked high and low for Nancy Pelosi and Mike Pence, wanting to seize the former and hang the latter, while Trump sat—for *hours*—at his dining table, watching the spectacle on television and obstinately refusing, in spite of his own family's urgent pleas, to come to his senses and call off his dogs.

Trump has so many negative personal qualities—or perhaps we should call them *conditions*—that it would take a dozen no. 2 pencils to list them all.

But hey! I've got plenty of pencils, so let's give it a try:

Trump is hyper-materialistic—a man obsessed with the accumulation of money, not for sharing with anyone in need but entirely for himself and his obscenely wealthy friends.

Trump is threatened by women, people with differently colored skin, and anyone who's getting more attention and praise than he is.

Trump is deeply insecure and pathologically defensive—a bully permanently trapped in the toddler stage of his severely abbreviated maturational history and less in control of his own behavior than many preschoolers.

Trump is culturally ill-informed, functionally illiterate, intellectually unadventurous, and chillingly void of any kind of humor that's not designed expressly to misrepresent, humiliate, or destroy anyone who doesn't unconditionally agree with him.

Trump is actively, blatantly racist and misogynistic.

Trump is the ultimate narcissist, head-over-heels in love with everything about himself. He's incapable of seeing anything beyond his own galloping hubris, his Dennis the Menace self-absorption, and what he imagines to be the inhumanly large size of his penis.

Trump is astonishingly limited in his appreciation of literature and the fine and performing arts.

Tellingly, he seems only to favor power, money, paintings of himself, the praise of dictators, and winning—at any cost, no matter how untenable are his arguments on the issues that mean so much to this country.

* * *

How in the world did Trump become those things? And why? My guess is atrocious parenting, the unrestrained privilege that is available to people of great wealth, and a vast army of friends, relatives, and business associates who have either admired his behavior or been willing to tolerate it.

Right now, off the top of my head, I can think of only two genuine rays of hope in the otherwise sordid, never-ending melodrama of the Trump family: Mary Trump and Fred Trump III.

Mary Trump, Donald's niece—how awkward, to be such a thing!—is a clinical psychologist, a widely followed podcaster, and a bestselling author. Her book *Too Much and Never Enough: How My Family Created the World's Most Dangerous Man* unapologetically hangs the better part of the Trump family's dirty laundry out for all to see. "Donald today is much as he was at three years old," she writes, "incapable of growing, learning, or evolving, unable to regulate his emotions, moderate his responses, or take in and synthesize information."[88] The sequel, *Who Could Ever Love You: A Family Memoir,* masterfully adds fuel to the fire by concentrating on the author's relationship with her uncle.

In the matter of what makes Donald Trump tick—a question being asked by tens of millions of people around the world—Mary Trump's insights as a psychologist are invaluable and, I believe, will be studied by historians for centuries to come.

Fred Trump III, the brother of Mary Trump, is an ardent supporter of people with disabilities. His youngest child, William, has intellectual and developmental disabilities due to a genetic seizure disorder. In his bestselling book *All in the Family: The Trumps and How We Got This Way,* Trump writes that when he went to his uncle Donald one day and asked him for help with the cost of William's medical care, Donald told him he should let his son die and then "move down to Florida."[89]

Offering help to *anyone* in need, including, apparently, his own flesh and blood, has never been one of Donald's strong points.

For compassionate people, generous of heart, these are dark times! Allow me to say once again, and with a growing sense of urgency: *Embracing Trumpism is a sure path to moral and ethical suicide.* Embrace him for *what*—being the Guru of Greed? And most importantly, what has having a white collar done for him when it comes to morality, ethics, professional competence, and plain human decency?

---

88. Mary L. Trump, *Too Much and Never Enough: How My Family Created the World's Most Dangerous Man,* Simon & Schuster, 2020, Kindle, chapt. 14.

89. Martin Pengelly, "Trump told nephew to let his disabled son die, then move to Florida, book says," *The Guardian,* July 24, 2024, https://www.theguardian.com/books/article/2024/jul/24/trump-nephew-book-disabled-son-die.

Detail from *The Garden of Earthly Delights,* painted around the year 1500 by Hieronymus Bosch.

I and millions of others gave the man a chance when, to our shock and dismay, he was elected president the first time. We looked and looked and looked, then looked the other way, repulsed, as he piled on indecency after indecency. But in the end, we found absolutely *nothing* in this deeply troubled man worth embracing. And now, to our enormous misfortune, we have to do it *all over again.*

ME AND MIKE:

White and Blue—and a Touch of Red, Too

"Words are easy, like the wind;
Faithful friends are hard to find."[90]
—William Shakespeare

Mike Plumer in one of our lighter
moments at Panera.

---

90. William Shakespeare, "The Passionate Pilgrim," poem XX.

In the beginning, the casual observer would have looked at **Mike Plumer** and me and judged us to be about as socially compatible as oil and water, the Red Sox and the Yankees, or hardcore atheists and true believers. And yet our friendship has lasted more than half a century.

How could such a thing have happened?

Maybe it was just the laws of physics, hard at work. But more likely, it was simply the result of an unlikely encounter between two utterly dissimilar objects—in this case human beings. And so it was with the two of us.

The year was 1974. I'd just moved with my wife, Marilyn, and our five-year-old daughter, Amy, to Berwick, Maine, after the two of us finished our graduate studies at Eastern Michigan University. We'd come to Berwick because Marilyn had just landed a job as a music teacher. I came along for the adventure, jobless but wildly optimistic in spite of it.

Colonial Cafeteria on School Street in Berwick, Maine, mid-1970s. Twenty-two-year-old Mike Plumer was the Colonial's owner, manager, and head chef. Today the site is occupied by a Cumberland Farms convenience store that sits farther back from the street.

I met Mike for the first time at the **Colonial Cafeteria** in Berwick—a small, tidy gathering place for locals. Since there was no other full-service, family-friendly breakfast and lunch establishment in the immediate area, and because both the food and the service were fantastic, the Colonial was often packed.

It's not as if Mike just happened to be sitting near me that day, making it easy for us to strike up a conversation while waiting for our meals to arrive. The reality is that while I was just another customer, Mike was, at the tender age of twenty-two, the Colonial's owner, manager, and head chef. And it wasn't the first place he'd managed. Obviously an early bloomer, he'd managed his first restaurant while only eighteen years old.

His father, George, was the chef for many years at Colby's Restaurant on Hanson Street in nearby Rochester, New Hampshire. Colby's was renowned for its small-town warmth and rich array of home-cooked meals and expertly baked pies. Mike had worked there himself, learning the ropes of the restaurant industry by observation and immersion, so he'd had plenty of incentive to follow in his father's footsteps.

What got things going for Mike and me right away as friends was the fact that we each had a no-holds-barred sense of humor. When it came to off-the-cuff jokes, we were a latter-day Abbott and Costello or, on some days, at least two of the Three Stooges. *Why bother with a third?* we must have wondered. *We're doin' just fine on our own!*

We had no problem, for instance, with the humor of comics like George Carlin and, eventually, Sarah Silverman. And if our laughs sometimes bubbled over into Gilbert Gottfried territory, we figured, *No problem; it's all in the family!*

But, aside from our inherently ribald, trigger-happy senses of humor, we were more different, occupationally speaking, than Redd Foxx and Mother Teresa.

Clearly, Mike's roots are profoundly, classically blue-collar. Who would ever think *white-collar* when envisioning a restaurant's back-of-the-house mayhem, tables turning over like cars on an assembly line, and the nonstop clatter of plates?

There's no better example of a blue-collar eatery's inner workings than the **Maine Diner** in tourist-packed Wells, known proudly as "The Friendliest Town in Maine." From Open for Business to Last Call, one can see all three functions at Maine Diner up close and personal, roaring along like Amtrak's Downeaster.

This, then, has been Mike Plumer's world for several consecutive decades. As of this writing, Mike, now in his early seventies, is still going strong as a chow slinger (AKA restaurant professional) after having owned and/or managed a long series of award-winning restaurants including the immensely popular **Jake's City Kitchen** in Dover, New Hampshire.

My roots, on the other hand, are a bittersweet tangle of blue-collar insecurity and white-collar yearnings. My circumstances were hardly unique. In the pervasively sexist and racist 1950s, every blue-collar White male came straight down the baby chute with an excellent chance of being financially secure and universally respected, even as, tragically, Blacks and other minorities came out wanting simply to *survive* with their dignity and their fundamental rights intact.

Sadly, the vast majority of blue-collar *women* wanted first and foremost to be *married* to a financially secure, universally respected male who looked like *them*. And if women had low aspirations, it was because, for centuries, whatever aspirations they *did* have were discouraged, ridiculed, and at every turn made next to impossible to achieve.

Yes, I had ambitions. But, as with a great many small-town, blue-collar teens of the time, my ambitions were modest. Did I want desperately to be a doctor, lawyer, or CEO? *None* of those! The thought that I might even be *capable* of such lofty achievements never entered my mind. Because I happened to be a skilled and enthusiastic musician, I studied privately and planned to become a music teacher. And as a child of blue-collar parents who themselves had only modest, seldom-mentioned ambitions, I followed suit without even *thinking* higher. Composer, conductor, or solo recitalist? Those possibilities were also beyond my imagination.

As I worked my way through high school, I managed to become band president, Future Teachers of America president, and finally student council president. Do these sound like blue-collar aspirations to you? Whether they do or not, they help tell the tale of where I felt certain I was headed after graduation. And as a young, White male—a smalltown child of the Eisenhower era—the cards were pretty much stacked in my favor.

So there you are: Mike Plumer, kitchen wizard, crack mechanic, and Yankee-born jack-of-all-trades vs. Ross Bachelder, small-town Midwesterner, classical musician, writer-in-embryo, and natural-born joiner.

And yet we had certain crucial traits in common: our remarkably compatible senses of humor and a relentless work ethic. And if all this isn't enough, each of us can claim a one-time New Hampshire governor as our distant relative: Democratic-Republican **William Plumer** of Epping and Farmer-Republican **Nahum Josiah Bachelder** of East Andover. I don't know if either gentleman's leadership abilities rubbed off on us, but I think it's safe to say we're both proud to have the affiliation, if only by name.

Bachelder was a full-time farmer before getting into politics, and indeed he continued to farm throughout his governorship. Plumer also came from a farming family, but he became a traveling preacher—an *exhorter*, in the common parlance of the time—after a persistent illness made him unfit for either farming or military service.

Can either Mike or I rightfully claim to be more blue-collar in our origins than the other? The answer, as I see it, is a tentative *no*, but with a few caveats worth mentioning.

Mike's mother and father were, he says, dirt poor. That suggests to me that even if they *wanted* more out of life, they were, for various reasons including their poverty, unlikely ever to achieve all of the goals they aspired to. In short, they were living what some would call a hardscrabble existence.

And while my parents couldn't really be described as dirt poor, they could hardly have claimed to live on Easy Street, either. For several years after moving out into the country, we had no hot water heater, which meant that we had to heat bathwater on our stove, then carry the bucket of water down the hall and into the bathroom. And for more than a decade, my brother and I slept in unfinished, wasp-infested attic bedrooms.

George Plumer surely had a work ethic every bit as strong as his son's, but beyond wanting to have a successful restaurant, it's unlikely he had any visions of grandeur about himself. And the same was true of my father. While at one time he was the co-owner of a grocery store, Van Camp and Bachelder, and then, for many years, a shop foreman in the auto industry, he never mentioned having greater ambitions than those. There's nothing wrong with those ambitions, of course! But, like so many survivors of World War II (my father took a bullet from a machine gun in Schwerstedt, Germany, in 1945), he was just thankful to be safely home and making ends meet.

Where the caveats come in is with the *spouses* of our respective fathers. I know from my many interactions with Mike's mother, Geneva, that she was a strong writer and an articulate speaker. She also had passionate, well-informed, left-leaning political convictions, along with a seldom-mentioned desire to accomplish a whole lot more than what she'd already accomplished in life.

It was the same with my mother, Anna Lee. She graduated from high school with a 4.0 average, was a devoted advocate of the FDR school of political thinking, was an avid reader, and at one time played the saxophone in an all-woman jazz ensemble.

But both women were clearly products of their time—a world in which the ambitions of husbands virtually always took precedence over those of their wives. And as I see it, that stubborn, deeply entrenched reality discouraged any intellectual ambitions our mothers may have had and virtually guaranteed they would spend most of their waking hours as sole caretakers of their respective homes and children.

These realities helped define Mike and me as undeniably blue-collar in our origins. My aspirations and work experiences after college were more white-collar than Mike's. And yet Mike has no small amount of what it's fair to call *white-collar* tastes and proclivities. Like his mother, Mike is an avid reader. He loves history and enjoys dining out.

In the never-ending battle between blue-collar and white-collar values—a battle which at the time of this writing is becoming more and more emotionally charged and irrational—each side thinks, either secretly or openly, that the other is dead wrong about both their convictions and the way they conduct themselves in their daily affairs. *Why do they waste their time on that horrible country music?* say the white-collars. *Why would anyone want to sit there and suffer through a bunch of overpaid fancy-pants musicians makin' honks 'n' squeals on those whackadoodle instruments of theirs?* say the blue-collars.

Lest you wonder, I can assure you I was being only *half* facetious with those characterizations. People on both sides of the political divide have, privately at least, said far worse things about each other than about each other's tastes in music. It's all about labeling, and the Trump Era's extreme right-wingers—especially the ones with white collars—have become remarkably adept at proudly slinging debilitating mud into the faces of their opponents, utterly indifferent to the fact that their assertions lack any credibility.

Politicians would like for us to believe that there is such a thing as blue-collar or white-collar values, but is there?

My friend Mike is a perfect subject for examining these complexities.

Mike is a reader. Today's right-leaning white-collar politicians encourage traditionally blue-collar voters to pooh-pooh book learning and the very notion of expertise and to view the public education system as a means of socialist indoctrination. Yet reading and learning used to be admired—viz., the admiration Americans had for people such as Ben Franklin, Abraham Lincoln, and Thomas Edison.

Mike respects human differences. Meanwhile, the party currently winning over the majority of blue-collar voters is encouraging people to accost, insult, deport, delegitimize, and otherwise reject people who are different from them.

Mike believes in playing fair—a quality that's at the very heart of his value system. In an ideal world, fairness should be accorded to everyone regardless of skin color or social status. No special treatment—no unwarranted forgiveness—for the rich and/ or powerful, just because they're rich and/or powerful.

When all is said and done, there really should be *no need at all* to label people as either blue-collar or white-collar. It becomes a lever by which to force people into voter blocs—often, I would argue, falsely.

Nor should there be a need for people from *either* camp to avoid social interaction with each other because of their own personal insecurities or notions of superiority. Why, for example, should carpenters, construction workers, or grocery store clerks deprive themselves of art galleries, museums, and concert halls just because—let's be honest—they're often crammed full of arrogant, over-dressed dilettantes pretending all the while to be experts? To the reluctant, I say don't cheat yourself out of an opportunity to expand your cultural horizons. Their pretentiousness is *their* problem, not yours!

And conversely, there can be no good reason for politicians, academics, and MBAs not to step away from their passions once in a while and get down and dirty with anything from carpentry and auto repair to pool halls and bingo.

One way to alleviate these stubborn, seldom-discussed lines of delineation would be for *both* sides to acknowledge and then embrace the best of what the other side has to offer. If you think there can be no good country music, attend a live performance and give it a chance! If you think chamber musicians are pointy-headed intellectuals, go to a concert and listen to the magic they can create (and ignore any snobs you might notice in the audience)!

A community in which everyone is encouraged to become skilled in both mind *and* body—adept at both the sharpening of their intellects and the sweat of their highly skilled brows—is by far the healthier community in every respect than one in which people are herded to opposite sides of a cultural fence.

Mike Plumer has read all of my books, entirely on his own initiative. And while he has no active interest in classical music—for many years my specialty, both during and well beyond college—he has come and supported me in several of my performances and, I should mention, lived to tell about it.

If Mike asks me to go with him to a car show or vintage diner—a chance to talk in depth about either what makes a car run or why a restaurant fails—I jump at the chance. And why? Because, like him, I love cars and diners and have no problem saying so.

I've spent many happy weekends with Mike over the years, either admiring vintage cars or chasing down diners. Think **Jay Leno** and **Anthony Bourdain**—"regular guys" with impressive creds! Whenever Plumer and I have breakfast together, I'm always presented with a golden opportunity to listen to a really knowledgeable restaurant professional as he explains to me the inner workings of the restaurant industry, one element at a time.

What it has taken for Mike to establish, maintain, and leave a lasting thumbprint on the many restaurants he's nurtured over the years is no less an accomplishment than what it has taken me to conceive, write, and publish a growing number of books, all of which I've written since turning seventy. Recently, we decided that in spite of the vast differences between our two endeavors, his restaurants are the equivalent of my books and my books the equivalent of his restaurants. Seen objectively, *both* of them deserve to stand as imposing monuments to their creators' hard-earned skills and prodigious work ethic.

Mike, by the way, has accomplished all of this—his top-to-bottom knowledge of cars and his wide-ranging expertise in the restaurant business—without ever setting foot in a college class-room. And while I had the good fortune to study literature and music in college—an enormous aid and incentive for anyone deter-mined to build a dual career as both writer and performer—I've also become a productive visual artist without ever having set foot in a college drawing class—without ever having subjected myself to those notorious "crits" that leave many art majors wondering why they ever signed up for college-level art instruction in the first place.

When it comes to restaurants and the visual arts, the two of us have gotten where we are entirely by the seat of our pants—by putting in countless hours of labor, guided by a fierce work ethic and a hidebound refusal to give up when the going gets tough.

White, Blue, and a Touch of Red, too? You bet!

As for that touch of red in our friendship, if being "red" means being patriotic, then the two of us are as patriotic as they come. The difference between our patriotism and the patriotism of the zeal-ots—the jingoists—is that we've always kept our patriotism close to our vests and have seldom if ever seen a need to brag about it or even *mention* it. Our lawns may be flagless, but our hearts, whether white or blue or a mixture of the two, are full of appreciation for being able to call a country with cultural diversity, a constitution, and a dyed-in-the-wool commitment to equality our home.

So *really* now: who can claim with any authority that our accom-plishments—Mike's in the restaurant industry, mine in the fine and performing arts—are more blue-collar than white-collar or more white-collar than blue-collar? Whatever you may think, one thing is undeniably true: we've done what we've done *our* way, and it's only strengthened our always solid, forever invincible friendship.

CONCLUSION:

Leaving Our Mark on an Ailing Planet

Yes, these are dark times!

So is it not time, *now*, for us, as both individuals and a country, to stop pretending?

Our planet is ailing, and in ways far too numerous to thoroughly list here, let alone properly address. And yet I very much hope you'll allow me to give it a shot anyway, just as you're more than welcome to do.

Women's rights have been bombed back into the Stone Age thanks to Donald Trump, his army of self-serving, pathologically obsessed, power-hungry sycophants, and the handpicked Supreme Court justices who disgraced themselves by going out of their way to dismantle Roe v. Wade.

Guns—far too many guns, the wrong kind of guns in the hands of all the wrong people—have taken over neighborhoods in cities small and large from coast to coast, and tens of thousand or people, including children, are dying thanks to the disgusting self-absorption and insensitivity of the gun lobbyists and their followers.

The obscene hoarding of wealth by the excessively rich—pinchers of everyone's pennies but their own—makes King Midas look like a rank amateur when it comes to blatant, unapologetic greed.

The costs of childcare, senior care, health care, and housing are skyrocketing, and lip service alone will never single-handedly improve the quality of our lives.

Corporations, in an effort to preserve and balloon their profit margins, are sucking the life out of this bruised and battered planet, one environmental atrocity at a time, in the service of the Almighty Dollar. *Their* Almighty Dollar, anyway—and the dollars of their shareholders (most of whom grew up hearing adults talk about stocks and investing, topics seldom discussed around blue-collar dinner tables).

Extreme right-wing politicians have either mislaid their morality or banished it altogether from the Golden Rule we once so ardently cherished as a culture. *Dog eat dog; me or you; your problem, not mine*: these unfortunate dicta have introduced into our daily lives a brand-new and yet ages-old dogma of self-preservation at any cost, including the loss of one's inviolable integrity and fundamental human decency.

The Citizens United decision of 2010 unleashed an obscene system of corporate lobbying and dark-money contributions, in which politicians on both sides of the aisle willingly participate.

Do we as reasoning, caring creatures really want to stand by and do nothing while watching others do all the work of mending the damage that outright avarice and indifference to suffering have done to our way of life?

Do we really want to be remembered by our friends, our family, our neighbors—and good people everywhere—as people who care only about ourselves and to hell with the less fortunate?

I, for one, prefer to be remembered for things noble, not nefarious; things constructive, not destructive; things compassionate, not cruel. And a great many people share my preferences wholeheartedly.

The only thing well-meaning people may be guilty of *not* doing is being proudly *vocal* about their values—of keeping the best parts of themselves *to themselves* when it would be far more productive for them to stand up and be heard, loudly and clearly, about their most treasured beliefs.

Ways You Can Make a Lasting Difference

Don't allow yourself to be deceived! Caring deeply about matters of individual and social improvement is *not* the exclusive province of the monied class—the white-collar crowd—the people of privilege. Caring deeply is not a luxury, it's a *responsibility*. And it certainly is not *socialism*. Like education, opportunity, health, and the ability to retire with dignity, caring belongs to *all* of us, whether our collars are white, blue, or an invigorating blend of the two.

No matter what Hollywood's endless flow of glitzy, hyper-materialistic fantasies seems to be telling us, the yearning to be fondly remembered after our passing is hardly an exclusively big-city, white-collar phenomenon. People from every walk of life want passionately to leave behind them some tangible, undeniable evidence of their active, meaningful engagement with the world. Having children is one sure way, but beyond parenthood, many of us don't know where to begin with a task this formidable—this ambitious—this intensely *personal*. Leave behind *what?*

Of course, there are all sorts of good and bad ways to make history. So desperate are some troubled souls to make a mark that they go out of their way to leave irrefutable evidence of their anger, both with themselves and the people around them, for the way the cards have played out for them.

Want to be remembered for a very long time? Try mass murder! Unfortunately, it appears to be all the rage these days in gun-worshiping America.

Before gun violence exploded, there was always the *noose*, wasn't there. We have an appallingly long and reprehensible history with *that* weapon of destruction, too.

Consider the countless African-Americans, lynched well into the Jim Crow Era and beyond simply for being the wrong color—of not looking enough like those in power—or for proudly, adamantly refusing to be enslaved. Did you know that the last lynching in America—of nineteen-year-old African-American **Michael Donald** of Mobile, Alabama—happened on March 21, *1981?* I audibly *gasped* when I learned about it while doing research for this essay. I'd thought, naively, that the last recorded lynching must surely have happened more than a century ago.

And consider the nineteen poor souls—fourteen women and five men—who, as a result of being unfairly branded as "witches," either died in prison or were swiftly and brutally hanged in front of a cheering, jeering crowd at Gallows Hill in Salem, Massachusetts. Oh, and don't forget the eighty-one-year-old man—also a Salemite—who was summarily pressed to death beneath a pile of stones for refusing to testify at the trial.

Guns! Rope! Mass murder! Not your cup of tea? Then just *one* heinous, isolated act against *one* unfortunate victim (or series of victims) would do the job, I suppose. Think Jack the Ripper! Lizzie Borden! Jeffrey Dahmer! For the record, only one of those three— the once-honorable (I suppose) Jeffrey Lionel Dahmer, eventually dubbed the Milwaukee Cannibal—is known for certain to have committed the crimes he was accused of. Perhaps you'll recall that Dahmer did not have an easy departure from his most unappetizing existence. Don't remember? Look it up. The brief time Dahmer spent in prison was no picnic.

I'm sure I don't have to remind any of you that there are *far better ways* than gratuitous violence and indescribable cruelty for you to make your mark on the world. So let's try on a few of the more constructive, more personally satisfying ways!

Are you an **elementary school teacher**, or perhaps a **childcare worker**? Then unless you wake up one morning and discover that, like W.C. Fields, you've chosen the wrong profession and can't stand children, *trust me:* you'll go down in any history that matters as one of the most admired, respected, and cherished public servants in your community. Now *that's* a status worth having!

Are you a **nursing home attendant** or **assisted living professional**? Then if you do your job lovingly, competently, and compassionately—if you genuinely *care* about the people you serve and show it with everything you do—you're worth your weight in gold and will be rewarded with undying love and deep, abiding appreciation. And that's *also* a status worthy of having!

If, on the other hand, you're more publicly ambitious—more inclined to share your skills with large groups or entire communities as, say, a **police officer**, a **social worker**, a **politician**, or a **military professional**—then you, too, are an enormously important cog in the great machine that serves us all: *civilization itself* in all of its multifaceted, awe-inspiring glory.

Not all contributors receive the applause they deserve. Some get way too much applause; others get way too little. And sometimes, no matter how hard they try and how life-affirming and life-enriching their contributions have been, they get *no applause at all*. Life is not always fair and will never be fully, permanently equitable. And because of it, there will always be people, including me, who on occasion fall painfully short of their aspirations—their fondest dreams.

Not fun, of course! But true courage means learning to be thankful, in spite of our failures, for the contributions we *did* make, no matter how modest they may have been.

* * *

I'll end this discussion with brief responses to each of the **Nine Critical Points** I addressed in this book's introduction.

If, as I did, you feel insecure about your blue-collar roots, you may wonder just what to do with those feelings.

To begin with, it's critically important for us to remember that feelings—whether they're about our social status, our personal insecurities, or other things too numerous to mention—are not written in stone. And because of that, it's far more constructive and more cleansing to *challenge* them instead of obsessing about them or running away from them. So let's go back to my earlier assertions about blue-collar thinking and *have at it!*

To be blue-collar is to drive by houses larger, more artfully designed, and more attractively situated than yours and wonder, "Will I ever be able live like that?"

Learn to curb your very human desire to "live better." Put your yearnings in perspective! Is the home you live in really all that bad? If so, then find creative, affordable ways to improve it. And remember, small is beautiful, too!

To be blue-collar is to choose the cheapest possible options, whether you're shopping for a home, a car, a shirt, or something as simple as a restaurant side dish.

Be proud of being frugal about your day-to-day expenditures. Excess is not an accomplishment; it's a failure of will—a loss of common sense. As a reward for your frugality, allow yourself carefully-chosen, well-deserved moments of indulgence.

To be blue-collar is to watch with envy as the more affluent people in your community travel to distant lands, frequently and without any apparent financial worry.

Remember that the allegedly more "glamorous" destinations often turn out to be anything but glamorous. And besides: who and what defines the idea of glamor, anyway? Once again, we're talking about a profoundly subjective idea! A small, tastefully furnished B&B in a colorful, out-of-the-way town not far from your home? That's glamor! A hulking, obscenely expensive, tastelessly decorated hotel? For me at least, gilded halls *à la* Mar-a-Lago would be a grotesque waste of my hard-earned travel funds. The wealth of experiences I crave when on vacation can't be found within such a place.

To be blue-collar is to assume that to travel to any destination beyond the local ones you've already been to is an unjustifiable waste of money.

If heavy smokers or those hooked on five-star restaurants, name-brand labels, exorbitantly priced liquors, and other luxuries were to systematically cut back on their big-ticket indulgences, they would have more than enough money available for foreign travel—especially if they were to avoid high-travel seasons. Using their public library or investing only in pre-owned books would help, too. Learning and enjoying do not have to be financially prohibitive indulgences. Ask Eric Hoffer!

To be blue-collar is to view highly successful people as "privileged" and "spoiled" and, because of it, most likely undeserving of their success.

If, like me, you're blue-collar in origin, it's likely you assume, at least subconsciously, that people more successful than yourself have earned their success by either silver-spoon privilege or outright dishonesty. *Don't waste your time comparing.* How others have become successful has nothing to do with the way you're more than likely destined to earn your own success.

To be blue-collar is to assume that any higher educational facility other than a state university or a community college is for the moneyed class and therefore unavailable to you.

Elite colleges have a centuries-old superiority complex—a frame of mind, perpetuated by heavy endowments, constant self-promotion, and exaggerated feelings of grandeur—that leads them to incessant academic braggadocio. Such schools may be financially and academically superior in many ways, but it doesn't mean that their instructors are automatically superior when compared to instructors at less prestigious, less heavily endowed institutions.

Even *community colleges*, which suffer the most from the public's erroneous presumption that they're inherently inferior to the elites, can have within their ranks instructors with fine minds, an excellent work history, and impressive skills as educators. Find the affordable school that impresses you the most and fits you best; check out the backgrounds and accomplishments of its faculty, tenured or not; and then show them what you're made of!

To be blue-collar is to assume that because you aren't living the high life, there's either something fundamentally wrong with you or you're simply not smart enough and skilled enough to have achieved such lofty goals.

Nonsense! Once again, what constitutes the "high life" is entirely a matter of opinion. To me, a small home decorated with fine-art prints, crammed full of books, and surrounded by thoughtful friends and beautiful music is the high life, while a thirty-room mansion without art and music, books and friends, and stimulating conversation—without any evidence of intellectual sophistication—would not be the "high life" at all. It would be the *low life,* and as far as I'm concerned, you can *keep* it!

To be blue-collar is to feel that if you were only more physically attractive, you'd be more successful.

The physical ideals you see paraded before you in movies—more often than not for the sole purpose of box-office enhancement—in no way reflect the wonderful diversity of appearances within the human community. Only a tiny handful of people actually look and behave like the people in movies and on television.

To see a powerful example of a more honest, true-to-life approach to cinema, watch Aki Kaurismäki's award-winning 2023 film, *Fallen Leaves.* In Kaurismäki's beautifully conceived, directed, and filmed story, the action is refreshingly slow-moving. The protagonists—two lonely Ukrainian blue-collar laborers struggling to stay employed, socially engaged, and happy with themselves—actually *look* like blue-collar laborers. The male love interest isn't incongruently slicked up and nattily dressed, and the female love interest is not a cinematic sex object caked with irrelevant, unnecessary cosmetics. They're just *people!* What can be wrong about *that?*

But perhaps the film's most impressive accomplishment is that, through sheer cinematic artistry, it shows what falling in love feels like without the use of either over-the-top sex scenes or hysterically fast-moving scene changes. We're talking an *authentic working-class romance*, not a Hollywood caricature of real people.

You have absolutely no obligation to buy into the print and electronic media's vision of you. Be *yourself*—save money, too!—and happiness will be yours to celebrate and cherish.

To be blue-collar is to feel that you'll never be able to escape fully from your less privileged, less-than-glamorous lifestyle.

To feel that you'll never be able to escape from what you consider to be a less-than-desirable station in life is to play the *victim*—an attitude that can only lead to failure. All of life is a series of intensely personal, potentially life-altering emergences. Together, patience and determination can help you find your path to self-fulfillment.

If you were born blue-collar and don't like how it feels, then consider it an *opportunity*, not a life sentence. On the other hand, if you happen to have been born white-collar and are happy with who you are—and assuming you don't flaunt your good fortune by playing the Superior One—then why rock the boat? Why change your circumstances? Go ahead and indulge, but find ways to *share* your good fortune.

Sometimes, no matter who you happen to be, just *staying put* is the greatest possible step forward.

* * *

It has taken me decades to sort out my feelings about my blue-collar heritage. And yet I'm now in what I consider to be a good place—happily married to a wonderfully supportive woman; active as a writer, artist, and musician, living in Maine, a state I'd always wanted to live in; and the father of our equally supportive, highly intelligent daughter, Amy. I've found not only peace with but *pride in* my blue-collar upbringing. And because I've spent so much time in both worlds—the blue *and* the white, in nearly equal proportion—I've more empathy, more all-around perspective, and a greater understanding of myself and the people I associate with. I've actually *grown enormously* because of my multifaceted life experiences, and who in their right mind would have reason to complain about *that*?

As people get deeper into their lives—*farther along*, one might say—they become more thoughtful, more habitually reflective. I'm often tempted to call these reflections my *Final Accounting*. My *Day of Reckoning*. My *Judgment Day*.

Actually, I kind o' *like* that last one! Singers and composers seem to like it, too. Want proof? People who study these things have discovered that 5,206 songs have the words *Judgment Day* in either their lyrics, their title, or both. However, since I'm not formally religious, I feel entirely, blissfully free to have this thing we're talking about—this Day of Reckoning—*my* way. And I'm not about to wait around to do it, either!

That's because I happen to see my "accounting" as anything but final. To me, it's an ongoing, never-ending process—a series of self-administered pop quizzes and mid-semester exams rather than one final, make-it-or-break-it exam. My own very personal, custom-designed version of a Day of Reckoning is not just a one-shot deal. As far as I'm concerned, *every day* is, in small and large ways, a reckoning!

So you've a right to wonder: what are *my* ambitions? What one mark, or series of marks, have I wanted most eagerly to make on this, our shared and eternally struggling planet? How do I want to be *remembered*?

Time now for me stop the hedging and lay down the facts.

First and foremost, I want people to remember what I stood for—what I *believed* in:

. . . that once we're mature adults, sane of mind and securely on the road to wisdom, then barring unforeseen disaster, **we're the authors of our fates.**

. . . that **men and women are *equal*** in everything they do or aspire to do.

. . . that **the separation of church and state** is at the very foundation of American democracy.

. . . that if we don't learn to **think for ourselves**, there will always be others more than eager to step in and do it for us.

. . . that, broadly speaking, there are two kinds of doers in the world—**specialists and generalists**—and that while both kinds play absolutely essential roles in society, *neither* kind is in any way superior to the other.

. . . that **active immersion in literature and the fine and performing arts**, as either creator, consumer, or both, is the best possible way to turn an impressionable child into a sensitive, caring, productive, intellectually aware adult.

. . . that a person without **an active, inventive sense of humor** is missing out on one of the best parts of the human experience.

. . . that women must have **full control over their bodies**, and that men have no business interfering with those rights.

. . . that **physical or emotional abuse** of men, women, children, animals, or the environment is inexcusable under any circumstances.

. . . that we must teach our children to **question authority** when they find themselves subjected to unjust and irrational rules and regulations—especially those imposed by people and organizations without the child's best interest in mind.

. . . that, to borrow the words of Martin Luther King, Jr., **the content of a person's *character***—not the color of his or her skin—is what matters.

. . . that without **the enormous contributions made by immigrants of every stripe**, the United States would never have succeeded.

. . . that **ALL** of this country's inhabitants have an absolute, inviolable right to life, liberty, and the pursuit of happiness.

. . . that **NO** American—including the president of the United States—can ever be above the law under any circumstances.

. . . that a true patriot sees no need—*no need at all*—**to flaunt his or her patriotism** with excessive, self-serving, self-congratulatory displays of his country's flag.

. . . that **an inquiring mind** is the most powerful weapon against the debilitating consequences of ignorance.

I want to be remembered for being a damn good writer, for caring deeply about the students I had the pleasure of teaching, and for being a good father, not just to my own daughter but to *all* children, wherever they lived, wherever they came from, and whatever they looked like.

I want to be remembered for my passion for all things beautiful and mysterious. Indeed, I have a computer file with a steadily growing list of those things I consider worthy of inclusion.

I want to be remembered for loving animals, for being a worthy companion to them, and for taking good care of them in sickness and in health.

I want to be remembered for being an avid reader; for being a strong, unceasing advocate for libraries and librarians; and for my heartfelt belief in the power of words carefully chosen and wisely spoken.

I want to be remembered for having chosen my friends not for the elegance of their homes or the labels on their clothing but for the strength of their character, the firmness of their convictions, and the kindness they showed to others.

I want to be remembered for being kind to strangers, for reaching out to people in distress, and for having done my best to forgive those who have wronged me, while asking forgiveness for those I may have wronged.

Finally, after having spent decades doubting my creative abilities, I want to be remembered for having vastly exceeded not only other people's expectations for me but *my* expectations for *myself.*

* * *

In closing, Fellow Inhabitants, I'd like to challenge every last one of you to . . .

Write down your own list of formative influences and how they affected your values and self-perceptions. I can promise you that you'll come away with a greater understanding of, and appreciation for, not just *who* you are but *why* you're the *way* you are.

Write down your own list of expectations for how you want to be remembered so that you can work your way systematically through them.

Now, go and make *your* marks! Whether you consider yourself to be blue-collar, white-collar, or an exciting, imaginative mixture of the two doesn't really matter; your job is simply to make your marks *good* and *lasting*. And while you're busy making them, set your expectations for yourself as high as you can reasonably make them. After all, what can possibly be wrong with shooting for the moon, then traveling farther into your very own personal cosmos than you ever thought possible?

ABOUT THE AUTHOR

Maine writer, artist, and musician **Ross Alan Bachelder** has been active for more than fifty years in the fine and performing arts in and beyond northern New England.

Now in his early eighties, Bachelder describes himself as a flaming idealist, a proud political progressive, a passionate lover of books, and a hard-driving ball of creative energy—a man whose goal, as far back as he can remember, has always been to live every day of his life as fully and imaginatively as possible.

Growing Up Blue-Collar is his fourth book.